Africa in the United Nations System, 1945-2005

Published by
Adonis & Abbey Publishers Ltd
P.O. Box 43418
London
SE11 4XZ
http://www.adonis-abbey.com

Copyright © 2006, **Issaka K. Souaré**

British Library Cataloguing-in-Publication Data
A catalogue record for this book is available from the British Library

ISBN 1-905068-34-4

Cover Design   Mega Graphix

Printed and bound in Great Britain

Africa in the United Nations System, 1945-2005

By

Issaka K. Souaré

Adonis & Abbey
Publishers Ltd

DEDICATION

To my beloved wife, Aicha; my daughter, Makagbe;
and my mother of the same name

CONTENTS

ABBREVIATIONS & ACRONYMS

ACABQ	[UN General Assembly's] Advisory Committee on Administrative and Budgetary Questions
AEF	*Afrique équoitoriale française*
AGC	African Groundnut Council
AGS-UN	African Group of States at the UN
ANC	African National Congress (South Africa)
AOF	*Afrique occidentale française*
ASEAN	Association of South-East Asian Nations
AU	African Union
BCEAO	*Banque Centrale des États d'Afrique de l'Ouest*
DDR	Disarmament, Demobilisation and Re-integration
DPI	Department of Public Information
DPKO	[UN] Department of Peace-keeping Operations
ECA	United Nations Economic Commission for Africa
ECOMOG	ECOWAS Monitoring Group (peace-keeping forces)
ECOSOC	Economic and Social Council
ECOWAS	Economic Community of West African States
EU	European Union
FANCI	*Forces armées nationales de Côte d'Ivoire*
FAO	Food and Agriculture Organization
FLN	*Front de libération nationale* (Algeria)
IAEA	International Atomic Energy Agency
IBRD	International Bank for Reconstruction and Development
ICAO	International Civil Aviation Agency
ICC	International Criminal Court

ICJ	International Court of Justice
ICSID	International Centre for Settlement of Investment Disputes
IDA	International Development Association
IDP	Internally Displaced Persons
IFC	International Finance Corporation
ILO	International Labour Organization
IMF	International Monetary Fund
IMO	International Maritime Organization
INSTRAW	International Research and Training for the Advancement of Women
ITU	International Telecommunication Union
KAIPTC	Kofi Annan International Peace-keeping Training Centre
LAS	League of Arab States
LN	League of Nations
LURD	Liberians United for Reconciliation and Democracy
MDGs	Millennium Development Goals
MIGA	Multilateral Investment Guarantee Agency
MINUCI	*Mission des Nations Unies en Côte d'Ivoire*
MONUC	United Nations Mission to the DRC (since Nov. 1999)
MPCI	*Mouvement patriotique de Côte d'Ivoire* (armed opposition group)
MRN	*Mouvement démocratique républicain* (Rwanda)
MRND	*Mouvement révolutionnaire national pour le développement* (Rwanda)
NATO	North Atlantic Treaty Organization
NEPAD	New Partnership for Africa's Development
NGO	Non-Governmental Organizations
NIEO	New International Economic Order
OAU	Organization of African Unity
OHCHR	Office of the United Nations High Commissioner for Human Rights
OIC	Organization of the Islamic Conference
ONUC	*Opération des Nations Unies au Congo* (1960-1964)

OSG	Office of the [UN] Secretary-General
PAC	Pan Africanist Congress of Azania (South Africa)
Parmehutu	*Parti du mouvement de l'émancipation hutu* (Rwanda)
PCIJ	Permanent Court for International Justice of the League of Nations
PMC	Permanent Mandates Commission of the League of Nations
PSC	[African Union's] Peace and Security Council
RPF	Rwandan Patriotic Front
RTLMC	*Radio télévision libre des mille collines* (Rwanda)
SAIC	South African Indian Congress
SDAS	Sovereign Diasporian African States
SRSG	Special Representative of the [UN] Secretary-General
SWAPO	South West Africa People's Organization (Namibia)
TOM	*Territoires d'outre mer* (France)
UDHR	Universal Declaration of Human Rights
UNAIDS	Joint United Nations Programme on HIV/AIDS
UNAMIR	United Nations Assistance Mission for Rwanda
UNAPAERD	United Nations Action Plan for African Economic Recovery and Development, 1986-1990
UNCORS	UN Commission on the Racial Situation in the Union of South Africa
UNCTAD	United Nations Conference on Trade and Development
UNDP	United Nations Development Programme
UNEF	United Nations Emergency Force (Palestine)
UNESCO	United Nations Educational, Scientific and Cultural Organization
UNHCR	United Nations High Commission for Refugees
UNHSP	Nations Human Settlements Programme

UNICEF	United Nations Children's Fund
UNIDO	United Nations Industrial Development Organization
UNITAF	United Task Force (Somalia)
UNITAR	United Nations Institute for Training and Research
UN	United Nations Organization
UNNADAF	United Nations New Agenda for the Development of Africa in the 1990s
UNOCI	United Nations Operation in Côte d'Ivoire
UNOG	UN regional office at Geneva
UNON	UN regional office at Nairobi
UNOSOM	United Nations Operation in Somalia
UNOV	UN regional office at Vienna
UNRCPDA	United Nations Regional Centre for Peace and Disarmament in Africa
UNSECOORD	Office of the High Representatives for the Least Developed Countries, Landlocked Developing Countries and Small Island Developing States
UNTAG	United Nations Transition Assistance Group (Namibia)
UPU	Universal Postal Union
USUN	United States Mission to the UN
WARDA	West African Rice Development Association
WFP	World Food Programme
WHO	World Health Organization
WIPO	World Intellectual Property Organization
WMO	World Meteorological Organization

FOREWORD

Today there is welcome resurgence for multilateralism. Multilateralism based on the principles of the United Nations (UN) Charter, must however be in its scope and content, a cooperative and democratic multilateralism. It must seek just, peaceful and durable solutions to conflicts and disputes and it must foster global development and prosperity. Such multilateralism would include a rule-based international order and strong international institutions capable of effectively addressing the inter-related issues of conflict, poverty, under development, HIV/AIDS and other infectious diseases, proliferation of small arms, terrorism, weapons of mass destruction and environmental degradation, in one word, one that is capable of ensuring human security and sustainable development for all nations and peoples of the world in a fair, equal and equitable manner.

In this regard, the UN Charter should always be a source and inspiration of the international community and all nations for the realization of the new international order. All our collective aspirations can best be pursued within this world organization but the UN must however be strengthened and revitalized to respond to the challenges of the 21st Century.

The Millennium Development Goals for their part represent our common vision and hope for a new global partnership for shared prosperity and security - an ideal at the very heart of the UN. Africa has a keen interest for the fulfilment of all commitments made in this respect by all concerned world actors. By all indications, the Continent is still way off the mark in meeting many of the stated goals. We must further strengthen our common resolve to act in their resolute pursuit.

Indeed, this calls for the enhancement of international cooperation and a multilateral system that would be more responsive and effective in meeting global threats and challenges and addressing the scourges of major economic, social, cultural, humanitarian and environmental issues that are gravely hampering a peaceful world and the dignity of our peoples.

From an organization whose birth was prompted by the need to give a coordinated response to specific integration objectives affecting the commonality of its members, the African Union (AU) has evolved and is today, slowly but steadily affirming itself as the embodiment of the most profound aspirations, principles and values of the peoples of the region, a vehicle for achieving peace, prosperity and regional integration and as a legitimate and consensual mouthpiece of its members on matters of common concern and mutual interest.

It is no gainsaying that the AU, with its 53 members in the UN can and will play an effective role in promoting multilateralism as we pursue our common goal of creating a just and equitable international order.

I commend the author for the instructive and comprehensive historical perspective to the contemporary debate on Africa's role and place in the reform of the UN and express deep gratification for the opportunity offered through this Foreword.

In restating my conviction that the UN is as relevant today as it was in 1945, it is my hope that the publication of this book will serve as a timely and useful resource on multilateralism and that as such, it will help ensure a safer, more prosperous, peaceful future for all life on earth.

Julia Dolly Joiner*
Commissioner for Political Affairs
African Union Commission, Addis Ababa

---

* Mrs. Joiner is absolved of responsibility for any shortcoming relating to the content of this publication

ACKNOWLEDGMENTS

I must thank Mrs Julia Dolly Joiner, Commissioner for Political Affairs of the African Union for accepting —despite her many engagements— to read the manuscript of this book and contribute a Foreword to it. The superb effort of her Special Assistant and Private Secretary in facilitating this was highly appreciated. Professor Peter Gowan of London Metropolitan University read the entire manuscript and kindly contributed an Afterword to it. I cannot thank him enough for this great service especially given its promptitude despite his busy programme. I would like to extend my thanks to other individuals who encouraged me and/or devoted part of their precious time to reading early drafts of all or parts of this book and commenting on the different aspects of it. In particular, I thank Abdoulaye Souaré, Aboubacar A. Cissé, Joe L. Washington, Shuaib A. Swaray, Arthur Egbuniwe, Ibrahim Hassan Traoré and Aboubacar S. Kanté.

The editorial service of Jonathan Derrick is duly acknowledged and I am very grateful to the intellectual guidance of Jideofor Adibe who encouraged me and kindly accepted to publish this book. The encouragements of Kenneth Omeje, of the Department of Peace Studies at the University of Bradford (UK) and Desmond Davies, formerly Editor of *West Africa* magazine and now of *Africa Week* were also another source of inspiration. My friends Baba M. Touré, Aboubacar Camara, Abdourahman Diallo and Sidiki Camara did not stint in their support and encouragement. I must thank them for this. I am equally grateful to the assistance of Dr. Adekeye Adebajo, Executive Director of the Institute for Security Studies at Cape Town.

I must finally acknowledge the incredible patience and support of my beloved wife who as always provided me with a loving and stable family environment conducive to intellectual work on this book.

The critical comments and valuable suggestions as well as the support these individuals lent me significantly helped improve the quality of this book. Any error that may still be found in this book is, of course, mine and I take responsibility for it.

London, March 2006
Issaka K. Souaré

INTRODUCTION

Since the early twentieth century warfare has been the midwife of the globalization of governance. And Africa has been caught up in these twin processes of warfare and the seeds of globalization.
—Ali A. Mazrui, Addis Ababa, 2004

Wars are doubtless destructive. But wars can also be constructive. Wars destroy lives and livelihoods. But wars also lead people to chart new ways to rebuild their lives and prevent new wars from occurring. In contemporary history, two great wars have led to the creation of the two greatest international organizations. The First World War, also known as the Great War (1914-1918), led to the formation of the League of Nations in 1920. The Second World War (1939-1945) led to the founding of the United Nations Organization in October 1945. Africa played a significant role in both these wars. Africa however did not play such a significant role in the founding of their resulting two organizations. While the impact of the first War and its resulting organization on Africa was limited, the second War and its resulting organization have had a profound impact on Africa. The continent of Africa, too, has come to play a significant role in the second organization.

The different European powers had just completed their shameful scramble for Africa when the First World War broke out. During the war therefore, Africans were armed by their different colonial masters to fight their fellow Africans under the rule of other colonial powers. Those under British, French and Belgian colonialism were brought to fight the Germans and Africans occupied by them in German occupied African territories in Togo, Cameroon, Tanganyika (now Tanzania), Ruanda-Urundi (now Burundi and Rwanda), and German South West Africa (now Namibia); other Africans were recruited to fight for the Germans. This war was ended by the Treaty of Versailles and the formation of the League of Nations. Only two African countries from the continent —Ethiopia and Liberia— were members of this organization. Haiti, from diasporian Africa, was the third African country. Why was the African membership so limited in humankind's first experiment with global organization? What role, if any, did the African members of the League play or what treatment did they get? Why was such the case? The invasion of Ethiopia in 1935-6 by fascist Italy led to the collapse of the League. Why did Benito Mussolini decide to invade Ethiopia? What role did the League and its powerful members play?

The Second World War broke out in 1939 and became a contest between Hitler's Germany and its allies and other European powers, assembled around France, Britain and Russia. To use Mazrui's words, it was this war that played midwife to the United Nations Organization in 1945. On the other hand, the Second World War turned out to be a liberating force for Africa. As in the first War, Africans were armed by their different European masters to fight other Europeans. This time round however, with Germany knocked out of Africa since the end of the First World War, in addition to their military service in the different parts of the continent, Africans were brought in huge numbers to Europe or Asia to fight Germany and its allies. After he had fought alongside the white man to kill another white man and seen the white man being killed and/or shivering with fear and seeking comfort and assurance from the African soldier, the psychological barrier that had led many Africans to believe that the white man was invincible faded away. Colonialism is naturally contradictory. However, the fact that while Africans were labouring under the choking yoke of European colonialism at home they had just been brought by the same colonial powers to defend "their" freedom and save "them" from occupation by another European power was even more contradictory and baffling. This left none of the African soldiers that fought this war in any doubt that they also had every right to re-conquer their freedom. Soon after the War, African voices calling for freedom rose and the newly founded United Nations Organization served as a partner with Africa in achieving this.

Apart from the fact that the War played midwife to it, there were other factors that led to the creation of the United Nations. In other words, the United States that mobilised other nations to set up another global organization in replacement of the League of Nations had some special motives. Other nations that joined had theirs too. Both small and large, poor and rich, weak and powerful nations that joined the United Nations had their motives and expectations. What were these motives? What motivated other nations, especially those that were considered as big powers at the time, to accept this American idea? What interest did smaller nations such as Liberia have when they appreciated this idea? What explains the creation of two kinds of membership in the key body of the United Nations — permanent and non permanent? Why were only five nations given the permanent member status? Why did the choice for this status fall on China, France, Russia, the United Kingdom, and the United States? Why is it that no African country was considered for this? Is it because Africa played a limited role in the formation of the UN? Or is it because there was a certain perception of Africa on the part of the main actors of the "act of creation"? What bearing do these founding structures (of the UN) and perceptions (of Africa in world affairs) have on the current activities of the United Nations and/or its partnership with Africa?

In October 2005, the United Nations celebrated the sixtieth anniversary of its creation. Though there has been an avalanche of studies on the United Nations, only a few have dealt comprehensively with its relationship with Africa. In this book, I propose to fill this lacuna by providing a systematic and analytical assessment of Africa's relationship with the world body, from its foundation in 1945 to its sixtieth anniversary in 2005. The relationship of Africa —as of any other region of the world —with the United Nations has been of two kinds: a genuine partnership characterised by mutual respect and ending in success; and another relationship that has led to frustration and disappointment. It is to this that I turn after attempting to answer the questions raised above, and in so doing I raise many more questions and strive to answer them. My analyses of these issues rang from the United Nations Secretariat, based at headquarters in New York, to the numerous funds, programmes and specialised agencies linked to the UN and scattered around the world.

The role of the United Nations in African decolonization and the dismantling of the Apartheid system and the white minority regimes in Southern Africa is generally regarded as an example of genuine partnership between Africa and the world body. On the other hand, the performance of UN peace-keeping in Africa, especially in Somalia and Rwanda, is generally regarded as an area where the UN failed Africa. Social and economic development in Africa has also been one of the main terrains of Africa-UN partnership, from the creation in 1958 of the United Nations Economic Commission for Africa (ECA) based in Addis Ababa with a mandate to "foster regional integration and promote international cooperation for Africa's development," to more recent initiatives. These include the United Nations Action Plan for African Economic Recovery and Development, 1986-1990 (UNAPAERD), adopted by the UN General Assembly in 1986, and the United Nations New Agenda for the Development of Africa in the 1990s (UNNADAF), adopted in December 1991. The assessment of many observers of these economic initiatives is that they have failed to achieve their intended objectives. Why is there such a mixture of results? Is it because the UN employed different strategies in the different areas of partnership? Or is the explanation to be found with Africa adopting different approaches to the world body with regard to the different areas of partnership or actually different approaches to these areas of partnership?

Notwithstanding the apparent unfair distribution of employment opportunities in the UN system, there have been a number of Africans who have risen to leadership positions. Amadou-Mahtar M'Bow of Senegal was the first African to lead a full UN specialised agency, when he became Director-General of the United Nations Educational, Cultural, and Scientific Organization (UNESCO) in 1974. He served two full six-year terms, ending in 1987. Of the seven Secretaries-General of the United Nations during the period covered by this book, two came from Africa. The first of those was Boutros Boutros-Ghali of Egypt, who was elected UN Secretary-General in December 1991 and assumed his position in January the following year. Unlike all the previous Secretaries-General however, Boutros-Ghali was not re-elected for a second term, owing chiefly if not solely to American opposition. But the failure of his re-election bid did not mean the loss of the post to Africa. The Ghanaian Kofi Annan who succeeded him became the second African Secretary-General and was still serving his second five-year term at the end of 2005. There have also been a number of Africans who have occupied or were still occupying (as of the completion date of this book) high-level policy positions in the UN system.

The United Nations is an Inter-Governmental Organization (IGO). Thus, it has two kinds of personnel. On the one hand, it has accredited diplomats sent by their national governments to represent them at the UN and campaign for and/or defend their interests. These are in effect ambassadors of their countries to the UN and their salaries and service are a matter for their national governments. There are on the other hand those that are directly recruited by the UN or its specialised agencies or elected to occupy the different leadership positions at the UN Secretariat or at the headquarters of the specialised agencies. These are the staff members of the UN or its specialised agencies and are paid by them. The loyalty of these staff members, as in any IGO, is expected to be to the organization and not to their home governments. It is however true that depending on the support the head of an IGO gets, he or she may be able, to a large extent, to influence the attention given by the concerned organization to its different priority issues or to make a particular issue a priority one. I will thus look at some of these African civil servants at the global level and their professional itineraries. I will enquire into their ability to defend Africa's interests at the institutions they have led, are leading or work for at a decision-making level. What can they do for Africa? If they can indeed do something, what have they done? If they have done something, has this meant a contribution to the fortunes of Africa from the world body? If not, what are the factors that can explain this?

Consisting of five chapters, the book begins by looking at the formation of the United Nations and the theoretical underpinnings of this "act of creation." This chapter looks at the motives and expectations of its different stakeholders at the time of its formation, and traces its origins to its predecessor —the League of Nations. It also looks at the structure of the world body and tries to explain why this came about and what impact this has on Africa's relationship with the UN. Chapter two looks at the areas of Africa-

UN partnership that are generally regarded as fruitful to Africa. The alliance of the world body with Africa, or Africa's use of the world body in its process of decolonization and struggle against white minority regimes in Southern Africa are given here as examples.

Chapter three ponders over the areas of Africa-UN relations that are generally assessed as a failure. The following chapter is devoted to Africans in the UN system: their itineraries and their service to Africa while in their positions. The concluding chapter begins by highlighting the world's need for the United Nations and its interest in preserving it and working to making it more effective. Acknowledging the desperate need for reform of the world body, the chapter also looks at this issue as it relates to Africa. Here I posit that Africa may have more interest in focusing its calls for UN reform on the many issues of big powers' abuse or monopoly of the world body that are nonetheless readily negotiable, rather than the controversial issue of Security Council expansion or the veto power —unfair and autocratic as the present set-up may be. I then look at the future of Africa-UN relations in the twenty-first century. I conclude that Africa's relationship with the world body has mainly worked to the advantage of the continent —and could still work better— where and when Africa sees this relationship in terms of complementary partnership instead of dependency.

Chapter 1

Conceptualising International Organizations:
An Overview of Early UN-Africa Relations

The United Nations shall establish under its authority an international
trusteeship system for the administration and supervision of such territories
as may be placed thereunder by subsequent individual agreements. These
territories are hereinafter referred to as trust territories.
—United Nations Charter

This chapter looks at the United Nations Organization (UN), its origins and the maze of its operational structures. It will begin by putting the process of its formation in various theoretical perspectives, according to the different schools of thought of International Relations. In this, the focus will be on the type of institution it is, and why such an institution, somewhat representing a world government, was created. This clearly entails looking at the motives and expectations of its different stakeholders at the time of its formation. Since it was preceded by another global institution with more or less the same objectives, the chapter will also ponder over the League of Nations, the predecessor of the United Nations. What role, if any, did Africa play in these processes? Or what place was it given by the actors of these processes? What bearing do these founding structures (of the League and the UN) and perceptions (of Africa in world affairs) have on the current activities of the United Nations and/or its partnership with Africa?

The Formation of the UN in Theoretical Perspective

The United Nations Organization (UN) is in International Relations theories generally studied under "international regimes," or "international institutions." To begin with, it should be noted that the study of international regimes is plagued by a myriad of

21

definitional issues and a significant lack of conceptual clarity. Most "international regime" theorists look at it from an economic rather than a political perspective. The definition of "international regimes" that has become almost proverbial is the definition offered by Stephen Krasner, who is generally thought of as a pioneering author on this issue. He defines "international regimes" as "sets of implicit or explicit principles, norms, rules, and decision-making procedures around which actors' expectations converge in a given area of international relations."[1] To Robert Keohane and Joseph Nye, regimes are "sets of governing arrangements." To those authors, those arrangements include "networks of rules, norms, and procedures that regularize behaviour and control its effects."[2]

As Susan Strange notes in the same volume edited by Krasner, the departing point of these confusions is the fact that authors mean different things when they use the concept of "international regime."[3] Clearly, if we limit ourselves to these two definitions and the like, we will risk being left with a vague understanding of the subject matter. Perhaps the definition provided by Young brings us a step closer to this understanding. In his article reviewing three books dealing with the concept, including Krasner's edited volume, Young contends that "international regimes are social institutions." His aim here is to differentiate between "international regimes" or "social institutions" and "organizations." Thus, he defines international regimes/social institutions as "practices composed of recognized roles coupled with sets of rules or conventions governing relations among the occupants of these roles." As for "organizations," he defines them as "physical entities possessing offices, personnel, equipment, budgets, and so forth."[4] Young's definition of what he calls "social institutions" is not very much different from the definition given by Krasner and Keohane and Nye. The novelty in his definition seems to be the differentiation between "regime" and "organization."

The author gives the International Monetary Fund (IMF) and the World Bank as examples of "organizations." He gives the Bretton Woods system, which gave birth to these two organizations, as an example of an "international institution" or "regime."[5] From this exercise, and to use Bull's brilliant conceptualisation of "rules," we can point at "regimes" as sets of rules that are made, communicated, interpreted, and administered by "organizations."[6] I have a problem however with Young's equation of "international institutions" with "regimes" rather than with "organizations." Would he and hence the reader not have been better off putting "international institutions" with "organizations" rather than with "regimes?" Would he insist that the UN for example is only an international organization and not an international institution? This would clearly defy common use of the term and not on the basis of any plausible argument. We shall thus, in this book, follow the latter use; not because it is common, but because it seems right and more logical.

We shall define "international institutions," which I equate with "international organizations" as synonyms, but differentiate from "international regimes," as physical entities possessing permanent offices, budget, personnel, and so forth and whose role is to communicate, interpret and administer a set of well defined rules and regulations for the shared benefit of all actors concerned. The UN, IMF, World Bank and the like are thus organizations/institutions and their respective treaties or charters are regimes whose interpretation, communication and administration amongst their members constitute their main role and duty. To make this clearer, let us take the example of the United Nations. The Charter of the institution that is the UN is a set of rules and regulations by which the UN (with its offices, budget, personnel and so on) works in order to achieve its main purpose of preserving and maintaining international peace and security.

Inasmuch as actors that come together to form organizations or institutions are different, there are different types of organizations with regard to the nature of their members or actors. There are organizations whose members or actors are individuals. If such organizations are based within the boundaries of a single country, they are generally described as "civil society groups" or "non-governmental organizations" (NGO), as opposed to government bodies. If a civil society group is not country-bound, either by its offices or activities, such organizations are generally described as "international non-governmental organizations." Such an NGO with a global reach tends to be a network of national NGOs either created by it or forming the basis of its creation. Organizations such as Amnesty International and Human Rights Watch are international NGOs. Nonetheless, if actors forming the organization are sovereign states or governments, such an organization is described as an "inter-governmental organization;" that it is an organization whose members are governments. Organizations such as the UN, the African Union (AU), the Association of South-East Asian Nations (ASEAN) or the Organization of the Islamic Conference (OIC) are examples of this.

While the above conceptual discussion about "international regimes" may seem rather philosophical than empirical, the exercise of defining the UN by the nature of its members or actors is quite directly connected to our understanding of its work, especially as it relates to Africa. The work of an inter-governmental organization (IGO), such as the UN, on an issue of concern to it, the quality of this work and its speed, depend to a large extent on the commitment and willingness of its members, which is also based on their self-defined interests, as we will see later. By understanding this, one would know for example where to put the blame in a perceived failure of a project of an IGO. It means that some members of an IGO —on the basis of their reading of its principles and charter— may expect it to do something and a good number of members call for that, but a powerful minority of its members decide otherwise and their decision prevails. In such a case, because the majority of the concerned IGO's members failed to call the rebellious minority to order and consequently either followed or kept quiet about the violation of their own principles and rules, the IGO as a whole, albeit rather unfairly, may be blamed for the failure. Likewise, if a majority of members of an IGO favours something in accordance with its principles and rules and succeeds in imposing that on a rebellious minority, the credit may also go to the IGO as a whole and all the members will generally share the credit, including the rebels or obstructionists.

It is on the basis of this that I consider, for example, the role of the United Nations in combating Apartheid and white minority regimes in Southern Africa as a success and credit the whole of the world body for it and consider it as an example of successful Africa-UN partnership. This is despite the fact that there were some members of the UN, indeed powerful members, whose action and behaviour often ran on different lines from those of the world body. Nonetheless, I credit the whole institution for it because the majority worked for it and, with their collective endeavour, managed to compel the obstructionists to play by the rules of the Organization and respect its principles and ideals (see *Chapter 2*). Likewise, I consider the UN's role in the genocide in Rwanda and the civil war in Somalia as a failure on the part of the world body because albeit there were some members of the Organization that reminded or attempted to remind others of their duty under the Charter, the obstructionists, although few, nonetheless succeeded in preventing the UN from doing its job and the conformists failed to compel them to order. I thus consider this an area where the UN — although this judgment is unfair on those states that urged proper action— failed and disappointed Africa (see *Chapter 3*).

This leads us to another pertinent question about the formation of international institutions such as the UN: Why are international institutions formed? As will be further elaborated later, there were fifty-one countries (i. e. sovereign states) that converged on San Francisco in April 1945 to found the United Nations Organization. What on earth urged these states to commit themselves to setting up such an enterprise? What were their motives? What were their expectations? How does this help us understand Africa's relationship with the UN in the first sixty years of the latter's existence?

Here, though some authors tend to reduce the debate and focus it between only two broad schools of thought,[7] virtually every theoretical school in international relations has had a word in explaining some aspect of international institutions.[8] To remain however within the purview of the questions posed above and in order not to burden the reader with a stack of theories more than he/she needs, we shall adopt here the former view and thus limit ourselves to two main schools: realism and liberal institutionalism.

Both these two schools depart from the same premise, that international institutions are an important feature of contemporary international system. They also agree that states are rational actors when committing themselves to creating international institutions as they facilitate cooperation between their members. Differences however emerge in their explanation of why states commit themselves to creating institutions. Realists contend that the anarchical nature of the international system does not encourage states to commit themselves to institution-building. They will only do this if their relative gains —their advantageous position vis-à-vis other states in the proposed institution— are assured. They argue that states' concerns about relative gains prevent them from intensive cooperation. This means that even if states did put substantial weight on such relative-gains concerns, the circumstances under which they would greatly inhibit cooperation are quite limited.[9]

To the liberal-institutionalists, states commit themselves to creating international institutions out of their realisation that they have an interest in institutions in that institutions help them overcome problems of collective action, high transaction costs and information deficits. They see their benefit in terms of absolute gains; that is what they expect to gain from their adherence to the institution proposed and not how they will be better off compared to others, which is what realists think is important to states. As a result of this, liberal-institutionalists argue, states, when deciding whether to cooperate in the formation of an organization or once the organization is created, evaluate what is in it for them, rather than how they will come out relative to others. Their main concern is therefore whether they will get the best deal possible. In other words, as Keohane put it, states deliberately enter into institutional arrangements through some sort of bargaining process so long as the marginal benefits of doing so outweigh the marginal costs.[10]

Looking at the United Nations and its history over the past sixty years, one may understand, through these theories, why some states tend to behave in a certain way in certain circumstances within the world body. The United States was the main ideological and financial sponsor of the project of the United Nations in 1945 and the years leading up to it. Looking at the composition of the Security Council, one may be tempted to equate the efforts of other permanent members, especially the Europeans, with those of the US to explain how they too acquired this status. But as Fassbender argues, although in a different context, without the United States, the Western European states, economically and militarily exhausted by the Second World War and thus greatly politically weakened, not only would not have been able to establish a world organization, but probably would not have even tried it.[11] The same goes for the Soviet Union, whose concerns were more about internal issues and the consolidation of the Soviet empire in Eastern Europe than anything else. What the US did therefore in the formation of the UN is what is commonly referred to, especially in the literature of international political economy, as the theory of hegemonic stability —that is, a situation where a powerful state with the necessary resources supports the formation of an institution and encourages or compels others to join it even if it has to bail some members out because they cannot afford the full cost of maintaining their membership.

A hegemon does this for two reasons. On the one hand, it does it to maintain a certain stability in the system by regulating it through the proposed regime or institution, without which its hegemonic status may not have any noticeable prestige or meaning. On the other hand, it commits itself in this way in order to advance its own self-defined interests. For this, the hegemon is ready to shoulder a relatively big responsibility, but also expects a privileged role in the concerned institution. From this, one can understand why the United States and other great powers insisted at the time of the formation of the UN on having the privilege of not only permanent membership in the key body of the UN (i. e. the Security Council), but also the power to stop any proposed decision of the world body that might not be to their liking (i. e. the veto power). This is not to deny however that it was the Soviets that first suggested the notion of veto power.

While this is clear in the case of the US as it was the main sponsor and thus the hegemon —speaking of leadership—, the granting of permanent membership and veto power to another four countries may need further explanation. This can be better explained by the fact that the US as the hegemon wanted not only a privileged status in the UN but also a status that was legitimised in the eyes of other great powers —albeit powers not as powerful as it was. The concept of "hegemony" is in fact void of any meaning if it does not have legitimacy; that is when others do not recognise it. Without such legitimacy, the US' hegemonic status would have been void of any meaning. Thus, it may have been able to set up the new organization but perhaps without some important powers, such as the USSR, especially when the latter became a power almost comparable to the US in the early 1950s. And this would not have been good for the organization. The Cold War constituted a serious impeding factor in good relations between the two superpowers despite the fact that both were members of the UN. One could thus imagine how terrible it would have been had the UN not been a meeting venue for them to negotiate and dialogue on common issues.

For this —despite differences of principle— the US could not afford to ignore the Soviets if it truly wanted the proposed organization to be a global one whose legitimacy was recognised by all states. In fact the organization has worked better, it must be stressed, as an effective instrument for advancing and/or protecting American capitalist interests around the world. As will be seen later, the Atlantic Charter adopted by the British Prime Minister, Winston Churchill, and the American president, Franklin D. Roosevelt during the Second World War is regarded as one of the founding documents that inspired the creation of the United Nations. For this reason, it would have been hard to see the United Nations founded without any privileged position for London so long as such privilege was available. But the Britain of 1945 with its vast colonial empire still intact, despite its economic and military weakness because of the war, was still a big power. Moreover, given that the US was the main sponsor of the new organization and had realised the necessity to invite the Soviets and give them a privileged position notwithstanding their mutual mistrust, inviting other powerful countries sharing its own political principles was a strategic necessity.

Assured of the unconditional loyalty of the majority of Latin American states that would also be members of the new organization, with the big power club of the organization thus composed, the US was assured of using the UN for its hegemonic interests. However, with the Soviet call for veto power, which was not necessary for the US to advance its hegemonic interests given the aforementioned setting of the proposed organization, the Americans sought to maximise their chances for American dominance. It was here that the China card was played by the

Americans. In 1945 China was under the Nationalist government of Chiang Kai-shek, and under that government allied to Washington China obtained a Security Council seat with veto power. But after the communist victory in China in 1949, the Nationalists who had fled to Formosa or Taiwan still held that seat, and not the effective government of China, the communist one in Beijing. Thus by allowing the pro-American venal and demoralized regime, as Gowan described it, in Taiwan to occupy the seat of China in the Security Council as opposed to Communist China, the Americans not only gave the Council a fake regional balance but also, and most importantly, ensured their dominance within the Council and, thus, over the whole organization. With the highly probable prospect of London's financial dependence on the United States for some years to come, this composition of the Council made the Soviet Union the only member that could potentially challenge the US.[12]

How to explain France's invitation on board? Gowan argues that it was by the insistence of Churchill that this was made possible and that Churchill, in insisting on this, was looking for an ally in the Council to shield Britain from outright American dominance.[13] One could substantiate this observation by the fact that France did not contribute to any preliminary effort for the creation of the UN, owing mainly to the long delay in the Roosevelt administration's recognition of de Gaulle's government during the war. France was not present in Washington for the "Declaration by the United Nations" (January 1942), or at the Moscow (October 1943) or Teheran (December 1943) conferences, though the countries that were to be the other four permanent members took part in one or more of these. Nor was France present at the Dumbarton Oaks conference (August-October 1944). France was not even a sponsor of the invitations for the San Francisco conference of April 1945.[14]

But one could also find another explanation for France's invitation by Britain and its acceptance, albeit grudgingly and lately, by Roosevelt. Both France and Britain had been seriously weakened by the war. The effect on France was more significant than on Britain because France had to endure heavy fighting on its own soil, which was not the case for Britain. Despite this, Britain knew that the gap between it and France was not that wide and that France, with its vast African empire, could catch up with it. Because of this and the history of rivalry between the two nations, Britain knew that France would contest, sooner or later, its privileged status if it were not offered one. France was a Western country with a big colonial empire and its contesting of Britain's privileged status would have affected the stability of this deal or expose it to constant and wider contestation by other members. One can clearly see such a development today in the repeated calls by countries such as Japan and Germany to have this setting reformed; both countries were considered in 1945 as "enemy states" and were not invited at San Francisco, but Japan and Germany of the twenty-first century are not the Japan and Germany of 1945. As a Western European capitalist country, France would be by an ally to both Britain and the US. And this proved very rewarding during the Cold War.

This is how the hegemonic theory helps us explain the composition of the Security Council. The logic behind this notion of privilege was that it was essential that there should be unanimity and consensus between the great powers. And in order to have that there had to be machinery and provision in the Charter that ensured it; otherwise, the UN would not last, as its predecessor the League of Nations did not last. The "big five" would then devote their will and power unitedly to the maintenance of international peace and security on behalf of, and in the interests of, all the UN family.

Thus, the US, in alliance with other big powers, ensured their privileged status within the UN. Amongst this club of big powers however, the same theories of institution-building would come to play. The motives of the US would always be to ensure relative gains, while others would have been motivated by absolute gains.

Other members of the UN, the remaining 46 countries that were present at San Francisco and signed the UN Charter, agreed with these arrangements, albeit grudgingly in some cases, because they had realised that despite this unfair and autocratic deal, they were not losing either. As they were relatively weak and poor —in the case of some very weak and terribly poor— an anarchic and lawless world order was not to their advantage. The promises of the new institution to guarantee and protect individual states' sovereignty was big a gain for a state in their situation, albeit this promise, as it turned out, was to be kept only if it was in the interest of the big powers. Thus while giving the permanent membership and veto privilege to the big powers was not fair to them, they nonetheless had secured a point. From here, liberal-institutionalists provide the better explanation. From this discussion, one could rightly argue that in the United Nations structure, the autocratic composition of the Security Council is more in tune with realist explanations, while the General Assembly is better analysed from a liberal-institutionalist approach.

Part of the arguments presented above may suggest that the United Nations, like any other international institution for that matter, reflects the interests of its powerful members. Indeed, and this leads to another question: why then do hegemonic powers so often undermine such institutions, as one could argue in the case of the US within the UN? Bruce Cronin attempts to answer this question in a thought-provoking essay. Cronin starts from the premise that there is a contradiction between the propensity for a powerful state to break rules in promoting or defending its self-defined interests and its desire to maintain long-term systemic stability through the institution in question at a minimal cost. To explain this apparent contradiction, he contends:

> On the one hand, as the strongest of the great powers, hegemons possess the capabilities and will to act unilaterally in pursuing their own interests. This raises expectations among domestic political actors and state officials that the government will pursue its own course when its interests are at stake. On the other hand, in their role as global or regional leaders, hegemons also have an interest in maintaining an international or regional order in which law and multilateral institutions provide for a set of stable expectations and constrains. [. . .] However, having socialized the key states into accepting the assumptions and norms underlying the order, the hegemon is placed in a position where it must follow the rules and institutions it had helped to establish, even when it is not in its interests to do so. To do otherwise, will undermine the very order it created.[15]

In reality, what Cronin's explanation shows, perhaps unconsciously on his part, is the rivalry between realist and liberal-institutionalist forces within a hegemonic country and their impact on that country's foreign policy, especially towards international institutions. The author's reference to "domestic political actors and state officials" cannot be used to imply that all domestic actors in a hegemonic or any other country believe that their country, however powerful and/or rich it may be, ought to ignore its international obligations whenever these obligations conflict with its self-defined narrow interests. The author cannot argue that there are not "domestic political actors" who oppose their government if it chooses to go down such a route and breach its international obligations. This is because these other forces recognise that their interest and that of their country may well be in the latter respecting its international obligations even if some segments of their society think otherwise. These are the liberals, and governments listen to them and find themselves acting in the way the second clause of Cronin's argument explains. The group he referred to in the first clause are those that follow the concepts of power as advocated by realists.

Perhaps a more plausible answer to the question posed above is to be found in Gowan's analysis of what he calls the "fundamental insight" hit by the Roosevelt administration during the formation of the UN. Gowan suggests that the American negotiators of the UN realised that international institutions could be constructed to face simultaneously in two radically different directions: mass popular politics and power or hegemonic politics. As regards the face turned in the direction of "mass popular politics," he explains this to be the "ethical face, offering promise for a better world." It is strikingly accurate to observe that each time the US has turned to the General Assembly for a resolution, it has generally done so on issues that could be defended —even hypocritically— by ethical arguments. Examples of this include the "Uniting for Peace" resolution of 1950 to authorise use of force in Korea. However, when an issue cannot be morally defended, the US has often had recourse to power politics or ignore the UN altogether, branding it as "irrelevant," as we saw in 2003 when George W. Bush invaded Iraq without UN approval.[16]

Big powers stay in line and respect the rules and principles of the UN if this does not contradict in any direct way their self-defined interests. On such issues, they cooperate fully with other members of the Organization. Here, the liberals are triumphant.

However, if they perceive staying in line as incompatible with their "interests," they do not hesitate to vindicate the realists and step out of the line. The frequency and boldness of such breaches depend however on the status of the state concerned. Those with real international power, (i. e. the US and Russia before the collapse of the Soviet Union) seldom pay much attention to the rules; for them, rather than international law being the framework which controls what they may do, it is their actions which shape the law.[17]

An Imperial Club or a League of Nations?

As the practice of African enslavement —which had started in the late fifteenth century and consisted of kidnapping Africans and taking them in inhuman conditions to the Americas where they were sold as objects and used for farming— was coming to an end, legitimate trading connections began to develop between Africans and Europeans, especially in the coastal areas of Africa. Soon this changed and the Europeans began looking, once again, at Africans as peoples better in servitude than in equal partnership. Aided by the advantage of firearms, they began a violent scramble for Africa that ended with the effective occupation of the continent.

Between 1876 and 1880, it became clear that the European powers, especially Britain, France, Germany and Portugal as well as "little" Belgium were now committed to shifting their hitherto peaceful residence for trading purposes to colonial expansion and the establishment of formal control in Africa. The time had come for the partition and consolidation of control over Africa. The Berlin Conference from November 1884 to February 1885 formalised this. Despite fierce African resistance,[18] by the beginning of the First World War in 1914, almost all of Africa, save Liberia and Ethiopia,[19] had effectively been occupied by the different European powers.[20]

The war was a world-wide war because Africans together with all other colonial peoples, especially in Asia, were affected by this essentially European war in one way or the other. It was the end of the war in 1918 that offered the opportunity to create the League of Nations, which formally came into existence on 10 January 1920 and had headquarters at Geneva in Switzerland. The First World War had been started by Germany which occupied a part of France in

33

the course of the war. Britain, France, Belgium and other western European countries were allies against Germany and its supporters. The Americans joined the War in 1917 on the side of the Allies which gave the latter a big boost given the emerging powerful status of the United States at the time. However, owing to the idealistic convictions of the then American president, Woodrow Wilson, and his apparent belief in peace, together with the prospect of victory of his chosen side, he provided his European allies with a set of principles which he intended should be the guiding principles of the subsequent peace treaty. These principles were included in what later became known as Wilson's "Fourteen Points."

It would seem that the American president believed that the creation of an international organization, based on the idea of "collective security" could prevent the recurrence of any new wars between the different European nations or be used to easily contain it and put an end to it. Thus, the last point of his document suggested the formation of a general association of nations to be formed to afford mutual guarantees of political independence and territorial integrity of all states. The new body was to have a permanent structure and a codified covenant. It is because of this that many authors tend to consider the League of Nations as Wilson's brainchild, albeit the United States did not adhere to the League of Nations as Congress rejected it. But the new organization was an Anglo-French affair more than anything else.

One thing that the League of Nations was inseparable from was the famous Treaty of Versailles, the peace treaty that the victors of the First World War adopted to codify their post-war relations. The link between the two was such that the Covenant of the League constituted the first of sixteen sections or chapters of the Versailles Treaty singed on 28 June 1919. The Treaty consists of a total of 440 articles and the first 26 articles (first section) are entitled: "The Covenant of the League of Nations." The second section that follows this deals with the "Boundaries of Germany" which is contained in just four articles (27-30).

As far as the League's relations with Africa are concerned, two main points may be retained. One point is the re-scrambling of the African territories that had been occupied by Germany and their distribution, under what the League's Covenant called the "mandate system," amongst the other colonial powers that had triumphed in the war or their allies. The other point concerned the perception and attitudes of the colonial powers that were members of the League towards the two independent and sovereign African territories at the time —Ethiopia and Liberia.

Africa and the League's Mandates System

In his theorisation of European imperialism, G. N. Sanderson discusses a number of theories. One of these theories was the one called "Social Darwinism", which sought to justify European colonialism, especially in Africa, on the grounds of the illusory assumption of the colonial strategists that Africans and other colonial peoples were backward peoples, immature in their thinking and uncivilised in their modes of life. They were described or thought of as "primitive nations." This was even the explicit assumption of the French and Belgian *mission civilisatrice*.[21] Looking at the conceptual and ideological foundations of the "mandates system" of the League of Nations, the only conclusion one may make is that it was mainly based on this illusory assumption of white supremacy.

In the Versailles Treaty, the mandates system is dealt with by two sections and ten articles in all. These are Article 22 of the Covenant of the League of Nations (first section), and Articles 119-127 of section IV of the Treaty, which deals with "German Rights and Interests Outside Germany." Before the defeat of Germany in the First World War, there were a number of African territories occupied by Germany. These were Togo (in West Africa), Cameroon or Kamerun as the Germans called it (in Central Africa), Ruanda (now Rwanda), Urundi (now Burundi) and Tanganyika (now part of the present-day Tanzania in East Africa), and German South West Africa (now Namibia in Southern Africa).

Article 119 of the Versailles Treaty forced defeated Germany to renounce "in favour of the Principal Allies and Associated Powers all her rights and titles over her overseas possessions." By this, Germany was obliged to renounce all rights, titles and privileges whatever in or over territory which belonged to it outside Germany in Africa or in the Asian-Pacific islands in favour of the victorious powers, namely Britain, France and Belgium, and their allies, namely the Union of South Africa and Australia (nominally on behalf of the British Imperial Crown) amongst other powers.

These territories formally occupied by Germany were to be put under the mandate of the different victorious nations and their allies. The concept of the mandates system meant, according to Article 22 of the League's Covenant, the administration of the conquered German colonies "inhabited by peoples *not yet able to stand by themselves* under the strenuous conditions of the modern world" by the victors of the First World War. These imperial nations were considered, or rather considered themselves, as they were the drafters of the Covenant, as "advanced nations who, by reason of their resources, their experience or their geographical position can best undertake this responsibility ... on behalf of the League." The administration of these territories was thus considered as a "sacred trust of civilisation," clearly in the same way as the colonial nations had claimed during their scramble for Africa a few decades back.

The imperialistic ethos (based on the classical superior attitude of colonial powers to the colonial peoples, especially Africans) of the League's mandates system could also be observed in the declarations of the different delegates of the colonial powers to its Assembly. For example, Arthur James Balfour, a former British Conservative Prime Minister (1902-1905) and the British Permanent Representative to the League, who was also one of the die-hard defenders of the British Empire, made a speech to the first meeting of the Assembly of the League of Nations in 1920. In that speech, he said amongst other things:

> The great object which we must have in view is to bring all these Colonial Powers into a common spirit of cooperation for the benefit of races which are not, and perhaps cannot in the course of any historic future that we can look forward to, be put on an equality with those whose duty and pride it ought to be to guide them as far as possible on the upward path.[22]

The League, through its Permanent Mandates Commission (PMC), classified the territories that were formerly occupied by Germany and the Ottoman Empire into three alphabetically labelled categories according to European definitions of "development" and "progress." While the various Arab provinces that were part of the

Ottoman (also known rather subjectively as Turkish) Empire were classified as "A" territories, the concerned African territories were put under the lower "B" and "C" categories. The class "A" territories were considered as having reached a stage of development where their existence as independent nations could be "provisionally recognized subject to the rendering of administrative advice and assistance by a Mandatory [European power] until such time as they are able to stand alone."

Again, one could argue that this provision was somehow influenced by the set of principles laid down by the American President in his "Fourteen Points." This was actually the provision of point XII of his Declaration.[23] Some respected authors such as Callahan and Coogan contend that the American President had an "anti-imperialist" view vis-à-vis the post-war settlement, as he was fiercely opposed to any straightforward annexation of "conquered German territories" in Africa by the European powers. They argue that Wilson's view was to put the African territories directly under the mandate of the League of Nations.[24] It does nonetheless seem that, even from his speech of 8 January 1918 in which his "Fourteen Points" were contained, Wilson never was greatly concerned about African territories under European occupation even when he talked about "imperialism," at least not as much as he did about European territories under German occupation or other territories such as the aforementioned Arab provinces. It is clearly obvious from this speech of January 1918 that whenever Wilson spoke of "imperialism," his reference was only to German occupation.

This argument can be substantiated by a close look at his speech and the territories he referred to in his "Fourteen Points." These were clearly limited, and those authors cited will agree with this, to the Russian territory (Point VI), Belgium (Point VII), all French territory (Point VIII), the peoples of Austria-Hungary "whose place among the nations we wish to see safeguarded and assured" (Point X), Rumania, Serbia and Montenegro (Point XI), the Turkish portion of the Ottoman Empire (Point XII), and "an independent Polish state" (Point XIII). There is no mention whatsoever of any African territory, either occupied by the victorious European nations or formerly occupied by the defeated Germany. And even if it were to be admitted that his "anti-imperial" stance extended to Africa by rejecting initial European ideas to annex these African territories to their colonies, his proposal to put those African territories under the direct supervision of the League suggests that he shared the European perception of African peoples as "backward races" whose administration needed to be entrusted in "advanced nations until they could stand by themselves." After all, African-Americans were still struggling for their basic rights in his country. In addition, Wilson sent Marines to occupy Haiti in 1915 and for 19 years, only withdrawing from the country in 1934 and having left a puppet government there.[25]

In any case, the African territories formerly occupied by Germany were classified under categories "B" and "C." German South West Africa (Namibia) was considered a "C" territory and put under the direct administration of the Union of South Africa, to be administered "under the laws of the Mandatory as integral portions of its territory." Togo, Cameroon and the East African territories formerly occupied by Germany were put under category "B." The first two were each divided into two parts, between France and Britain, with France obtaining the bulk of Cameroon and half of Togo. In East Africa, while the territory of Tanganyika put under British trusteeship, Urundi and Ruanda were put under Belgian administration. While it is fair to acknowledge that there seemed to be some differences in the early years of the mandates system between their administration and that of what the European powers called "colonies," with the inhabitants of the mandated territories being relatively better treated, the fact remains that by taking such an approach towards Africa, the League of Nations acted mainly as an imperial club as far as Africa is concerned.

True, the mandates system laid down some principles and guidelines by which the mandatory powers had to abide in their administration of the mandated territories, albeit such guidelines were different from a territory to another, based on the category under which it was put by the PMC. In any event, the mandatory powers were prohibited, under Article 22 of the League's Covenant, from subjecting the inhabitants of their administered territories to certain "abuses" such as enslavement, and obliged to protect them from arms and liquor traffic, forced labour and conscription for military service "other than police purposes and the defence of the territory." The mandatory powers were asked to submit a periodic report to the PMC to measure their observance of these principles.

The only exception to these requirements in Africa was the relationship between the Union of South Africa and Namibia, as the latter was to be governed according to the laws of the mandatory power. This meant racial discrimination against the indigenous people by the white minority regime in Pretoria. And, as will be seen later (see *Chapter 2*), the relationship between these two entities became a major source of controversy in international relations after the end of the Second World War and the replacement of the League with the United Nations in 1945. But even in the case of Namibia and those territories in its category, the mandatory power was asked to look after the interests of the indigenous population.

This notwithstanding, it must be noted that of all the guidelines and rules governing the mandates system, the most observed rules seem to have been the ones concerning freedom of movement in the mandated territories and the right of nationals of all member states of the League of Nations. This was certainly because there were some other European countries that insisted on this since it had been included in the texts regulating the system. This was particularly the case of Italy, whose officials did not quite appreciate the way the former German territories were distributed, and Germany, after its admittance to the League in September 1926. This was not a surprise given Germany's enduring colonial grievances as the whole system concerned the territories formerly occupied by Germany or Turkey and confiscated by the Allied Powers by virtue of the Versailles Treaty, refused to return to her.

Apart from this, all the other guidelines seem to have been more in theory than in practice —doubtless because the colonial powers were themselves both the players and the referees in the mandates game. The periodic reports that were sent to the PMC were drafted by the colonial officers of the mandatory power and their findings were taken at face value. The PMC itself was mainly composed of people who had worked in the colonial administration of their respective countries. As Callahan notes for example, seven of the eleven members of the PMC in 1929 were nationals of colonizing or mandatory states, but only three were from states without overseas empires. The Chairman himself was Alberto

Theodoli, Italy's former Under-Secretary of state for the colonies.[26] This being the case, it does not come as a surprise that whenever Africans petitioned the League about infringements by the mandatory power of their rights under the texts supposedly governing the mandates system, the PMC rejected their complaints.

For example, the Duala people of Cameroon counted a good number of educated individuals amongst them in the period between the two world wars. Aware of what was going on in world affairs and determined to defend their dignity and regain their sovereignty, the Duala people oftentimes addressed petitions to the League of Nations throughout the 1920s. In these petitions, they demanded the return of their lands seized by the Germans in 1914 and then retained by the French mandate government. They accused the French colonial officers of abuses, such as torture and forced labour, and other serious breaches of the mandates system.

They implied the rightful existence of a sovereign Cameroon Kingdom that was able to govern the people of Cameroon without need of any "tutelage" of outside powers. After all, they had finely governed themselves, as had many other African peoples, well before their territories were invaded by the Germans. This clearly and rightly flew in the face of the conceptual foundations of the mandates system itself. Thus, because the dispute was at this stage between the Duala people and the French colonial administration, the League's PMC accepted France's public explanations that all land transactions had been legal and that the petitioners were either "unrepresentative" or "victims of self-serving outsiders" and therefore should not be taken seriously.[27]

Such was the relationship, in a nutshell, between the League of Nations and Africa on the issue of African territories formerly occupied by Germany. The other characteristic of this relationship was to be found in the perception of European members of the League of the independent African states that were also members of the League. The cat-and-mouse relationship ended with the invasion of Ethiopia by the fascist dictator of Italy in 1935.

Liberia and Ethiopia: Two Independent African States in the League of Nations

Of the 42 founding countries of the League of Nations (i.e. those that were members as of 10 January 1920, the date on which the League officially came into existence), Liberia was the only independent country from continental Africa. With Haiti from Diasporian Africa, one could argue that Africa was represented only by two countries. The presence of the Union of South Africa as from this date does not count here for obvious reasons. Other African countries later joined the league in different categories. First to join was Ethiopia on 23 September 1923 despite the opposition of some European countries, and Britain in particular.[28] Egypt joined in 1937 but it was still under effective British domination. In reality thus, only Liberia and Ethiopia came from continental Africa and it is their relationship with the League that constitutes the thrust of these lines.

The debate in the European countries surrounding the two independent African states at the time reveals much about Africa's complicated relationship with the League of Nations as well as the European conceptions of race and civilisation and thus of Africans in this period. Whilst Liberia survived the myriad European attempts to extend the colonial rule over it under the League's mandates system, if not through pure annexation, Ethiopia succumbed to the European colonial ambitions over it, when Italy's ambition was achieved by the fascist regime.

Liberia was founded in 1847 by freed Africans who had been enslaved and brought to America and Europe during the so-called slave trade, or their descendants, as well as some who were intercepted at sea on their way to the Americas after the abolition of the practice of enslavement. These were added to the indigenous African populations that were already in Liberia and had welcomed them. The erstwhile-enslaved Liberians became known as the Americo-Liberians or Congos, as ordinary Liberians called them. Astonishingly enough, having suffered all kinds of racial discrimination in America and having been warmly welcomed by their African cousins who had considered them as their kin that had been forcibly and illegally taken away from them, the Congos established an Apartheid-like rule over the indigenous people. They described them as "hinterlanders" and "countrymen." They formed the True Whig Party that ruled the country from 1878 until its overthrow in a brutal coup d'état in 1980.

Under this corrupt and nepotistic oligarchy, indigenous people were regarded as "uncivilised" and unworthy of full civic rights, until they had assimilated what they regarded as civilised values. These could be summed up as professing Christianity, being literate in English language and having an American pedigree. Those people from the "hinterland" who did acquire these so-called civilized values still had a lower status.[29] In 1926, an American company called the Firestone Tire and Rubber Co. lent Liberia US$ 5 million in exchange for a concession of about one million acres of land and other exclusive privileges that gave the company a great influence in the country. Indigenous workers that were recruited to work for this company worked in conditions that amounted to pure forced labour, as it was practised in the neighbouring European colonies, especially French ones. This was the humiliating paradox in the Liberian case for an African observer. Here was an independent African state ruled by Africans expected to voice against maltreatment of Africans in territories occupied by European colonialists, yet acted as pure imperialists against a huge chunk of their brethren.

Being a founding member of the League theoretically shielded Liberia from outright invasion and annexation. There were calls in the West for Liberia to be put under the League's mandate, possibly under Germany or Italy or even the US, albeit the United States' Congress had refused to allow the country to join the League despite the efforts of its president, as mentioned above. These suggestions were reinforced by European conceptions of "race," "equality" and "civilization," where black people were considered as "backward" races or peoples, not to be equated with the whites who were considered the "civilized nations."

In 1929, the League of Nations sent to Liberia a commission of enquiry led by an English dentist, Dr. Cuthbert Christy, to investigate the allegations of maltreatment, including practices of enslavement, of the indigenous people by the ruling Americo-Liberian oligarchy. These allegations had made the headlines of

British and American papers. One may argue that it was actually these reports, together with the political pressures in some colonial capitals that gave the impetus to the League's investigations. The Christy Commission rendered its findings to the League in September 1930 and confirmed some of these allegations. This led to the resignation of many top Liberian officials, including President King and his vice-president, Allen Yancy. The new government led by Edwin J. Barclay promised to take on many of the Commission's recommendations for reform and, between 1931 and 1932, promulgated many laws aimed at putting an end to some of the serious allegations, especially the practice of slavery.[30]

Meanwhile, at this time, a great deal of effort and debate went on in Britain and the US about the possibility, if not the necessity, of putting Liberia under the League's supervision, possibly through a colonial power or the United States. For Britain, apart from the findings of the Christy Commission (which was a mere pretext), and her own colonial ambitions and European perceptions of race and equality, there was also an internal European problem. This internal issue was twofold. On the one hand, there was a great economic crisis that became known as the Great Depression which was having a serious impact on European economies and, by extension, political stability.[31] On the other hand, perhaps partly due to the first factor, there was the gradual rise of Germany in Europe and Germans nostalgic of their colonial past were calling for the return of their former occupied territories to them or a fair share in the mandates system. This was threatening the European balance of power at home which could eventually, as it actually did, lead to a recurrence of war between the European nations. In the course of negotiations with Germany and an ambitious Italy, the British thought that a piece of the colonial cake could be a bargaining counter.

Thus, Philip Noel-Baker, the principle private secretary to the British Foreign Secretary in Macdonald's Labour government, Arthur Henderson, hoped that two pieces (states or territories) of Africa could be found to be "handed over simultaneously under [the League's] mandate to Germany and Italy respectively." It is quite legitimate to assume that the two pieces referred to here were Liberia and Ethiopia, since all the other African territories were at this time under the colonial occupation of one European country or the other and it was inconceivable that one would have relinquished any of their so-called "African possessions." In fact, Liberia is almost explicitly mentioned in the rest of this opinion of Noel-Baker. To justify this colonial enterprise, and while waiting to go to a Disarmament Conference with other European powers, the Private Secretary argued:

> This would not only place the mandates system on a broader basis —in itself desirable— but if skilfully used it would probably help us thro[w] the very difficult position in which the Disarmament Conference is going to place [us] vis-à-vis these two powers.

However, mindful of the sheer illegality of this enterprise vis-à-vis a sovereign and founding member country of the League, the British official provided a caveat in his opinion:

> But at the moment, this seems a difficult manoeuvre to carry through; and there are obstacles to suppression of the sovereignty of a Member of the League for such an ulterior purpose . . . I therefore favour adherence to the present plan [of pressing the Liberian government to accept sweeping reorganization of the country under the supervision of foreign advisors], unless a very ambitious political arrangement can be come to.[32]

Curiously, the Liberia Committee that the League established after receiving the report of the Christy Commission was chaired by a certain Lord Robert Cecil, a member of the British delegation to the League. Cecil was one of the most fervent advocates of the idea of placing Liberia under white supervision through the League of Nations. Lord Lugard, for many years a member of the PMC and a prominent member of the British House of Lords, but otherwise famous for his former post as a British Governor-General of Nigeria, was also strongly in favour of this idea. Perhaps he was even more so than Cecil and this can be seen in a personal letter he wrote to his ally Cecil on 23 January 1932 about the question of Liberia:

> I suggest that Monrovia should be organised as a Municipality [under the current black government], and the rest of the country should be placed under a Commissioner appointed by the League

of Nations and the United States. He [the Commissioner] should report annually to the Council [of the League . . .]. It is essential that the [Liberian] Frontier Force should be officered by white men under the control of the League Commissioner, and that white administrative officials should not be under the Liberian Government.[33]

It would seem also that the American Secretary of State at the time, Henry Stimson, was of the same view. Such were the perceptions of race, equality and civilisation and such was the debate in some European capitals about Liberia and its relationship with the League of Nations. It was these already-cooked ideas that the British officials, backed by some other European countries, took to the League concerning Liberia. They intended sending another commission of inquiry to Liberia so that this second commission could confirm that nothing had changed in the country since the first commission. Before that however, some European officials at the League, led by the British, tried in vain to persuade the Liberian government to agree to these ideas, which the latter found unacceptable and an attack on its sovereignty.[34]

Faced with this "legitimate" position of the Liberian government, Lugard suggested the expulsion of Liberia from the League so that the apparent immunity from international law that its membership in the League conferred upon it could be withdrawn, which would open the door for any colonial annexation anyone could wish. Lugard's friend, Cecil, opined that the best thing was for Liberia to be left for "some civilised country to take over the thing" under the supervision of the League.[35] Eventually, the second commission was sent to Liberia to investigate further.

This commission, as expected, concluded that lasting improvements in the country required comprehensive and substantial outside assistance. Without surprise again, the Liberian government refused the most radical points of the recommendations of this commission, especially those pertaining to its sovereignty. However, while it refused such recommendations that it quite rightly perceived as a threat to its independent existence, the Liberian government agreed to engage with the American government with regard to the reform of its 1926 accord with the Firestone Company. With the good relations that resulted from this between Monrovia and Washington under Franklin D. Roosevelt, Liberia remained shielded from the European colonial ambitions. This continued while Mussolini invaded Ethiopia and eventually the Second World War kept the European powers busy with something bigger than the Liberian question.

Nonetheless, while Liberia survived in the end, the fate of Ethiopia was different and its unfortunate fate partly led to the collapse of the whole League system. Like Liberia, Ethiopia, then called Abyssinia, was the other independent African state member of the League of Nations, albeit its membership came at a later date than that of Liberia, as mentioned above. While Liberia's history as a modern state was novel and its ruling class depended hugely on the United States from whence that ruling class had come, Ethiopia had a history spanning centuries and a civilisation arguably superior to that of many European countries. Abyssinians were more mobile in the surrounding African territories than the Liberians were. As nationals of a member of the League of Nations, Abyssinian nationals were to be treated in the mandated territories in the same way as people from any member country of the League.

This clearly challenged European conceptions of race and definitions of "civilisation" and "equality." This was more noticeable in the presence of Ethiopian nationals in the neighbouring territory of Tanganyika, which was under British mandate, and their demands to be treated in the same way as British nationals and citizens of any other League member state.

By and large, Ethiopia's relations with the League and its powerful European nations, including Italy before and for some time after the rise of Mussolini, were rather amicable. During the European scramble for Africa in the 19th century, Italy had occupied Libya and two relatively small African territories —Eritrea and part of Somalia, which became known as the Italian Somaliland, as opposed to the other parts of the country occupied by Britain and France. The Italians had attempted to occupy the Abyssinian kingdom but they were crushed by the Ethiopian forces at Adwa in 1896. Thus, seeking revenge for the Adwa defeat, ambitious to build a new Roman empire, angry at not having been offered any mandated territory, and preoccupied by the Great economic Depression, Mussolini thought that occupying Ethiopia would be the best solution of his problems and ambitions. He thought that controlling Ethiopia's economic resources and agricultural wealth would help solve the economic problems of Italy. A successful colonial conquest, he thought, would also divert attentions from Italy's own internal problems and glorify his fascist regime. Mussolini thus started preparing to invade Ethiopia as early as 1932.

He eventually attacked Ethiopia in October 1935 without any declaration of war, which was a flagrant violation of the Covenant of the League of Nations. Of course, the outraged Ethiopian government took the matter to Geneva and, the League ruled in its favour and declared Italy the aggressor. Such a favourable ruling was doubtless made possible because other European members of the League were fearful of Fascist Italy and other members of the League, especially from Latin America, were concerned about their own sovereignty had Italy's action been left unchallenged. Faced with Italy's obduracy in refusing to comply with calls for withdrawal and a peaceful settlement, the League proposed economic sanctions against Italy. However, fearful of a deterioration of the political situation in Europe itself, London and Paris did not support some of the measures that were likely to have a real effect on the Italians and force them to comply with international law.

The British and French positions with regard to Italy were very contradictory. While they did not want Italy to succeed, as that might give it more power and thus affect the balance of power which was in their favour in Europe, they refrained from taking effective measures against Italy for fear of a backlash in Europe. Eventually, after a fierce seven months' battle, in which the Italians used poison gas against the Ethiopians, the colonial forces entered Addis Ababa and effectively controlled the strategic areas of the country and made it an Italian colony until they were defeated during the early years of the Second World War in 1941 and Ethiopia returned once again under African rule after five years of foreign occupation.[36]

The League of Nations failed to protect one of its members from foreign aggression. The Second World War soon commenced on European soil. All these events and the inability of the League to effectively deal with them further discredited the League and eventually led to its collapse. The last meeting of its Assembly was held in December 1939 and it was dissolved in 1945-6 to give way to the United Nations Organization. Such was the itinerary of Africa within the League of Nations.

From the League of Nations to the United Nations

In the same way as the First World War gave birth to the League of Nations, so did the Second World War to the United Nations Organization. And while the philosophical thinking of an American president, Woodrow Wilson, was very instrumental in the founding of the League, albeit America never adhered to it, so was that of Franklin D. Roosevelt for the United Nations. In the same way as Africa was very poorly and marginally represented in the League, so it was at the founding of the United Nations. The role of the big powers, the victors of the Second World War, in the formation of the United Nations was also as significant as that of the victors of the First World War for the formation of the League. And finally, as it will be seen later (see *Chapter 2*), while the League invented the system of mandates and placed a number of African territories under it, the United Nations continued the same policy under its trusteeship system and transferred the same African territories to this system. These are some of the main similarities between the League of Nations and the United Nations. Nonetheless, while Africa's status in the League never evolved for good, the continent's itinerary in the United Nations has been quite different from this.

The UN's roots go back to a bilateral declaration that became known as the Atlantic Charter. The declaration was adopted by the British Prime Minister, Winston Churchill, and the American President, Franklin D. Roosevelt, meeting "somewhere at sea" on 14 August 1941. This document was not a treaty between the two men. Nor was it a final and formal expression of peace aims. It was only an affirmation, as the preamble of the document stated, of a number of "common principles in the national policies of their respective countries on which they based their hopes for a better future for the world." The Americans had not yet entered the Second World War in any direct way, which they only did after the Japanese attack on

Pearl Harbour in Hawaii on 7 December 1941. The war was still raging and much to the advantage of Germany and its allies known as the Axis powers.

The Charter contained eight points or clauses. Of its eight points, one may argue that two bear directly on what later became the United Nations. In the fifth point, the two leaders expressed their desire to "bring about the fullest collaboration between all nations in the economic field with the object of securing, for all, improved labour standards, economic advancement and social security." In the following point, they declared that: "After the final destruction of Nazi tyranny, they hope to see established a peace which will afford to all nations the means of dwelling in safety within their own boundaries, and which will afford assurance that all the men in all the lands may live out their lives in freedom from fear and want."

In the last clause of the Charter, the two leaders proposed the establishment of "a wider and permanent system of general security." In late 1941, delegations of twenty-six nations (albeit some were still linked to the British Empire) that were fighting against the Axis powers met in the American capital, Washington, DC. On 1 January 1942, they signed the "Declaration by the United Nations." It was from this Declaration that the future organization took its name, which had been suggested by the American President. This Declaration made the Atlantic Charter its main reference. Apart from Haiti —again the Union of South Africa does not count here— there was no African country amongst these twenty-six countries. Nor was France, which later became a permanent member of the UN Security Council, present at the Conference. Paris and the north of France had been occupied by Germany and the unoccupied parts of the country under Marshall Pétain had no real independence, indeed one could say that region was a mere German protectorate. Since the Declaration was signed by sovereign governments, the exiled French officials, including General de Gaulle, could not be a signatory to this Declaration. Not long after this however, three African states, Egypt (under British domination), Liberia and Ethiopia adhered to the Declaration.[37]

The following year, on 30 October, the representatives of China, the United Kingdom, the United States of America, and the Soviet

Union met in the Soviet capital, Moscow and agreed to the establishment, after the war, of "a general international organization based on the principle of the sovereign equality of all peace-loving states." They agreed that membership of this organization should be open to all sovereign peace-loving nations, large and small, for the purpose of maintaining international peace and security. About a month later, the leaders of the four countries, minus China, met again in the Iranian capital, Tehran, where they affirmed their readiness to go ahead with the establishment of the proposed international organization.

The first concrete steps towards the creation of the UN came in the second half of 1944 by which time the German and Italian forces had almost been defeated. This was during a month-long conference from 21 August to 7 October 1944 in a mansion called Dumbarton Oaks in Washington, DC. By the end of the Conference, the leaders of the four nations that had met in Moscow finally reached agreements which were embodied in proposals for the establishment of the United Nations Organization. This Conference was mainly concerned with agreeing to the principles and purposes of the international organization, its membership and principal organs. Following to a great extent the structure of the League of Nations, they agreed that the key body of the Organization would be called the Security Council, since maintaining international peace and security was to be its main purpose. Though it was agreed at this conference that there would be some permanent members sitting on the Security Council, no agreement was reached about the voting procedures. As mentioned above, the issue of permanent membership of "big powers" derived from the realist theory that if the big powers were not given a privileged position, the UN would not work. The issue of voting procedures, among others, was dealt with by Roosevelt, Churchill and the Soviet Premier, Stalin, at a conference at Yalta, in the Soviet Union, in February 1945.

It was agreed that the five permanent members would be China, France, UK, USA and USSR. These five countries were to be given, at their insistence, the undemocratic privilege of being able to stop any resolution of the world body that might jeopardise their direct or indirect interests. It is this autocratic privilege that became known as the "veto" power. Freed by this time, France had now been considered for one of the permanent seats. No African country was thought of to occupy any of these five seats. The Council was to have a further six non-permanent members sitting alongside the veto bearers. It was further agreed that a general conference would be convened at the American city of San Francisco for all those nations that had declared war on Germany or Japan and had signed the 1942 Declaration by the United Nations. Thus, neither Japan nor Germany was invited to the proposed conference. Such was the influence of the Second World War on the UN that the drafters of the Charter referred to these nations as "enemy states," which can be found in Articles 53, 77 and 107; this is now being challenged by a number of people from the two countries as part of the package of their demands for UN reform.[38] The San Francisco Conference was to be held in April 1945 to present all these proposals to the wider membership and agree on a Charter for the new organization.

In the final account, delegates of fifty-one nations, including the aforementioned three or four African nations, converged on the American city on 25 April. Despite some initial opposition to the veto privilege by some delegates, especially a group of Latin American delegates spearheaded by Brazil, most of the proposals of Dumbarton Oaks and Yalta were adopted, which led to the drafting of the 111-article Charter of the United Nations. The Charter was finally adopted at another meeting at San Francisco in June. New York was chosen to host the headquarters and the Charter finally came into force on 24 October 1945 when the five permanent members of the Security Council and a majority of the other signatory nations had ratified it. In a resolution of the General Assembly passed in October 1947, this date was adopted to be officially known as the "United Nations Day."

This is the history of the foundation of the United Nations and such was the marginalisation if not the non-existence of Africa in the whole process. This marginalisation was further asserted when the United Nations, doubtless influenced by the colonial powers in it as we will see in the next chapter, decided not to return to the people of the African League of Nations mandated territories their sovereignty, or to return sovereignty to those under pure colonial occupation. Instead, the new organization set up its own Trusteeship Council to which it transferred the concerned African territories. In so doing, the UN clearly continued the same collective colonial role of the League towards Africa. The gradual increase in the number of African states in the UN system as a result of their regaining of sovereignty and the dismantling of European colonial empires somehow changed this marginalization. But has this absolutely changed Africa's marginalization in wider international relations? If not, what are the practical steps to be taken to ensure such a change? This is the thrust of the concluding chapter of this book.

Administrative and Operational Structures of the United Nations

As mentioned above, the United Nations is in many regards based on the model of the League of Nations, especially as regards its operational structures. Article 7 (1) of the Charter of the United Nations established six principal organs. These are the General Assembly, the Security Council, the Economic and Social Council, the International Trusteeship Council, the International Court of Justice (ICJ) and the Secretariat. Except for the ICJ, which is based at The Hague in the Netherlands, all these organs are based at the UN's headquarters in New York. Of the 19 chapters of the Charter, ten (Ch. III — Ch. XII) are devoted to setting forth the structures, functions, powers, voting procedures, membership and activities of these different organs.

The General Assembly

In a way, the General Assembly is the real United Nations. It is here that all the member states, large and small, poor and rich are represented with no privilege in voting procedure for one nation over another. It is also based on a real democratic procedure. Each member state has one vote. The Assembly may discuss any matters within the scope of the Charter or relating to the powers and functions of any organs. It may discuss any questions relating to the maintenance of international peace and security brought before it by any member state or by the Security Council and may make recommendations on any such issues to the concerned states or to the Security Council. The Assembly may initiate studies and make recommendations for the purposes of promoting international cooperation in the political, economic, social, educational, and health fields. Its initiatives may also be aimed at assisting in the establishment of human rights and the development of international law and its codification. The Assembly also receives an annual report from all the main bodies (organs) of the UN regarding their activities in the previous year. It is the Assembly also that considers and approves the budget of the UN system. The election of non-permanent members of the Security Council and the members of the Economic and Social Council is also part of its powers. It is the body also that is entrusted with the task of recommending the admission of new members and suspending or expelling existing ones.

The Assembly meets once a year in regular sessions, traditionally in the third quarter of the year, commencing on the third Tuesday of September. Special sessions may be called at the request of the Security Council, the majority of the Assembly's members or one member state with the approval of a majority of others. It elects a President and a Vice-President for each session. Thus, because there is no limit to special and emergency sessions, the Assembly may at times elect four presidents in a year; they could be the same person but could also be different people. There may be no special or emergency session in a year and this will allow the elected president to continue for the whole year and even be re-elected at the following special or emergency sessions and thus serve for more than a year, but not two full years. However, if there is more than one president in a year, it is only the one elected at the regular annual session that is ranked in the main category, for instance as the sixth. Others are ranked as sixth special, sixth emergency special or resumed, so that the ranking of Assembly presidents is based on an annual calculation.

In the first sixty years of the UN, which is up until the end of 2005, the period considered by this book, there were sixty presidents of the Assembly. Of those, ten Presidents came from continental Africa.[39] The first African to be elected President of the General Assembly was Mongi Slim of Tunisia, who was elected in 1961 as the sixteenth President of the Assembly. The last African president of the Assembly in the period considered was Jean Ping of Gabon who served part of 2004 as the fifty-ninth President. The longest serving African presidents of the Assembly have been the

Tanzanian, Salim Ahmed Salim, who served in 1979 as the thirty-fourth president, and as the sixth and seventh emergency special president in 1980; the Nigerian, Joseph Nanven Garba, who served in 1989 as the forty-fourth president, and as the sixteenth, seventeenth and eighteenth special president in 1990; and the Namibian, Mr. Theo-Ben Gurirab, who served as the fifty-fourth president in 1999 and the twenty-second, twenty-third and twenty-fourth special president in the following year. Two of these African presidents of the General Assembly have gone on to become Secretaries-General of the Organization of African Unity (OAU). The first one to do so was the Tanzanian Salim A. Salim, while the second was the Ivorian, Amara Essy, who had served in 1994 as the forty-ninth president of the Assembly before going on to become the acting Secretary-General of the OAU to oversee its transformation to the African Union (AU) in 2002. The other African presidents of the Assembly in this period came from Ghana, Liberia, Algeria and Zambia. The Algerian, Abdelaziz Bouteflika, went on to become the president of his country and was still serving in this capacity as this book went to press.

In the UN system, the General Assembly oversees and is directly responsible for a number of programmes and funds, research and training institutes as well as other UN entities. Amongst the programmes and funds that report directly to the Assembly are the United Nations Conference on Trade and Development (UNCTAD), the United Nations Children's Fund (UNICEF), the United Nations Development Programme (UNDP), the United Nations High Commission for Refugees (UNHCR), and the Nairobi-based United Nations Human Settlements Programme (UNHSP, otherwise known as UN-HABITAT). Of the research and training institutes that report to it, one may count the United Nations Institute for Training and Research (UNITAR) and the International Research and Training for the Advancement of Women (INSTRAW). The Office of the United Nations High Commissioner for Human Rights (OHCHR) and the Joint United Nations Programme on HIV/AIDS (UNAIDS) are also some of the UN entities that report to the General Assembly.

This structure makes the General Assembly appear very powerful, which it is to some extent and as regards certain issues.

Its resolutions are however not binding apart from the budgetary issues. Besides, Article 12 (1) of the UN Charter makes it subordinate to the Security Council. Under this Article, the Assembly is requested to refrain from considering any dispute pertaining to international peace and security that is under the consideration of the Council unless the latter so requests. Given this, the powerful members of the Security Council tend, and this was very noticeable on the part of the Western countries during the Cold War, either to ignore the Assembly's resolutions and recommendations or not to take them seriously since their adoption was not obligatory as were those of the Council.

The Security Council

The way in which the UN is structured doubtless makes the Security Council the most powerful and influential body of the UN, as the founding powers had wished in 1945. Apart from the veto power that its five powerful and permanent members have, which could nullify any proposed decision of not only of any other organ of the UN, but also of the Council itself, the resolutions passed by the council, especially under Chapter VII, are binding upon all member states. After the amendment of 17 December 1963,[40] Article 23 of the UN Charter provides that the Security Council consists of five permanent members —China, France, UK, USA and USSR (now the Russian Federation) — and ten non-permanent members. The non-permanent members are elected for two-year terms not renewable immediately. They are elected by the General Assembly on the basis of first, their contributions to the maintenance of international peace and security and second, geographical distribution. This has given Africa two non-permanent members at any one time since the amendment took effect on 31 August 1965.

The first African country to sit on the Security Council was Egypt from January 1946 to December 1947. Without being interrupted by, and without any other African state sitting on it at that time, Egypt sat again on the Council from January 1949 to December 1950. It took almost ten years after this before another African country was admitted to the Council. That was Tunisia from January 1959 to December 1960. The first time when two

African states met in the Council was when Egypt again (but then merged with Syria as the United Arab Republic) and Liberia were non-permanent members of the Council from January 1961 to December of the same year. While Egypt continued to December 1962, Liberia served only one year that time round. After the amendment of the membership of the Council, however, Africa benefited from increased membership. This materialised for Africa for the first time in the two-year period from January 1966 to December 1967. Then three African countries (Mali, Nigeria and Uganda) sat simultaneously on the Council. Uganda had to resign however at the end of 1966. In 2005, which is the end of the period covered by this book, Africa was represented on the Council by Algeria, Benin and the United Republic of Tanzania. While the two-year terms of the first two came to an end in December 2005, Tanzania continued into 2006 and was joined, in January of that year, by Ghana and the Republic of Congo. While Tanzania's term is due to finish in December 2006, Ghana and Congo will remain on the Council until December 2007.[41]

According to the Charter, the Security Council has the primary responsibility for the maintenance of international peace and security. Disputes and situations which may endanger international peace and security may be brought to its attention by any member state, by a non-member state which accepts in advance the obligation of pacific settlement contained in the UN Charter, by the General Assembly, or by the Secretary-General. It is the only body that may decide to take military action against an aggressor when pacific measures of settlement fail. It is on the Council's recommendation that the General Assembly elects the Secretary-General of the United Nations.

Unlike the General Assembly, the Security Council is in almost continuous session. Thus, representatives of each of its members (permanent or non-permanent) must be present at all times at the UN Headquarters in New York. Article 28 (3) of the Charter provides that the Council may meet elsewhere than at Headquarters. In the period considered, this happened four times. The first time it did was at Addis Ababa (Ethiopia) in 1972, and the second time came the following year in Panama City in Panama.

The Council also sat at Geneva in 1990 and at Nairobi on 18-19 November 2004 to discuss the Sudanese crisis.

The Economic and Social Council

The Economic and Social Council (ECOSOC), under the authority of the General Assembly for the economic activities of the UN, with the specialised agencies linked to it, is the organ of the United Nations that has had almost the closest relationship with Africa. Under the UN Charter, ECOSOC may make or initiate studies and reports with respect to international economic, social, cultural, educational, health, and related matters and may make recommendations with respect to any such matters to the General Assembly, to the members of the UN, and to the specialised agencies concerned. It is through the ECOSOC that international non-governmental organizations working on matters related to economic, social, educational, and other matters, and which are desirous to work with the United Nations may submit their applications for consideration. Once approved by it and by the General Assembly, such organizations become known as "specialised agencies."

Being the liaison organ between the United Nations and the specialised agencies, the ECOSOC may take appropriate steps to obtain regular reports from these agencies about their activities as they relate to the UN. Taking advantage of the provisions of Article 68 of the UN Charter, which allows it to set up commissions in economic and social fields, ECOSOC has set up five regional economic commissions, including the Economic Commission for Africa (ECA), which was set up in 1958 to work with African states and regional economic communities for economic and social development on the continent (see *Chapter 2*).

Of the UN specialised agencies with a non-subsidiary relationship with ECOSOC, one may count the International Labour Organization (ILO), the United Nations Educational, Scientific and Cultural Organization (UNESCO), the World Health Organization (WHO), the United Nations Industrial Development Organization (UNIDO), and the World Intellectual Property Organization (WIPO). It is also through the ECOSOC that the World Bank group of institutions (i. e. the International Bank for Reconstruction and

Development (IBRD) also known as the World Bank for short, the International Development Association (IDA), the International Finance Corporation (IFC), the Multilateral Investment Guarantee Agency (MIGA), the International Centre for Settlement of Investment Disputes (ICSID), and the IMF (International Monetary Fund) are connected to the United Nations.

The International Court of Justice, the Trusteeship Council and the Secretariat

Two of the current UN organs are almost the identical replicas of similar bodies of the League of Nations. These are the International Court of Justice (ICJ) and the Trusteeship Council. The ICJ is the principal judicial organ of the UN as was the Permanent Court for International Justice (PCIJ) for the League of Nations. Like the PCIJ, the ICJ is based at The Hague in the Netherlands. As the former had fifteen judges, so has the ICJ. In this regard in fact, the ICJ's work is still based on the revised version of the Statutes of the PCIJ that came into force in 1936. Neither of these two bodies is to be confused with the International Criminal Court (ICC). The ICC, though also based at The Hague, is an independent international organization. It was established by the Rome Treaty, which came into force on 1 July 2002. According to Article 2 of the Rome Statute, which is the Charter of the ICC, the organization is linked with the United Nations by an agreement, signed at the UN headquarters in New York in October 2004 by the president of the ICC and the UN Secretary-General.[42]

Though an organ of the UN, the ICJ has its own 70-article Statute as an appendix to the UN Charter. It is this Statute, and not the UN Charter, that sets forth its functions, powers and rules of procedure. Article 4 of this Statute stipulates that "the members of the Court shall be elected by the General Assembly and by the Security Council from a list of persons nominated by the national groups in the Permanent Court of Arbitration." Of the fifteen judges of the Court, not more than one judge may come from a single country at any one time. The judges are elected for nine-year renewable terms. By the end of 2005, there were three African judges amongst the fifteen judges of the Court. These were Raymond Ranjeva of Madagascar, Abdul G. Koroma of Sierra

Leone, and Mohamed Bennouna of Morocco. Judge Bennouna was the newest elected judge from Africa, having been elected on 7 November 2005 to start his nine-year term on 6 February 2006.[43]

The other UN organ that has its roots in the League of Nations is the International Trusteeship Council. This is the organ that took over the work of the League's Permanent Mandates Commission (PMC) in the so-called supervision of trust territories, a number of which, as we have mentioned above, were in Africa. Nonetheless, the Trusteeship Council suspended its operations on 1 November 1994, following the independence of the Republic of Palau, the last remaining trust territory, a month earlier. Palau is an island country in the Pacific Ocean located some 500 km east of the Philippines, and it was under the trusteeship of the United States until that time.

The Secretariat is the general and the main administrative body of the United Nations. Its head is the Secretary-General who is elected for a five-year term renewable by the General Assembly upon the recommendation of the Security Council. The Secretary-General is the UN chief administrator and world's highest ranking diplomat. He or she acts in this capacity in all meetings of the different organs of the UN. Between 1945 and 2005, there were seven Secretaries-General of the United Nations. Of those, two were from Africa: Boutros Boutros-Ghali of Egypt, who served a single five-year term as the sixth Secretary-General from 1991 to 1996, and Kofi Annan of Ghana, who began serving as the seventh Secretary-General in January 1997. His first five-year term was renewed in December 2001 for the second term to run out in December 2007 (see *Chapter 4*). The first Secretary-General was Trygve Lie from Norway, who served from February 1946 to November 1952 when he resigned. The first five-year term of his successor, Dag Hammarskjöld of Sweden expired in 1957 and he was re-elected for a second five-year term as of 26 September 1957. However, half way into this term, in September 1961, he died in a mysterious plane crash in Southern Africa while on a mission to mediate in the Congolese crisis (see *Chapter 2*).

The Office of the Secretary-General (OSG) aside, the Secretariat comprises such other administrative departments and offices as the Department of Peace-keeping Operations (DPKO), the Office for the Coordination of Humanitarian Affairs (OCHA), the Office of the

High Representatives for the Least Developed Countries, Landlocked Developing Countries and Small Island Developing States (UNSECOORD), and the Department of Public Information (DPI), the department responsible for UN publications. It is also the Secretariat that oversees and receives reports from the three UN regional offices at Geneva (UNOG), at Vienna (UNOV), and at Nairobi (UNON).

Conclusion

In this chapter, I sought to provide a general overview of the United Nations Organization. The chapter began by a concise theorisation of international organizations such as the UN. Providing this theoretical hook on which to hang the subsequent observations and arguments seemed necessary in that it facilitated, so I hope, the understanding of those observations. While it is true that almost every school of thought in international relations has something to say about an aspect of international institutions, for the sake of simplification, the theoretical discussion in this regard was limited to two broad schools of thought: realism and liberal-institutionalism. While realists tend to shine in explaining states' behaviour within international institutions, the liberal explanations of why states commit themselves to institution-building are far more plausible than those of realists. Both were thus used to explain the formation of the United Nations and especially the reservation of the privilege of permanent membership and veto power to a few states.

This was followed by a study of the League of Nations and its relationship with Africa. The mandates system being the League's project that linked it most to Africa, this system was studied and scrutinized. Given the many imperial characteristics of the mandates system, the conclusion was that as far as Africa was concerned, the League was more a colonial club for the continent than a partner organization. The only instance where an African state benefited from its link with the League, albeit accidentally, was when Liberia was spared from outright colonial annexation because of its membership of the League. Ethiopia however, which was the other independent state from continental Africa in the

League, did not benefit from its membership in the organization in this regard, as it was invaded by Italy and the League failed to either prevent Italy's action or to halt it.

The chapter then pondered the UN itself. The world body was studied from its history to its operation structures, through its decision-making mechanism. In all these, Africa's position was the focus of the analyses. I observed that Africa was very poorly represented in the UN during its formation as it was in the League of Nations. In contrast to the latter, however, African membership in the UN grew and with this growth, Africa's marginalization was reduced. A number of African states have assumed, through their permanent representatives to the UN, the presidency of the General Assembly of the UN. Almost all of them have taken turns in the non-permanent membership of the Security Council since the creation of the UN. The Trusteeship Council of the UN that made the UN's relationship with Africa somewhat imperialistic has suspended its work. Africa's relations now with the UN are more of partnership than they were in the formative years of the world body. But this has not fulfilled all the expectations of Africa. It is to these twin issues, Africa's partnership with the UN and its disappointment by the world body, that we will now turn in the next two chapters.

Notes

1. See Stephen D. Krasner (ed.), *International Regimes* (Itacha, NY.: Cornell University Press, 1983), p. 2.

2. Robert O. Keohane and Joseph S. Nye, *Power and Interdependence* (Boston: Little & Brown, 1977), p. 19. See also Robert O. Keohane, *After Hegemony: Cooperation and Discord in the World Political Economy* (Princeton, NJ.: Princeton University Press, 1984).

3. Susan Strange, "Cavelic dragons: a critique of regime analysis," in Stephen D. Krasner (ed.), *International Regimes* (Itacha, NY.: Cornell University Press, 1983), pp. 337-55.

4. See Oran R. Young, "International Regimes: Toward a New Theory of Institutions," *World Politics*, Vol. 38, no. 1 (October 1986): 104-22.

5. Ibid. See particularly p. 108.

6. Hedley Bull, *The Anarchical Society: A Study of Order in World Politics*, 2nd ed. with a new foreword by Stanley Hoffmann (London: Macmillan Press, 1977), pp. 51-54.

7. This is the view for instance of Richard Little, "International Regimes," in John Baylis and Steve Smith (eds.), *The Globalization of World Politics: An Introduction to international relations* (New York: Oxford University Press, 2001), pp. 299-316.

8. Andreas Hasenclever, Peter Mayer, and Volker Rittberger, "Integrating theories of international regimes," *Review of International Studies*, Vol. 26, no. 1 (2000): 3-33; and Eric Brahm, "International Regimes," *Beyond Intractability*, Guy Burgess and Heidi Burgess (eds.), Conflict Research Consortium, University of Colorado, Boulder <http://www.beyondintracatability.org/m/international_regimes.jsp.> (September 2005.)

9. Brahm, *International Regimes*, op cit.; Lisa L. Martin and Beth A. Simmons, "Theories of Empirical Studies of International Institutions," *International Organization*, Vol. 52, no. 4 (Autumn 1998): 729-58.

10. Keohane, *After Hegemony*, p. 76.

11. Bardo Fassbender, "The Better Peoples of the United Nations? Europe's Practice and the United Nations," *European Journal of International Law*, Vol. 15, no. 5 (2004): 857-84.

12. See Peter Gowan, "US: UN," *New Left Review*, no. 24, November/December (2003): 5-28.

13. Ibid. See particularly p. 12.

14. For a comprehensive and a detailed study of these preliminary conferences, see Robert Hilderbrand, *Dumbarton Oaks: The Origins of the United Nations and the Search for Postwar Security* (Chapel Hill, NC.: University of North Carolina Press, 1990); United Nations, *Everyone's United Nations: A complete handbook of the activities and evolution of the United Nations during its first twenty years, 1945-1963* (New York: Department of Public Information, 1968); John G. Stoessinger, *The United Nations & the Superpowers: China, Russia & America* (New York: Random House, 1977); and Stephen Schlesinger, *Act of Creation: The Untold Story of the Founding of the United Nations* (Boulder. CO.: Westview Press, 2003).

15. Bruce Cronin, "The Paradox of Hegemony: America's Ambiguous Relationship with the United Nations," *European Journal of International Relations*, Vol. 7, no. 1 (2001):103-130.

16. Gowan, *US: UN*, p. 9. Examples are mine.

17. See Arthur Watts, "The Importance of International Law," in Michael Byers (ed.), *The Role of Law in International Politics: Essays in International Relations and International Law* (Oxford: Oxford University Press, 2000), pp. 5-16, especially p. 6.

18. John D. Hargreaves, *Decolonization in Africa* (London: Longman group, 1994), pp. 73-99.

19. See M. B. Akpan, "Liberia and Ethiopia, 1881 – 1914: the survival of two African states," in A. Adu Boahen (ed.), *General History of Africa – VII: Africa under colonial domination 1880 – 1935* (Paris and Berkeley: Unesco and University of California Press, 1985), pp. 143 – 52.

20. For a detailed account of the partition of Africa and the reaction and resistance of African people, see, for instance, A. Adu Boahen (ed.), *General History of Africa*, Vol. VII; Joseph Ki-Zerbo, *Histoire de l'Afrique Noire: D'Hier à Demain* (Paris: Hatier, 1978), pp. 401-28; A. S. Kanya-Forstner, "Military Expansion in the Western Sudan — French and British Style" in Prosser Gifford and W. M. Rogers Louis (eds.), *France and Britain in Africa: Imperial Rivalry and Colonial Rule* (New Haven and London: Yale University Press, 1971), pp. 409 – 42; Basil Davidson, *Modern Africa: A social and political history* (London: Penguin Books, 1978), pp. 13-14; and Bill Freund, *The Making of Contemporary Africa: The Development of African Society since 1800* (London: Macmillan Press, 1998).

21. See G. N. Sanderson, "The European Partition of Africa: Coincidence or Conjuncture?" in E. F. Penrose (ed.), *European Imperialism and the Partition of Africa* (London: Frank Cass, 1975). See also Étienne Bebbé-Njoh, *"Mentalité africaine" et problématique du développement* (Paris: l'Harmattan, 2002) for a detailed and somewhat philosophical discussion of primordial and primitive theories about Africa and the Africans.

22. Cited in Michael D. Callahan, *A Sacred Trust: The League of Nations and Africa, 1929-1946* (Brighton: Sussex Academic Press, 2004), p. 1.

23. In this Point, the American President contended that: "The Turkish portion of the present Ottoman Empire should be assured a secure sovereignty, but the other nationalities which are now under Turkish rule should be assured an undoubted security of life and an absolutely unmolested opportunity of autonomous development . . . ."

24. See Callahan, *A Sacred Trust*, p. 16; and John W. Coogan, "Wilsonian Diplomacy in War and Peace," in Gordon Marten (ed.), *American Foreign Relations Reconsidered 1890-1993* (London & New York: Routledge, 1994).

25. See Edwidge Danticat, "Ghosts of the 1915 US Invasion Still Haunt Haiti's People," Miami Herald, 25 July 2005; and Hyppolite Pierre, *Haiti, Rising Flames from Burning Ashes* (Lanham, MD.: University Press of America, 2006).

26. Callahan, *A Sacred Trust*, p. 19.

27. Ibid., p. 48.

28. See M. B. Akpan and R. Pankhurst, "Ethiopia and Liberia, 1914-1935: Two Independent African States in the Colonial Era," in A. Adu Boahen (ed.), *General History of Africa – VII: Africa under colonial domination 1880 – 1935* (Paris and Berkeley: Unesco and University of California Press, 1985).

29. Stephen Ellis, The Mask of Anarchy: The Destruction of Liberia and the Religious Dimension of an African Civil War (London: C. Hurst & Co., 2001), p. 42; and Issaka K. Souaré, Civil Wars and Coups d'Etat in West Africa: An Attempt to Understand the Roots and Prescribe Possible Solutions (Lanham, MD.: University Press of America, 2006), pp. 44-6.

30. Akpan and Panhurst, *Ethiopia and Liberia.*

31. For a good analysis of the Great economic Depression in Europe of the 1930s, its origin, course and consequences, see Patricia Clavin, *The Great Depression in Europe, 1929-1939* (New York: Palgrave Macmillan, 2000); John Stevenson & Chris Cook, *Britain in the Depression: Society and Politics, 1929-39* (London: Longman, 1994), especially chapters 7 &11; Dietmar Rothermund, *The Global Impact of the Great Depression, 1929-39* (London and New York: Routledge, 1996); and Harold James, *The End of Globalization: Lessons from the Great Depression* (Cambridge, MA.: Harvard University Press, 2002).

32. Quoted in Callahan, *A Sacred Trust*, p. 57.

33. Cited in Callahan, Ibid, p. 58.

34. Ibid., p. 59; and Akpan and Panhurst, *Ethiopia and Liberia.*

35. Callahan, *A Sacred Trust*, p. 59.

36. Ibid., pp. 6-7; and Akpan and Panhurst, *Ethiopia and Liberia.*

37. There is an abundant literature on the history and origins of the United Nations. See for example, United Nations, *Everyone's United Nations*; Thomas G. Weiss, David P. Forsythe, and Roger A. Coate, *The United Nations and Changing World Politics* (Boulder, CO.: Westview Press, 2004); Sven Bernhard Gareis and Johannes Varwick, *The United Nations: An Introduction* (New York: Palgrave Macmillan, 2005); Peter R. Baehr and Leon Gordenker, *The United Nations: Reality and Ideal* (New York: Palgrave

Macmillan, 2005); and Linda Fasulo, *An Insider's Guide to the UN* (New Haven: Yale University Press, 2005).

38. See for example Arima Tatsuo, *Future Role of United Nations within the Framework of Global Security: Japan's Perspective* (Paper presented at the 41st Munich Conference on Security Policy, February 2005).

39. In the rest of the book, "Africa" and "Africans" will stand for continental Africa, unless otherwise expressly stated. This will be purely for convenience. It is my view however that Africa is not and should not be limited to the 53 or so countries that make up the African Union. It includes what I call Sovereign Diaporian African States (SDAS) such as Haiti, Jamaica and Barbados. The seas and oceans should not be a barrier here as they are not between Washington and Hawaii or France and, though strangely, Martinique and Guadeloupe.

40. Prior to this amendment, the Council consisted of five permanent members and six non permanent members only, which made the total of its members eleven. This changed following the adoption by the General Assembly of Resolution 1991 A (XVIII) (1963), which was ratified by the majority of its members as well as the five permanent members of the Security Council. It was decided that of the ten non-permanent members, five should come from Africa and Asia (thus each could be guaranteed two members at any one time), one from Eastern Europe, two from Latin America and Caribbean, and two from Western Europe and other areas.

41. For a list of elected members of the Security Council since 1946, visit <http://www.globalpolicy.org/security/membership/mem2.htm.> (12 February 2006.)

42. See ICC Press Release 20041004-78-En of 4 October 2004.

43. See International Court of Justice, Press Release 2005/23 of 8 November 2005.

Chapter 2

Africa in Partnership with the UN

When the United Nations Organization was founded in 1945, Asian and African nationalism was of little consequence. Since then, however, so many former colonies have achieved independence that Afro-Asian countries now form the most influential single group within the United Nations.
—Kwame Nkrumah, *Africa Must Unite*, p. 194

In the previous chapter, we provided a conceptualisation of international organizations in international relations theories and in particular the United Nations. We also had an overview of the main structures of the UN as well as the status and role of Africa during the formation of the world body. In this chapter, we will look at one specific aspect of Africa-UN relations —partnership between the two entities. In retrospect, one could argue that on issues such as decolonization (including the dismantling of the white minority regimes in Southern Africa) and attempts at restructuring the unfair international economic order, the United Nations has been a partner and an ally of Africa.

As we will see below, this does not exclude some obvious contradictions in some works of the world body on a number of these issues. Nor does it assert that all the efforts that may have led to any successful outcome in one area or another of this partnership have been at the behest of the UN itself. Indeed, many if not all of UN efforts on these issues were only, and could only have been, complementary to those of Africa. The initiative came mainly from Africa who then sought the support of the world body. Noteworthy also is that many efforts were futile owing, on the one hand, to the lack of this role being played by Africa and, on the other, to the frictions and differences of view between the different bodies of the

UN itself —namely the Security Council and the General Assembly. We shall now look at some of these issues in more detail.

The UN and African Decolonization

On the question of decolonization in Africa, one finds the actions of the United Nations quite contradictory in the first fifteen years of its existence. For until 1960, it seems legitimate to argue that the world body acted as a collective imperial power, inheriting that role from the League of Nations, as seen in the previous chapter.[1]

Article 1 (2) of the UN Charter provides that one of the purposes and principles of the United Nations is to "develop friendly relations among nations based on respect for the principle of equal rights and self-determination of peoples." In relation to economic and social cooperation amongst nations, Article 55 instructs the member states of the United Nations, through the Organization, to promote universal respect for human rights and fundamental freedoms for all peoples without distinction as to race, sex, language or religion. The Charter contends that "respect of the principle of equal rights and self-determination of peoples" is a necessary condition for the creation of conditions of stability and well-being of peoples, which is almost the main *raison d'être* of the United Nations.

In December 1948, the United Nations adopted the Universal Declaration of Human Rights (UDHR). Article 1 of the Declaration stipulates that "all human beings are born free and equal in dignity and rights. They are endowed with reason and conscience and should act towards one another in a spirit of brotherhood." Yet Article 73 of the UN Charter makes for two readings. On the one hand, it implicitly ascertains, not to say condones, the practice of colonialism by recognising and not condemning the existence of "territories whose peoples have not yet attained a full measure of self-government." On the other hand, the article, especially in paragraph B, calls upon those countries which have or assume responsibilities for the administration of these dependent territories to "develop self-government, to take due account of the political aspirations of the peoples, and to assist them in the progressive development of their free political institutions."

This first reading of the article is even more disappointing, at least from an African perspective, if one considers the argument of some well-known international lawyers that the "peoples" referred to in this Article are not even those that were at the time under colonialism. The actions of the United Nations also confirmed this. Moreover, even if the provision of this article concerned colonial peoples, in legal terms, the wording fell quite short of what today is generally thought of as "self-determination" or "independence."[2] Denying thus or not recognising in the Charter of the United Nations the right of those peoples under colonial rule to freedom from such subjugation is contrary to the proclaimed aims and objectives of the United Nations. It is more so if viewed in light of the meaning of the UDHR, especially its article 1.

The justification of the whole system of trusteeship was that the dependent peoples were not politically and intellectually mature enough to assume responsibility and govern themselves. In other words, Africans and other peoples under European colonialism were considered to possess a lower level of intelligence than their masters —not far from saying that they were considered as sub-humans. The absurdity of this assumption needs no efforts to establish. The regrettable fact is however that the United Nations maintained this—without doubt because it was dominated by those that had invented such arguments (i. e. the imperial nations). The contradiction here again is that subjugation of some people by others being contrary to all human logic, the system of trusteeship flew in the face of article 1 of the UDHR, as we quoted above.

Perhaps this was due to the fact that those commanding the United Nations at the time did not think that the Declaration applied to the colonial peoples. Indeed this is what we understand from the interpretation of the then British Prime Minister, Winston Churchill of the Atlantic Charter signed between him and the American President, Franklin D. Roosevelt in August 1941.[3]

As regards the second clause of the article which calls upon the colonial powers to strive to promote the well-being of the dependent peoples to the utmost, this can only be explained in the context of the "happy slave" theory. Following this theory one condones the subjugation of a person by another but yet calls upon the master to look after his slave so as to appear nice. But can anything be equated with one's freedom?

This said, albeit it was by the initiative and through the efforts of the colonial peoples themselves, the United Nations came to be a major partner and ally with Africa and all the dependent peoples in their struggle to regain their independence and sovereignty despite the counter efforts of the colonial powers. As noted in the previous chapter, Africa was poorly represented at the United Nations in the first fifteen years after its founding. One might even argue that until the accession of Ghana (1957) and Guinea (1958) to the world body with two staunch believers in Pan-Africanism and African emancipation as their heads, Nkrumah in Ghana and Sékou Touré in Guinea, Africa's presence was symbolised by only a few theoretically independent but practically dependent states. All this changed dramatically in 1960.

The year 1960 saw the entry of newly independent African countries into the United Nations en masse. Of the seventeen countries admitted to the world body in this year, all but one came from Africa. This dramatically changed the balance of power in New York. The UN is run by two main organs: the Security Council and the General Assembly. The former was and is still dominated by its five permanent members. Of those, two (Britain and France) were colonial powers at the time. The most powerful Security Council member, the United States, had more common ground with these two than differences, especially with regard to Southern Africa. China's seat was until 1971 occupied by Formosa (Taiwan) and not the communist mainland China in Beijing. Formosa was almost a Western protégé. Thus, within the Security Council, only the Soviet Union could sympathise with the colonial peoples. The number of non permanent members was limited to just six, with very little, if any, power to counter the permanent members.

The General Assembly is the organ where all member states are represented. Unlike the Security Council, its representation and voting procedures are "democratic." While membership of the UN did not give an automatic tribunal to the new members at the level of the Security Council, the General Assembly provided them with just that. At the Assembly, the newly independent African states struck a deal with their Asian and Latin American counterparts to defend their interests and make themselves heard. This way, there was far more discussion of African and Asian affairs than ever before.[4] And whilst it is true that the bulk of the work was done by the liberation movements on the ground and their struggle against the colonial powers, the efforts of the former dependent territories which had become members of the UN through the Organization was very instrumental in that they accorded the liberation fighters international support that they might not have been able to lobby for on their own. Those at the UN also strove to press the colonial powers on the issue of decolonization by always reminding them of the contradiction of their actions with the declared mission of the UN. Because it was the UN tribunal and system that they used to achieve this, the United Nations was therefore a partner in the liberation struggles of the colonial peoples.[5]

Thanks to the efforts of those members in the General Assembly, the United Nations passed, in December 1960, a historic and unequivocal Declaration on the Granting of Independence to Colonial Countries and Peoples. In this Declaration, the Assembly affirmed that the "subjugation of peoples to alien subjugation, domination and exploitation constitutes a denial of fundamental human rights" and that it was "contrary to the Charter of the United Nations." It solemnly proclaimed the necessity of bringing to speedy and unconditional end colonialism in all its forms and manifestations. To debunk one of the main arguments of the colonial powers in justifying their actions against all human logic, the Declaration boldly stated that claims of "inadequacy of political, economic, social or educational preparedness should never serve as a pretext for delaying independence." It further stated that immediate steps should be taken in Trust Territories and non-self-governing territories and all other territories which had not yet regained their independence to transfer all powers to the peoples of those territories, without any distinction as to race, creed or colour, or indeed enable them to enjoy complete independence and freedom.[6]

The Africa-UN partnership on the subject of decolonization could be illustrated by a number of examples. Perhaps the decolonization of Algeria and the four Portuguese colonies provides

71

the best illustration of this point. Of all the colonial powers, France and Portugal were the two powers that resisted the process of decolonization more ardently in all or part of their occupied African territories. And of all the African territories occupied by France, Algeria proved the greatest obsession in French colonial thinking.

It is instructive to recall that after the Second World War and in a bid to counter the rising nationalism in the French African colonies and yet determined to maintain them under French rule, a conference called by General de Gaulle, in 1944 at Brazzaville, made proposals leading to a *Union Française* with the French colonies in sub-Saharan Africa. These had been grouped in two blocs for administrative convenience: French West Africa (*Afrique occidentale française*, AOF) with its capital in Dakar, and French Equatorial Africa (*Afrique équatoriale française* —AEF), with its base in Brazzaville.

In this union, indigenous Africans would have more say in the running of their territories. They would no longer be technically considered as colonies, but as French overseas departments or territories (*Territoires d'outre mer* —TOM). Their inhabitants would be considered as French overseas citizens. They would thus delegate representatives to the National Assembly in Paris. It was clear from this formula that total independence for these territories was not envisaged and executive authority would still be vested in the French governor in the territory or the federal governor in Dakar or Brazzaville. White supremacy would be maintained, as white settlers in these territories would still have more votes, and thus more say in the running of the territory, than the majority black inhabitants and owners of the territory. This policy was thus implemented as a substitute for independence and a strategy to calm the dissident voices calling for a revision of the colonial system.

However, with the turn of events in the late 1950s, General de Gaulle, who had been returned to power in May 1958 to save France from plunging into a full-scale civil war between the imperialists and those in favour of French withdrawal from Algeria, proposed another constitution. In addition to the union formula now in place since 1944, the new constitution provided another choice for the French African colonies. The latter could now opt for "secession" from France. And in that case, the "separatist" territory would have its independence with "its consequences," starting from the immediate suspension of any French assistance. Thus, at a referendum held in September 1958 aimed at adopting the new constitution, only Guinea opted for immediate independence or "separation," to use the terms conveyed by the constitution, and it chose this with its consequences. All the other territories voted to remain "French," or so they thought. This is not to dispute the fact that "no" campaigners were subjected to intimidations in some territories.

The case of Algeria was a different matter. The North African country was considered by many French as part and parcel of metropolitan France —hence the slogan of *Algérie française*. Yet, apart from the issue of the so-called Trust Territories, the Algerian case provided one of the first occasions of UN-Africa partnership on African decolonization. In 1954, demands for Algerian independence degenerated into open warfare between the Algerian liberation movements on the one hand and the French government and French settlers in Algeria on the other. The French were determined never to negotiate the Algerian question. Since they thought that Algeria was part of France, they proclaimed that any kind of revolt on the soil of Algeria was "treason." The then French Interior Minister, François Mitterrand, who later became president, was quoted as saying that "the only negotiation is war."[7] And war, bloody war it was.

It was not long before the Algerian case was brought to the attention of the UN General Assembly. For seven years (i.e. from 1955 to 1962), the Algerian question came up regularly in the different sessions of the Assembly. Such was the impact of the UN deliberations on the Algerian case that many French gestures of apparent good will coincided with, if they were not influenced by, the way the affair went in the General Assembly. In 1957 for example, as Kouassi argues, the French parliament, after lengthy debates, adopted more liberal laws for Algeria, which were purely designed to counterbalance the effect on international opinion of France's intensification of the war in Algeria, which, in turn, was being influenced by the General Assembly's resolutions and condemnations of some French actions.[8]

The Algerian question was first brought to the attention of the General Assembly in September 1955. It was the Afro-Asian group of countries that brought the matter to the United Nations for the General Assembly to consider it as a potential threat to international peace and security. The French government angrily protested at this. Misinterpreting Article 2 (7) of the UN Charter, they argued that the world body did not have any right to debate the Algerian question as it was "an internal issue." To back that misinterpretation, they rather shamelessly argued that Algeria had, for 125 years, been "legally" part of France, without mentioning however how it became so and what feelings the oppressed and dispossessed people of Algeria had about that. And when a majority of General Assembly members voted in favour of tabling the issue for the Assembly's consideration, France, like Apartheid South Africa later, slammed the door and, for some time, adopted a policy of staying away and letting it be known that it might even leave the United Nations altogether. This apparent threat, backed by other colonial powers, led the Assembly to remove the Algerian question from its agenda and France resumed its seat.[9]

Nonetheless, as the session of 1956 approached, the Afro-Asian Group succeeded in getting the question once again on the General Assembly's agenda. They had used the war crimes committed by the French in Algeria to argue that France was waging "a war of extermination" or genocide, and that this brought the case under the provisions of the Universal Declaration of Human Rights, which prohibits such acts. With the admission of Ghana (1957) and Guinea, to whose admission in 1958 France was ferociously opposed,[10] the African Group at the UN was formed and a radical one it was as far as the fight against colonialism was concerned. This meant more heat over the French and all other colonial powers. A big boost had been given to the Algerian liberation movement which was already represented at the UN by the National Liberation Front (FLN, *Front de libération nationale*). Eventually, the Algerian issue was settled by the victory of the liberation movements. This was due to the combined efforts of the latter on the ground and the tremendous international support they got at the United Nations, thanks to the hard work of the small African Group and its Asian allies at the UN.

The Algerian case is thus particularly illustrative of the role played by the UN-Africa partnership on the issue of decolonization in Africa. Ahmed Ben Bella, the first president of independent Algeria, solemnly acknowledged this. In his first speech to the General Assembly, in October 1962, after the unanimous vote accepting his country's admission to the United Nations, he stated amongst other things:

> For seven years the Algerian question came up regularly at every session of the Assembly. The debates to which it gave rise marked out the changing course of the conflict, and delegations [at the United Nations] were in a position to appreciate the dimensions of this conflict and to become familiar with its circumstances.[11]

Connected to decolonization but yet different from it were the efforts made to dismantle the system of Apartheid and white minority regimes in Southern Africa. It is to this delicate issue and the role played by the UN-Africa partnership in this that we now turn.

Dismantling Apartheid and White Minority Regimes in Southern Africa

In a way, this heading should have been merged with the one above. However, Apartheid was quite a different form of colonialism. It was an extreme kind of foreign domination. Its cruelty and contradiction with healthy human logic were unpalatable. The system of Apartheid was what one may call "second hand colonialism," that is land seizure and occupation by colonial settlers independently of —albeit in alliance with— the original colonial power, the so-called metropolis. It is this peculiarity of its nature and the fact that it was practised only in one region of the continent (Southern Africa) that led me to justify studying it under a separate heading of its own.

The system of Apartheid, considered by its racist and segregationist methods and policies, was more or less used in three countries of Southern Africa: the Republic of South Africa, Zimbabwe and Namibia. The term however was only used in the South African case and rather loosely in Namibia. The white minority regime in Zimbabwe, then called Southern Rhodesia, was hardly described as such. Yet, the policy of racial segregation in favour of the white minority that characterised the system of Apartheid was there, albeit at a lesser degree compared to what it was in South Africa. The official name of Nelson Mandela's country was at the time the Union of South Africa. The system in Namibia was an extension of what was going on in South Africa —Namibia having been re-colonized by the Union of South Africa in 1915.

Namibia had been a German colony until the First World War. Soul-searching in the war, as it came to the brink of defeat; Germany could not defend its overseas colonies. South African troops thus forced their way into Namibia —then called German South West Africa. This move was certainly made possible with the help of Britain, which was the colonial power or at least the former colonial power with some residual power, even over South Africa. South Africa was to be Britain's policeman in Namibia, which meant that Namibians had only changed hands between two colonial powers. The new one was just as cruel and wicked, if not more so. One can imagine the extent of this cruelty if one remembers that the Germans were also responsible for genocides in the country, especially against the Herero community who are now seeking reparations from Germany for the suffering experienced during their short colonial rule over them. Under the Apartheid regime in South Africa, Namibians laboured under the choking yoke of the Afrikaners until the country's independence in March 1990, thanks to the joint efforts of the Organisation of African Unity (OAU) and the United Nations.

The genuine concern of the independent African states about the situation in Namibia in particular and in all the dependent African territories at the time was natural. The OAU's *ad hoc* committee and the different commissions on the eradication of Apartheid were very instrumental. The efforts of the African Group at the UN in keeping the momentum at the international level proved also to be a very effective diplomatic tool in combating white minority rule in Southern Africa. Again, it is Africa's partnership with the United Nations on this issue that concerns us here.

The involvement of the United Nations in the question of Namibia dates almost immediately after the founding of the world body in 1945. Having succeeded the League of Nations, the UN, as mentioned above, sought to continue the work of the League by turning the League of Nations Mandated Territories into UN Trust Territories. As mentioned earlier (see *Chapter 1*), the League had placed Namibia under the mandate of the Union of South Africa on 17 December 1920, after the First World War. South Africa was doing this on behalf of the British Crown. Determined to annex the territory to the Union of South Africa, Pretoria refused to place Namibia under UN trusteeship. As a member of the UN, it claimed that the world body did not have any legal right to deal with the Namibian question, as it was an internal issue. It insisted that UN's continuous attempts to deal with the Namibian issue were contrary to the provisions of Article 2 (7) of the UN Charter.[12]

In a resolution of 6 December 1949, the General Assembly referred the case of Namibia, then called South West Africa (South Africa had removed the prefix "German" and the territory had not yet been named "Namibia"), to the International Court of Justice (ICJ) in The Hague. On 11 July 1950, the ICJ, by 12 votes to 2, gave an advisory opinion upholding that the UN had legal right to deal with the matter and thus called for the territory to be placed under the United Nations' trusteeship system since it was the body that succeeded the League of Nations. South Africa declined to recognise this opinion. This was not surprising as the Court, dominated by Western powers more or less complacent with South Africa, also mentioned in the same Advisory Opinion that "the Charter did not impose on the Union of South Africa a legal obligation to place the Territory under Trusteeship."

Despite this apparent setback, the General Assembly did not wane in its efforts to be a real partner with Africa in the latter's endeavours to rid the continent of colonialism and particularly white minority rule in Southern Africa. Thus, in October 1966, the Assembly adopted Resolution 2145 (XXI) in which it sought to revoke South Africa's mandate and place Namibia under UN trusteeship. A South West Africa People's Organization (SWAPO) had been formed by the majority black Namibians in April 1960. The purpose was to regain their sovereignty by armed struggle, since all the peaceful means had apparently failed. They nonetheless remained open to dialogue as the events of the 1980s showed. The General Assembly decided to recognise this organization as the sole legitimate representative of the Namibian people. In 1968, SWAPO suggested that the country be named "Namibia" instead of South West Africa. In June of that year, the UN officially adopted this name. Eventually, partly through the United Nations Transition Assistance Group (UNTAG), [13] formed by Security Council Resolution 435 (29 September 1978), South African troops withdrew from Namibia. In March 1990, Namibia regained its sovereignty and the country became a member of the United Nations on 23 April 1990.

As mentioned above, the system of Apartheid came to Namibia by extension. The inventor of this abhorrent system was the Union of South Africa. To put it more precisely, more than any other section of the white settlers, it was the Afrikaners[14] —these extremist racists and strong advocates of the pathological illusion of white supremacy— that advocated this repulsive system and, when they came to power in 1948, adopted it as official state policy.

Southern Africa in general and South Africa in particular is a very rich area in Africa —perhaps the richest and the most strategically important sub-region of the continent. South Africa was invaded and occupied by Britain in the 19th century through a number of bloody confrontations with the resistance fighters of the local African people. For its strategic position, the country in particular and the sub-region in general were flooded with white settlers from the different European countries, especially Britain and Holland. As in the case of other British colonies with a significant white settler community such as Canada (1867), Australia (1900), New Zealand (1907), and the Irish Free State (1921), South Africa was transformed into a self-governing "Dominion" under the British Crown in 1910, with the state power in the hands of the minority white settlers.

As a continuation of colonialism, the settlers oppressed the local people and, by force, seized their farm lands. The indigenous black people naturally resisted these practices which, in turn, invited more oppression and wickedness over them. As a quasi sovereign state, South Africa became a founding member of the League of

Nations at the end of the First World War. This situation of systematic oppression of black peoples remained unabated all the way through to the time of founding of the United Nations in 1945, of which South Africa was also a founding member. The organized black resistance had seen, in 1912, the birth of the African National Congress (ANC), followed in 1921 by the South African Communist Party, as well as the ANC Youth League. The latter was formed in 1943 led by such prominent personalities as Nelson Mandela. With the passing of time, these organizations became more militant in their demands and demonstrations for change.

In 1948, the extremist Afrikaner National Party came to power. Its leader was a certain Dr Daniel Malan. The Afrikaner party coined the word and introduced or rather constitutionalised the system of Apartheid. The ideology of this evil system is put succinctly by Nelson Mandela in his acclaimed autobiography:

> Malan's platform was *apartheid*. Apartheid was a new term but an old idea. [...] it represented the codification in one repressive system of all the laws and regulations that had kept Africans in an inferior position to whites for centuries. What had been more or less *de facto* was to become relentlessly *de jure*. The often haphazard segregation of the past three hundred years was to be consolidated into a monolithic system that was diabolical in its detail, inescapable in its reach and overwhelming in its power.[15]

Determined to uphold the pathological myths of white supremacy over the blacks and in the face of black unity and militancy, the extremist government applied further repressive and reactionary measures on black people in an unprecedented way in the country. With the support of other white political parties, the all-white parliament passed a number of repressive laws whose content and application baffled human logic. In 1950, they passed the so-called "Group Areas Act." This required the classification of all South Africans by race and colour. Three years later, they passed the Native Labour Act, which legally abolished the rights of freedom of association and collective bargaining for black workers. In the same year of 1953, the Criminal Law Amendment Act was passed. This made it an offence for black people to protest against or support any campaign against any of these oppressive laws. And in 1956, the Mines and Works Act came to confirm prohibition of Africans from exercising skilled work in the mining sector.[16]

For the 46 years from 1948 to 1994 that the system of Apartheid lasted as the official policy of the Government of South Africa, the United Nations' partnership with Africa in combating this political evil was instrumental. The work of the UN may be divided into three distinct phases. The first phase spanned about two decades from the official adoption of the system of Apartheid as a state policy in 1948 to 1966. There were only few African members at the UN at this time. The Western powers, some of which tended to be more or less sympathetic to if not supportive of the regime in Pretoria, overwhelmingly dominated the Security Council. Thus, the UN's work, which was mainly through the General Assembly, was more or less limited to appealing to the South African government to reconsider and renounce its Apartheid and racial segregationist policies.

The second phase of UN-Africa partnership in combating the system of Apartheid was the period from 1967 to 1989. This was when the UN and independent African states launched an international campaign, which appealed to the world public opinion, especially in the Western countries whose governments were not very supportive of UN actions. The aim was to persuade the ordinary masses to pressurise their governments in a bid to put pressure on the Apartheid regime in South Africa and eventually isolate it in most of its international relations. The third and last phase of UN-Africa partnership against Apartheid is the period from 1990 to 1994. This was when a new leadership came to power in Pretoria and recognised that the white settlers could not eternally defeat the growing anti-Apartheid movements in the world, especially as almost all the African territories had regained their sovereignty. It was in this period that imprisoned liberation leaders, such as Mandela, were set free and the unjust ban on black political parties was lifted. In this phase, the United Nations worked with South Africans, the black majority and the white minority government of de Klerk, to promote negotiation and dialogue and organise free and fair general elections which led to the formation of the first legitimate and majority government in South Africa.[17]

The very first consideration by the UN of the issue of racial discrimination in South Africa came during the very first session of the General Assembly in 1946, barely a year after the formation of the world body. It was to consider a complaint lodged by India against South Africa's increasing discrimination against people of Indian origin.[18] India did not regain its sovereignty from Britain until 1947, but owing to some special arrangements, it had been allowed to send delegates to the founding conference of the UN at San Francisco, as it was a member of the League of Nations. This allowed India to be a founding member of the UN. On the other hand, South Africa harboured many people of Indian origin, including, at one time, the great Indian liberation campaigner by peaceful means, the Mahatma Gandhi.[19] The settlement of Indians and other Asians in such colonies as South Africa and Kenya was an official British colonial policy in a bid to exclude the indigenous black people from exercising any skilled work, even at the most subaltern levels, to ensure their continuous servitude status and also to anticipate any competition between the majority blacks and the minority white settlers that would naturally be to the advantage of the majority should they be skilful.

Notwithstanding India's complaint and the Assembly's consideration of it, nothing concrete was apparently done. The first resolution of the Assembly specifically aimed at Apartheid was adopted in 1952, about four years after the official adoption of the dreadful doctrine in South Africa. This came after the ANC and the South African Indian Congress (SAIC), together with organizations representing the Coloured people (people having been classified by the regime as white, black or Bantu, Indian and coloured people) as well as some white opponents of the system of Apartheid launched, on 26 June 1952, a non-violent "Campaign for the Defiance of Unjust Laws." As one of the leaders of the campaign, Mandela recalls:

> Two stages of defiance were proposed. In the first stage, a small number of well-trained volunteers would break selected laws in a handful of urban areas. They would enter prescribed areas without permits, use Whites Only facilities such as toilets, Whites Only railway compartments, waiting rooms and post office entrances. They would deliberately remain in town after curfew. [Knowing that their action would at least lead them to prison but determined

to express their natural legal rights in the most peaceful way possible,] each batch of defiers would have a leader who would inform the police in advance of the act of disobedience so that the arrests could take place with a minimum of disturbance. The second stage was envisioned as mass defiance, accompanied by strikes and industrial actions across the country.[20]

Not surprising, the Apartheid regime reacted very angrily to the protest by arresting thousands of people and subjecting many to different types of physical violence such as flogging. The following month, the ANC, under the leadership of Walter Sisulu, sent a letter to Trygve Lie, the then Norwegian Secretary General of the UN, asking for an opportunity to put their grievance to the General Assembly. The letter was signed by Professor Z. K. Matthews, the ANC Representative in Cape Town, who was also to be the ANC's speaker before the UN should the request be granted.[21]

Moreover, following the publicity that this protest generated and its role in helping to focus world public opinion on the system of Apartheid, together with the angry and repressive reaction of the regime in Pretoria, the governments of Egypt and 12 Asian countries (Afghanistan, Burma now Myanmar, India, Indonesia, Iran, Iraq, Lebanon, Pakistan, the Philippines, Saudi Arabia, Syria and Yemen) requested the insertion in the agenda of the 7th session of the Assembly held in September 1952 an item entitled: "The question of race conflict in South Africa resulting from the policies of apartheid of the Government of the Union of South Africa."[22]

On 5 December 1952, the General Assembly adopted a resolution establishing a three-member UN Commission on the Racial Situation in the Union of South Africa (UNCORS) to study the problem "in the light of Purposes and Principles of the [UN] Charter ... and the resolutions of the United Nations racial persecution and discrimination." The Assembly instructed the Commission to report its conclusions to it at its eighth session, to be held the following year. In a separate resolution, the Assembly contended that "in a multi-racial society harmony and respect for human rights and freedoms and the peaceful development of a unified community are best assured when patterns of legislation and practice are directed towards ensuring equality before the law of all persons, regardless of race, creed or colour ...."[23]

The three members of the Commission were from Chile (Chairman), Haiti and France. The Commission submitted three annual reports (in 1953, 54 and 55) to the General Assembly. In each of them, it concluded that the racial policies of the government of South Africa were in contravention with the Charter of the UN as well as with the provisions of the Universal Declaration of Human Rights.

The year 1960 marked a turning point in the UN-Africa partnership in their joint fight against Apartheid. Three separate factors married to make this turning point. The first one originated from within South Africa. A second factor came from the wider African continent. These two joined to take the battle further to the United Nations, which produced the third turning point. As regards the factors from within South Africa, it is instructive to note that the year began with mass protests across the country against the unjust and humiliating pass laws, which required Africans to carry an internal passport on them to enable them to travel within their home country. 21 March marked the climax of the resistance against the pass laws. On this fateful day, the predominantly Afrikaner police received orders to deliberately fire at peaceful African demonstrators at Sharpeville, killing 68 and wounding more than 200. Instead of giving comfort to the Afrikaners by giving in, as they had surely hoped, the resistance took a new surge throughout the country, comforted by the international outrage at the actions of the Apartheid regime. Seemingly frightened by the turn of events but blinded from recognising the truth and reality by its racist convictions, the Malan regime declared a state of emergency on 30 March and, in April, banned the ANC and the Pan Africanist Congress of Azania (PAC) and detained their leaders, tried them and gave them heavy prison sentences.

In reaction to these events came the wider African factor. As previously mentioned, 1960 was and remains to this day the year that saw the largest entrance in a single year of new members to the United Nations. Yet 16 of the 17 new states that were admitted to the UN in this year came from Africa. By this, two African forces came to play. The African Group of States at the UN was strengthened and, in alliance with other Third World regions, they became a powerful voice. They thus began to press the UN not only to take stronger UN actions against Apartheid, but also to consider wider African issues more seriously. The other African force, which was to lend even more strength to the African Group at the UN, was the serious efforts that were being made at home to form an organization of all independent African states. These efforts eventually succeeded in creating the Organisation of African Unity (OAU) in Addis Ababa in May 1963.

In June 1960, about three months after the Sharpeville massacre, independent African states held their Second Conference at Addis Ababa. Before this, the UN Security Council had pondered over the events of March. At the urgent request of nine independent African states (Egypt, Ethiopia, Ghana, Guinea, Liberia, Libya, Morocco, Sudan and Tunisia) and 20 Asian countries, the Security Council considered the "situation arising out of the large-scale killings of unarmed and peaceful demonstrators against racial discrimination and segregation in the Union of South Africa."[24] This was another turning point in UN-Africa partnership in combating apartheid, as almost all the previous considerations of the matter had been done by the General Assembly and not the most influential Security Council. On 1 April, the Council adopted Resolution 134 by 9 votes in favour and none against, with Britain and France abstaining. In this resolution, composed of five paragraphs, the Council recognised that the situation in South Africa was one that had "led to international friction and if continued might endanger international peace and security." It called upon the regime in Pretoria to abandon its policies of Apartheid and racial discrimination.

Thus, at the Conference at Addis Ababa, after paying homage to the victims of the "shameful policy of apartheid and racial discrimination" in South Africa, the Independent African States decided to assist these victims and promised to furnish them with all the means necessary to attain their political objectives of liberty and democracy. The Conference then called for tough economic and diplomatic sanctions against the Apartheid regime. In particular, they invited the oil-rich Arab states (that were and remain to this day the closest allies of Africa in the UN) to prevent their oil from getting into South Africa. They also invited the Independent African States that were members of the British Commonwealth "to take all possible steps to secure the exclusion of the Union of South Africa" from the organization. With regard to the UN, the Conference recommended approaching the UN in order for it to take the appropriate measures against South Africa in accordance with Article 41 of the UN Charter.[25] This Article permits the Security Council to call upon member states to adopt coercive measures against an astray member state, such as economic sanctions and the severance of diplomatic relations.

In the face of the Afrikaners' unshakable obduracy and the lenience of some permanent members of the Security Council vis-à-vis the application of myriad resolutions adopted, especially by the General Assembly, calling for the abandonment of the system of Apartheid, the Assembly further toughened its language at its 7th session held in 1962. On 6 November, it passed resolution 1761 (XVII) in which it deplored the failure of the regime in Pretoria to comply with the repeated requests and demands of the UN by refusing to abandon its racial policies. In paragraph 4 of the resolution, the Assembly requested UN member states to take some specific measures, either individually or collectively, to bring about the desired change of policy in South Africa. It proposed, *inter alia*, breaking off diplomatic relations with the regime or refraining from establishing such relations, closing their sea-ports to all vessels flying the South African flag, boycotting all South African goods, and refusing landing and passage facilities to all aircraft belonging to the government of the Union of South Africa. It was in this year also that the Assembly established the "Special Committee on the Policies of Apartheid of the Government of the Union of South Africa." The name of this Committee was shortened in 1971 for it to be known as the "Special Committee on Apartheid;" it was renamed in 1974 as the "Special Committee against Apartheid."

As noted above, the second phase of UN-Africa partnership in their joint fight against Apartheid was the nearly two decades from 1967 to 1989. In this period, with the notable exception of Namibia, virtually all African states regained their sovereignty and became members of the United Nations. The African Group of States at the UN (AGS-UN) had grown even stronger. Of course, by this time, the OAU had also been born. By this, not only did African states benefit hugely from the coordinating role of the AGS-UN, but also the fact that African states could even coordinate their positions at home and during a single meeting at Addis Ababa before coming to New York was a veritable bright development. The Security Council too expanded in 1963 from just eleven members to fifteen with at least two non-permanent member seats for Africa at any single time. Albeit the increase only affected the non-permanent membership of the Council as the five permanent members retained their status, it did have a significant bearing on the Council voting records, procedures and the way it began to consider matters brought to its attention. The increase meant that the non-permanent members were now in the majority. And because any proposed resolution rejected by at least nine members, even non-permanent, cannot be adopted by the Council, the non-permanent members could now use their collective vote as either a stick or a carrot vis-à-vis the big powers.

Moreover, 1971 saw Formosa (Taiwan) give up its permanent seat with veto power on the Council to mainland China with its capital in Beijing. From 1945 to 1971, the permanent member seat of China was occupied by the pro-Western Taiwan because the Western members of the Council did not want to see the seat of China occupied by the Communists of Beijing. The Soviet Union was thus isolated in the Council by the Western powers during this period. Yet, albeit it could be attributed to a number of factors, the Soviets were the most sympathetic to African issues of all big powers. The Chinese voice added to that.

Thus in this period, the UN moved from merely appealing to the South African government to renounce its policies of racial discrimination to real action and taking practical measures. These actions included, for example, imposing some of the aforementioned economic and diplomatic sanctions on South Africa and excluding the country from international sporting competitions and exposing the evil nature of the Apartheid system to the world public opinion. Obviously, this proved to be the most delicate of all the three phases of UN-Africa partnership against Apartheid. It was so because the Apartheid regime did not lack powerful sympathisers, not to say supporters, amongst the big powers.

The Western powers were particularly uncooperative with UN actions and unsympathetic to African positions with regard to the

South African regime. Britain (the former colonial power of South Africa), France and the United States —three permanent members of the Security Council— were particularly uncooperative and at times obstructionist. The regrettable attitude of these three countries in particular and some other Western countries was to the point that the General Assembly found itself compelled, in a resolution it passed in 1966, to publicly condemn their "failure to cooperate in implementing resolutions of the General Assembly." It also deplored their refusal to join the Special Committee against Apartheid. In sum, the Assembly was disappointed at their obstructionist and frustrating attitude towards the proposed actions of the wider membership of the United Nations.[26]

The attitude of these three permanent members of the UN Security Council was indeed disappointing. This was even more when they used or rather misused their veto power not only to block proposed actions of the UN, but also to prevent the world body from even criticising the Apartheid policy in South Africa and those of other white minority regimes in the region. It is for example unfortunate to note that of the 32 or so vetoes cast by Britain by the end of 2005, nine (five with the US and four with the US and France) were used to back the Apartheid regime in South Africa. A further nine (twice with the US) were used to back the minority white racist regime in Zimbabwe, while, worst still, Britain used a further seven (six with the US and France) to support the South African government in its racist policies in Namibia. This is a total of 25 vetoes, or 78 percent of all British vetoes cast.

It seems intriguing for many people why some Western powers acted in the way they did towards the Apartheid and other white minority regimes in Southern Africa. Two explanations may be found to this. One is that some leaders in these countries more or less shared the racist convictions of these regimes, albeit they tended to be careful not to show this publicly to the international community and world public opinion. The other factor was what was called the strategic and economic considerations. It was this latter one, which was to some extent, albeit immorally, explicable and demonstrable, that the uncooperative governments used to justify their refusal or unwillingness to cooperate with the international community or even to heed the principles of human conscience and morality. The former British Prime Minister (1979-1990), Margaret Thatcher, was one of the staunchest supporters of the Apartheid regime in South Africa, and her stance may well have been motivated by both the two aforementioned factors. However, it was to the latter one (the economic and strategic one) that she turned to provide her self-justification when she wrote:

> South Africa had by far the richest and most varied range of natural resources of any African country. It was the world's largest supplier of gold, platinum ... and other vital materials [...] Even if it had been morally acceptable to pursue a policy which would have led to the collapse of South Africa, it would not therefore have made strategic sense.[27]

Thatcher claims that this was the only explanation for her failure to cooperate with the international community and take heed of the moral implications of her support for the Apartheid regime. Yet, the racist underpinnings of her stance can be spotted even in her carefully written autobiography. To her, "[Apartheid] South Africa could not fulfil its economic potential unless black labour was *brought* to the cities and trained [to serve their white masters.]"[28] Thatcher never acknowledged that what the oppressed people were engaged in Southern Africa was a legitimate resistance. Her preferred word to describe the situation was always, "the need to stop *violence.*" She is even reported to have described Nelson Mandela as a "terrorist." Similarly, with France's record of racism and discrimination against black people, even to this day, the stance taken by Paris with regard to Apartheid South Africa and other white minority regimes was not a surprise.[29]

Such was UN-Africa partnership in combating the political evil of racial discrimination in South Africa in this period. It is the attitude of these Western countries rather than a failure of the wider UN system that better explains the relative ineffectiveness of UN actions against the Apartheid regime in Pretoria and why it took so long for the system of Apartheid to collapse. It also explains why the bulk of UN work on the issue was done by the General Assembly instead of the Security Council. Despite all this however, the South African resistance movements spearheaded by the ANC and African and other members of the United Nations, especially through the General Assembly and the UN specialised agencies, continued their efforts in order to have a real change of policy in South Africa in particular and the Southern African sub-region in general. It was these efforts that paid dividends in the last and third phase (1990-1994) of UN-Africa partnership in the fight against Apartheid. It was these efforts also that eventually resulted in the total collapse and dismantling of the wickedest and the most evil political doctrine of the twentieth century.

Conflict Resolution and Peace-building in Africa

On the basis of the three logical phases of armed conflicts — pre-conflict, conflict period and post-conflict period— one can identify three main concepts of conflict management. These are: conflict prevention or preventive diplomacy; conflict settlement, peace-making and peace-keeping; and conflict transformation and post-conflict peace-building.

Arguably, it is the report of the former and first African UN Secretary-General, Boutros Boutros-Ghali, entitled *An Agenda for Peace* that made the term "conflict prevention" very popular in the conflict management research community. Boutros-Ghali defined it as the "action to prevent disputes from arising between parties, to prevent existing disputes from escalating into conflicts and to limit the spread of the latter when they occur."[30] The main aims of this will be "to seek to identify at the earliest possible stage situations that could produce conflict, and to try through diplomacy to remove the sources of danger before violence results."[31] His successor, Kofi Annan, another African, confirmed this in a similar report to the Security Council in June 2001.[32]

The terms "conflict settlement," "peace-making" and "peace-keeping" refer to the range of actions undertaken or that ought to be undertaken to bring hostilities to a halt and bring the warring factions to the negotiating table. It also includes the deployment of peace-keeping troops by a third party such as UN peace-keeping troops. At this stage of armed conflict, with a cease-fire in place, efforts are made to seek to address the deep-rooted sources of the conflict in an attempt to reach a durable solution to the conflict, which is why the term "conflict resolution" can also be used here.

The third and final concept is conflict transformation or post-conflict peace-building. Albeit the term "peace-building" got its pre-eminence in the conflict management research community after its use by Boutros-Ghali in his *An Agenda for Peace*, it had been used by Johan Galtung about two decades earlier and possibly by many others.[33] According to Boutros-Ghali, post-conflict peace-building consists of the "comprehensive efforts [made or to be made] to identify and support structures which will tend to consolidate peace and advance a sense of confidence and well-being among people." These efforts "may include disarming the previously warring parties and the restoration of order, the custody and possible destruction of weapons, repatriating refugees, [providing] advisory and training support for security personnel, monitoring elections, advancing efforts to protect human rights, reforming or strengthening government institutions and [consolidating the democratic process in general]." Thus, to Boutros-Ghali, the concept of post-conflict peace-building should be viewed as the counterpart of preventive diplomacy in that preventive diplomacy is to avoid a crisis and post-conflict peace-building is to prevent a recurrence [of conflict once peace has been restored through the measures of peace settlement.[34]

Maintaining international peace and security is the prime cause and the main *raison d'être* of the United Nations. At least in theory, it was partly the determination of the peoples of the world "to save succeeding generations from the scourge of war" that led them to consider forming and eventually pool their resources and political will to form the United Nations Organization in 1945. Therefore, peace-keeping is or ought to be the main activity of the United Nations. This is partly why its main executive organ was given the name "Security Council."

However, on the basis of the concepts mentioned above and considering UN involvement in conflict resolution in Africa, it is quite right to conclude that as far as the first phase, conflict prevention is concerned, the world body has by and large failed Africa, as we will see later (see *Chapter 3*). The involvement of the UN in the second phase, peace-keeping, can be said to have so far been a mixture of relative success and outright failure. We will look at some of those that were relatively successful while reserving the analysis of the disastrous ones for the next chapter. It is however in the phase of peace-building that the record of the world body seems to be generally positive in Africa. This is not a surprise given the enormous resources and technical expertise that it has. A few case studies may better put these remarks in perspective. For this, I have chosen the very first UN peace-keeping mission in Sub-Saharan Africa (ONUC) sent to the Congo in 1960, and the most recent one, the still ongoing (as of February 2006) United Nations Operation in Côte d'Ivoire (UNOCI). The UN peace-building efforts in support of those of the Economic Community of West African States (ECOWAS) in Liberia and Sierra Leone could also be shown as an example of successful UN conflict management effort in Africa. We have mentioned above the case of the United Nations Transition Group (UNTAG) sent to Namibia in 1989. This is regarded, at least according to Zacarias, one of the closest observers of the mission, as an "almost total success."[35]

In the Congo

The United Nations Operation in the Congo (ONUC, from its French name *Opération des Nations Unies au Congo*) which was sent in 1960 to the present-day Democratic Republic of Congo (DRC), then called Congo-Léopoldville, was a remarkable peace-keeping mission in at least three regards. First, it was by far the largest peace-keeping force in UN history. It comprised at its peak some 20,000 civilian and military officers on the ground. Secondly, it was the first time the United Nations had intervened in a situation of internal or intra-state conflict as opposed to inter-state conflicts, its classical and preferred field of operation. In fact, despite the Congo experience, most UN peace-keeping operations remained limited to international conflicts until the recrudescence of internal conflicts (civil wars) in the 1990s. Like almost all the other civil war situations that have attracted UN attention, the Congolese crisis, albeit internal in origin and in appearance, had many international dimensions that justified UN intervention, for it had become a threat to international peace and security. The third remarkable aspect of the ONUC is that even before its formation, two of the leading actors in the crisis for whose resolution it was established lost their lives in the vicissitudes of the situation: Patrice Lumumba, the Congolese Prime Minister, was tragically assassinated in early 1961 and Dag Hammarskjöld, the UN Secretary General died in a still unexplained plane crash while on mission in the area later in the same year.[36]

In the European scramble for Africa, the "giant" Congo had been colonised by the "little" Belgium.[37] The Belgian occupation of the Congo turned out to be one of the most neglectful and exploitative colonial regimes in Africa. In retrospect, although it was not very different from other colonial powers in general, one can conclude that all that the Belgians were interested in was to pillage the country's vast natural resources and exploit its people to the full with an exceptional arrogant attitude that can rarely be imagined between two peoples. At the dawn of independence in 1960, of the 14 million Congolese, there were only 17 university graduates. There was no single indigenous doctor in the whole country. There were no lawyers or engineers. Yet the Congolese people were eager to regain their independence.

In December 1959, Congolese leaders held a round-table conference with Belgian officials in Brussels. Partly influenced by the march of other African territories towards independence and pressed by the nationalist forces on the ground, Belgium agreed in January 1960 to grant independence to the Congo, but gave no time for preparations on the ground. Perhaps to force the newly independent state to be entirely dependent on it for assistance, it insisted that the Congo's independence would be given as of 30 June that same year, and so it was.

Came Independence Day and the Congolese celebrated their regaining of sovereignty. On 23 June, barely six days before D-Day, Joseph Kasavubu was elected President of the new state, while Patrice Lumumba won the position of Prime Minister. The two Congolese figures were of different political persuasions. Unlike the President, Lumumba wanted to assert full independence for the country and was more vocal towards the Belgian imperialists. It is for this and the tragic circumstances of his assassination that he is still to this day remembered as one of the heroes of African independence.

Independence came but the Belgians maintained most of the administrative and technical personnel of the colonial administration. Two military bases in Kamina and Kitona remained in the country with the pretext that the Belgian government could, at the request of the Congolese government, call out the Belgian troops from the two bases to assist the latter in maintaining law and order. The two military bases had a few thousand all-white officers commanded by the Belgian Lieutenant-General Emile Janssens. The Belgian general also remained the commander of the new Congolese army. Of course, such provisions had been enshrined in a dictated "treaty of friendship" signed by the representatives of the two Governments just one day before independence. The treaty never was ratified.[38]

Other military camps had a few African officers but were still dominated by the Belgians. In his speech delivered on Independence Day in the presence of the king of the Belgians, Lumumba referred to these realities and the exploitative nature of Belgian occupation in a way that the Congolese were not used to seeing a black man do in front of the white man, let alone a king of the whites. It was partly this speech that alerted many Congolese about the state of affairs in their country. The Congolese offices petitioned General Jenssens for more promotion opportunities. The Belgian general, in a daily order of 5 July 1960, bluntly dismissed their petition arrogantly stating that "before 30 June you had white officers. ... Nothing has changed."[39] Given this arrogant reaction of the Belgian officers, mutiny broke out in the few military camps where there was a mixture of white and Congolese soldiers. Congolese officers called for the Africanization of senior ranks in the gendarmerie.

This revolt was the starting point of the whole affair. In the night of 5 July, Lumumba strove to restore calm in the mutinous camps. He dismissed the Belgian general Jenssens the following day and replaced him with Victor Lundula, a Congolese, with the rank of Major-General. He appointed the man who later became Mobutu Sese Seko, a Congolese officer, as the military Chief of Staff with the rank of Colonel. He promoted all the Congolese non-commissioned officers. However, the disturbances continued and intensified.

The UN Secretary General at the time, Dag Hammarskjöld, had visited the Congo in January 1960. During the celebrations of Congolese independence, he had sent his Under-Secretary for

Special Political Affairs, Ralph J. Bunche, to attend the events as his personal representative. Bunch arrived in Léopoldville (now Kinshasa) four days before Independence Day and was still there when these disturbances commenced. Bunche was in the country to discuss opportunities for United Nations technical assistance for the new Congolese government. Thus, when he felt that the Belgians intended on sending Belgian troops to the Congo, he strongly advised the Belgian ambassador to the Congo not to go ahead with that without the consent of the Congolese government. This was the beginning of the United Nations' involvement in the Congolese crisis and the start of another phase of UN-Africa partnership in conflict resolution. Having sensed the fragility of the Congolese army and the obduracy of the Belgians to continue with their neo-colonial plans, Bunche urged the Congolese authorities to seek UN technical assistance of a military nature in order to help the government control and strengthen the army.

The Congolese authorities agreed to this suggestion and, on 10 July, submitted a formal request to the UN Secretary-General for technical assistance of a military nature, including military advisors, military experts and technicians.[40]

Nonetheless, the Belgians unilaterally reinforced their presence in the country the following day (11 July). With no prior agreement with the Congolese government as the UN envoy had advised, the Belgian government sent several battalions of parachutists to a number of major Congolese cities, including Léopoldville. Their pretext was to restore law and order and protect the Belgian nationals that had remained in the Congo after independence. This illegal intervention of the Belgians in the country increased tension and disorder throughout the country. On 11 July, possibly at the instigation of the Belgians, Moïse Tchombe, the provincial president of Katanga, proclaimed the secession and independence of the province from the federal government of Léopoldville on the ground of a breakdown of civil order and the disintegration of the country's administrative system. This province was the richest region of the country, which provided the country with more than half of its revenues and had the biggest concentration of Belgian investment.

Henceforth, the United Nations was to have a major role in the Congolese crisis especially that the number of independent African states now in the world body had dramatically increased. Thus, the day after the arrival of the Belgian troops in the country, the Congolese authorities sent a telegram (jointly signed by President Kasavubu and Prime Minister Lumumba) to the UN Secretary-General for urgent UN military assistance. Their major preoccupation was to preserve the national integrity of the country in the face of foreign aggression which, as they contended in the telegram, constitutes "a threat to international peace."[41]

Using his powers under Article 99 of the UN Charter, Hammarskjöld summoned the Security Council to consider the crisis in the Congo.[42] He asked to be authorised to take the necessary measures to provide the Congolese government with UN military and technical assistance. During the night of 13/14 July, the Council sat and eventually adopted resolution 143 (1960). In this resolution, the Council simply appealed to Belgium "to withdraw its troops" from the Congo and agreed to offer UN military assistance to the Congolese government "until ...the [Congolese] national security forces might be able . . . to meet fully their tasks." The resolution was adopted by eight votes in favour to none against, with three abstentions. The abstainers included Britain and France, as these two countries remained loyal to Brussels in its time of struggle on their common denominator (i.e. colonialism and neo-colonialism.)

In any case, it is clear that the wording of this resolution fell quite short of what the Congolese authorities had requested. Whereas their concern was the illegal presence of the Belgian troops on their soil, the wording of the resolution related only to the internal situation in the Congo. Thus, in their second telegram to the Secretary-General, they explicitly wrote: "assistance sought aims not restore internal situation in Congo but rather protect national territory against act aggression by troops from metropolitan Belgium."[43]

Eventually however, the UN force (ONUC) was sent to the Congo. It was formed mainly of African contingents. Ethiopia, Ghana, Guinea, Mali, Morocco and Tunisia had offered to send troops and the Council agreed to that. Seven military battalions from these countries together with a Swedish battalion from the United Nations Emergency Force (UNEF) based in Gaza (Palestine) arrived in the Congo in steps beginning on 15 July. The force reached nearly 20,000 officers at its peak in July 1961. Hammarskjöld appointed the Swedish Lieutenant-General Carl C. von Horn as supreme commander of the force while he designated Bunche as his Special Representative in the country.

This notwithstanding and partly owing to the ambiguity in the mandate of the UN force, the security situation worsened in the country. In fact, despite the presence of UN troops, the secession of Katanga was being consolidated by Belgian and other mercenary support and Belgian troops remained in the country. This necessitated further Security Council efforts. The Council adopted a second resolution on 22 July but almost reiterating what it had already said in the previous resolution.[44] It took another meeting of the Security Council in August and another resolution (S/4406) before the UN troops would be authorized to enter Katanga. However, the classical principle of not getting involved in the internal issues of any country was upheld, for the resolution stipulated that ONUC "will not take part in any internal conflict, will not intervene in such a conflict in any way, and will not be used to influence its outcome."

In the meantime, the Congolese troops received orders from Lumumba, the Prime Minister, to launch their own military operation against the secessionist province of Katanga in September. However, a constitutional crisis or rather dissensions emerged within the Congolese ruling class owing mainly to differences of view between the two top men in the country, President Kasavubu and Prime Minister Lumumba.

Amidst these turbulent moments, the UN Secretary-General made a grand mistake. It is unclear whether he was simply naïve or whether he was just being influenced by the Council members that were allied to Belgium, or was it a bit of both? One cannot tell. What is certain however is that his decision to "directly" telegraph Moïse Tchombe to discuss with him the terms "for deploying United Nations troops to Katanga" was a gross political and diplomatic error. No country, even Belgium, had officially recognised Katanga's independence. Yet by this action the Secretary-General sent a very bad signal by implicitly implying that the rebellious province could somehow be regarded as sovereign to the point that the UN chief administrator could deal with it directly. Hammarskjöld set off for Katanga and arrived at Elizabethville (now Lubumbashi), the capital of Katanga, on 12 August accompanied by some 300 Swedish ONUC troops. At the end of a two-day meeting with Tchombe, the latter got him to agree to his own terms as conditions for the deployment of UN troops in the province, including respect of the *status quo*.

By accepting those terms, Hammarskjöld greatly angered Lumumba and many of his supporters amongst the Pan-African movement. The Soviet Union, already at odds with the UN Secretary-General, supported Lumumba in his disagreement with the UN chief administrator. Hammarskjöld's role and with him that of the UN was now being regarded as imperialistic.

This further worsened the crisis, especially between Kasavubu and Lumumba. On 5 September, after a meeting with two Belgian officers and some neo-imperialist elements of the UN force, Kasavubu suddenly declared on the radio the dismissal of Lumumba from his post as Prime Minister. By the end of the year, Lumumba was arrested, and in January 1961 he was handed over to Tshombe's forces and murdered. The head of the only Congolese government to have been legally invested by the parliament had been eliminated. A tragic end had been put to the life of one of the most aspiring sons of Africa. The Katangese secession was continuing. The Belgian troops were still in the country. UN's efforts up to this day were almost a complete failure and disappointment, if not in complicity with the imperialist forces. Fortunately, from a tragedy came a blessing.

Soon after the regrettable murder of Lumumba, which was only publicly announced on 13 February 1961, and following the outrage which it caused in world public opinion, the UN Security Council found itself compelled to give precise instructions to the Secretary-General, instead of leaving him to take his own decisions. With further Security Council resolutions and new and reinforced mandate for the ONUC, the UN force began by making commendable progress. Starting from the beginning of the last quarter of the year, UN troops began disarming and/or arresting scores of non-African mercenaries. By mid-April 1961, the tasks of the UN force in the Congo now included, according to General Assembly resolution 1600 (XV), such tough tasks as investigation into the circumstances of Lumumba's death, the resumption of efforts to reorganise and control the Congolese army (*Armée nationale congolaise* — ANC), removal of Belgian troops and political presence, and convening of a Congolese parliament. It seemed that the main remaining task of the UN troops was now the internal issue, particularly the Katangese secession. For this, the UN Secretary-General thought that a further negotiation with Tchombe was needed. He thus sought and obtained the promise of a cease-fire and discussions from the rebel leader. He soon set off to meet Tshombe, but in the night of 17 September, the aeroplane taking him and his Swedish crew crashed after a sharp turn over the aerodrome near Ndola in present-day Zambia.The Secretary-General and all the crew members died, thereby opening a new page in UN involvement in the Congo. Again, as in the case of Lumumba's death, Hammarskjöld's was not to be in vain either.

The UN chief's death led to the world body taking a firmer stance on the issue of Congo and ONUC's mandate. A new Secretary-General was appointed in the person of U Thant of Burma now Myanmar. In November, the Security Council adopted a new resolution authorising ONUC to use force if necessary.[45] New measures were adopted to crush the secession, disarm the mercenaries and get Belgium to withdraw its troops. With this success in the apparent unification of the country, ONUC began a phased withdrawal of its troops until their mission was terminated in June 1964. By the time UN troops finally left the Congo at the end of June, the civil strife in the country had not yet come to a complete end. However, as Kouassi contends, given their role in ending the Belgian occupation and the defeat of the mercenary troops, all this despite the fact that some Western powers had sided with both Belgium and through it the destabilising secessionist forces in the country, it would appear that the UN helped to save the Congo from disintegrating.[46] One could also argue that albeit Hammarskjöld appeared to be naïve and, because of this, committed some serious political and judgemental errors, he did have good intentions with regard to the UN mission in the country.

About three decades after the end of this mission, the UN returned to the Congo in 1999, after the signing of the Lusaka Agreement. This Agreement was signed in the Zambian capital, Lusaka, on 10 July 1999, following an active mediation by the OAU and the Southern African Development Community (SADC). It was signed between the government of Laurent-Désiré Kabila of the Democratic Republic of the Congo (DRC) and the governments of Angola, Namibia, Rwanda, Uganda and Zimbabwe, the countries that had been assisting one or the other belligerent in the conflict that was going on in the DRC since or shortly after the overthrow of the dictatorial, kleptocratic and nepotistic regime of Mobutu Sese Seko in May 1997 by the forces of Laurent-Désiré who was assassinated in power in January 2001, allowing his son, Joseph Kabila to be appointed the new President. As provided by this Agreement, the Security Council established, in November 1999, the United Nations Mission in the Democratic Republic of the Congo (MONUC) and Kofi Annan appointed Kamel Morjane of Tunisia as his Special Representative in the country. This mission was still ongoing by the end of 2005.

The case of Côte d'Ivoire

The most recent example of UN's involvement in peace-keeping in Africa is the UN peace-keeping mission in Côte d'Ivoire. The conflict in Côte d'Ivoire started on 19 September 2002. It was first an insurrection by some army officers allegedly unhappy with their proposed demobilisation from the army while the Head of State, President Laurent Gbagbo, was away. The officers had taken up arms in an uprising that led to fighting in Abidjan —the country's economic capital— in which about 300 people were killed, including the Interior Minister, Émile Boga Doudou, and the erstwhile military Head of State, General Robert Gueï. It soon became clear that the country was heading for a full-scale civil war. And civil war it became. Quickly, the insurgents changed their first claim to that of protest against what they called discriminatory policies that the government was applying or maintaining against some groups of the population identified as those from the North. They then formed themselves into the *Mouvement patriotique de Côte*

99

d'Ivoire (Patriotic movement of Côte d'Ivoire —MPCI). A former leader of the Ivorian national students' union, Guillaume Soro, in his mid-thirties, became their declared leader. Two other factions later joined this main rebel group, as always in civil wars.

The UN's involvement in Côte d'Ivoire dates back to 2001, well before the start of the current civil war which started in the country on 19 September 2002. This was after the events of October 2000 following popular protests on the streets of Abidjan to prevent the military from clinging onto power, in which many people died amid allegations of massacre and extra-judicial killings. After Laurent Gbagbo assumed the presidency, the UN sent an International Commission of Inquiry to Côte d'Ivoire between February and May 2001. Later in the year, this Commission presented to the UN Secretary-General its findings and recommendations in a final report of 80 pages including annexes.[47]

After the outbreak of the civil war in September 2002, the UN was not very quick in its response. However, it seems that the hiatus between the start of hostilities in the country and its first reaction was spent in observing the situation and hoping that the mediation efforts of the Economic Community of West African States (ECOWAS) and the African Union (AU) would succeed in controlling the situation. The first reaction of the United Nations to the crisis came from a statement by the President of the Security Council on 20 December 2002. In this statement, "the Council condemn[ed] attempts to use force to influence the political situation in Côte d'Ivoire and to overthrow the elected Government." The statement also made it clear that the Security Council strongly supported the efforts of ECOWAS to promote a peaceful solution to the conflict. It urged ECOWAS leaders to continue their efforts in a coordinated manner.[48] Ever since this statement, Côte d'Ivoire has hardly been absent from the deliberations of the different bodies of the United Nations — without doubt because France has been pushing for this.

From the start of the conflict to the end of 2005, the UN Security Council passed 14 resolutions (four in 2003, three in 2004, and seven in 2005) on the situation in Côte d'Ivoire. In the same period, there were ten statements from Council presidents on the situation, including the aforesaid debut statement. Moreover, by the end of

2005, the UN Secretary General had submitted to the Council as many as 12 reports on the UN Operation in Côte d'Ivoire. Even the General Assembly had to deal with the Ivorian issue in three of its plenary sessions in 2003, 2004, and 2005.[49] While Security Council resolutions and statements of its presidents dealt with operational issues of the peace process on the ground, the concerns of the Assembly's deliberations were mainly about "the financial situation with regard to peace-keeping activities, in particular as regards the reimbursements to troop contributors that bear additional burdens owing to overdue payments by Member States of their assessments."

The first Security Council resolution with regard to the Ivorian crisis was adopted on 4 February 2003.[50] In this resolution, the Council reiterated its support to ECOWAS and African Union mediation efforts. It endorsed the Linas-Marcoussis Agreement that had been mediated by the French and signed in France the previous month and welcomed the deployment of ECOWAS peace-keeping forces (ECOMOG) and French troops in the country. It requested both ECOWAS and France to report periodically to the Council on all aspects of the implementation of their respective mandates. Three months later, on 13 May, the Council passed resolution 1479, which established, "for an initial period of six months, a United Nations Mission in Côte d'Ivoire (MINUCI), with a mandate to facilitate the implementation by the Ivorian parties of the Linas-Marcoussis Agreement." In August of the same year, the Security Council decided to renew for a period of six months the authorisation given to the ECOWAS and French forces in the country.[51]

Following a request by the ECOWAS to establish a peace-keeping force in Côte d'Ivoire, the Security Council, in its resolution 1528 of 27 February 2004, decided to establish the United Nations Operation in Côte d'Ivoire (UNOCI) for an initial period of 12 months as from 4 April 2004 and requested the transfer of authority from MINUCI to the new force. ECOWAS leaders were also requested to merge their peace-keeping troops into the new force. Interestingly, France did not allow the merger of its forces into the UN operation and the Council accepted this. The initial military strength of UNOCI was hoped to be 6,240 people, including 200 military observers and 120 staff officers, and up to 350 civilian police officers. However, owing to arguments between France and the US, the deployment of this force was significantly delayed, so that by September 2004, it had not reached the initial number of soldiers and it only reached this number in March 2005. To many observers, the US was hindering the deployment of the force in an apparent revenge for France's stance when Washington sought Security Council's backing for its invasion of Iraq in 2002/2003.

This, in a nutshell, is the involvement of the UN in the Ivorian civil war. While this shows a real partnership between the UN and Africa in this case, especially with ECOWAS, one observes however the significant influence that France has had on the world body's actions and the frequency, speed and wordings of many of its resolutions. A few examples could illustrate this. First, despite the fact that the Linas-Marcoussis Agreement was preceded (Accra I) and followed by many peace efforts and agreements (the Accra II & III and Pretoria Agreements), the United Nations made the Marcoussis Agreement the main reference in all its resolutions about the Ivorian crisis. Second, there is no denying that there were some media organs, especially in the government-controlled areas in Côte d'Ivoire that used, at times, deplorable xenophobic expressions amounting to incitement of religious and ethnic hatred. However, the frequent appearance of this issue in the Security Council's resolutions cannot be attributed to any party but France.

For example, in the fifth paragraph of the preamble to resolution 1572 of 15 November 2004, the Council expressed its deep concern "by the use of the media, in particular radio and television broadcasts, to incite hatred and violence against foreigners in Côte d'Ivoire." In reality, the foreigners concerned here are French nationals and this came after a bloody confrontation between the French troops and supporters of President Gbagbo in Abidjan in November 2004 in which several Ivorian protesters were killed. This incident, following the French destruction of the Ivorian air force, and the apparent arrogant response of the French authorities, especially the Defence Minister, led to anti-French demonstrations across government-controlled areas. In such circumstances, negative media reporting, albeit regrettable, may be inevitable.

The third example of French influence on UN decisions can be found in the same resolution and in two instances. First, the resolution "condemns the air strikes committed by the national armed forces of Côte d'Ivoire (FANCI)"on 4 November and regarded it as constituting "flagrant violations of the cease-fire agreement." In the following paragraph (para. 2), the Council "reiterates its full support for the action undertaken by UNOCI and French forces" in reaction to these illegal air strikes by the FANCI. To be sure, UNOCI had little if anything to do with this. The reaction was almost entirely by the French forces and was, one may argue, quite disproportionate and deliberately aimed at weakening the military capacity of the Ivorian government, which it succeeded in doing, at least partially by destroying the entire capacity of the token Ivorian air force. The second instance of French influence in this resolution relates to the travel ban and freezing of assets of those "who constitute a threat to the peace and national reconciliation process in Côte d'Ivoire." Knowing that members of the rebel forces do not need travelling as much as those of the Government or the entourage of President Gbagbo may need, but also because the former may not have any assets abroad at all, the target is clearly visible. In fact the hostility of the French authorities towards the government of Laurent Gbagbo in Abidjan is known.

Finally, one may note the fact that whenever the Security Council mentioned the UNOCI and the French forces in Côte d'Ivoire, the wording always emphasised the authorisation of the French forces to "use all necessary means in order to support UNOCI in accordance with the agreement *to be reached between UNOCI and the French authorities.*"[52] Despite this, the determination shown by African actors, particularly ECOWAS and the AU, made it, to a large extent, difficult for the UN to blindly subscribe to France's dictates. This was the case for example when the AU mediator in the Ivorian crisis, President Thabo Mbeki of South Africa, managed to put the application of the sanctions and travel bans on hold while he carried out his mediation efforts. This remained the case as this book was finalized. Likewise, towards the expiry of President Gbagbo's term of office on 30 October 2005, many senior French officials favoured having a transition without President Gbagbo. However, following the decision of the Peace and Security Council (PSC) of the African Union in early October to allow Gbagbo to remain in power up to 12 months in view of the impossibility of organising the presidential elections on the date scheduled, the UN endorsed this decision in its resolution 1633 of 21 October 2005. Unless something dramatic happens to disturb this fine partnership between Africa and the world body, the Ivorian crisis should serve as one of the finest examples of UN-Africa partnership in peace-keeping on the continent.

Arms Control and Refugee Protection

Related to peace-keeping in Africa but quite different from it is the control of small arms and light weapons that have become the preferred weapon of warring factions in the different armed conflicts that occur on the continent. The flow of refugees being almost an intrinsic consequence of armed conflicts, care for them while in foreign countries and their repatriation at the end of hostilities back to their home countries is part of any successful peace settlement. Here again, Africa and the United Nations have worked hand in hand despite some disappointing results.

As regards arms control, it is instructive to note that the first initiative on this issue came from Mali. In October 1993, President Alpha Oumar Konaré of Mali, now the President of the Commission of the African Union, sent a letter to the United Nations Secretary-General, Boutros Boutros-Ghali. In the letter, Konaré sought the world body's assistance, through its Secretary-General, in collecting small arms that were abundantly circulating in his country and in the sub-region even one year after the end of a protracted civil war in the north of his country. For the first time the issue of small arms was taken up by the UN. The Secretary-General talked about this letter at a meeting of the UN Secretary-General's Advisory Board on Disarmament Matters held in Geneva in January 1994.

In August 1994, the UN dispatched a fact-finding mission to Mali headed by a former Secretary-General of the OAU. In his report *Supplement to an Agenda for Peace* published in January 1995, Boutros-Ghali gave a further boost to the idea of finding solutions to the issue of small arms, especially when he argued: "I believe strongly that the search should begin now." Another Advisory mission was sent to a number of neighbouring countries to Mali in February/March 1995.[53]

At the fiftieth session of the General Assembly, held in December 1995, it was requested from Boutros-Ghali to prepare a report on small arms with the assistance of a panel group of qualified governmental experts.[54] At the fifty-second session of the Assembly in 1997, this Panel of Governmental Experts on Small Arms submitted its report. According to this report, small arms and light weapons are defined as "anything that can be carried up a hill by two adults, or transported on the back of a jeep." Small arms include revolvers and self-loading pistols, rifles and carbines, assault rifles, sub-machine guns, and light machine guns. As for light weapons, they include heavy machine guns, hand-held under barrel and mounted grenade launchers, portable anti-tank and anti-aircraft systems, as well as mortars of less than 100 mm calibre.[55] In September 1999, a joint workshop was held on the Establishment of a Database and an Arms Register on Light Weapons in Africa.[56] This came out of recommendations made in Bamako, Mali, in March 1999 during the ECOWAS Ministerial meeting on the modalities for the implementation of the Programme for Co-ordination and Assistance for Security and Development (PCASED), drawn up by a meeting of the United Nations Regional Centre for Peace and Disarmament in Africa (UNRCPDA) and ECOWAS organised in the Ghanaian capital, Accra.

It is true that despite these efforts, the African continent is still awash with small arms and light weapons. As I have argued elsewhere,[57] the problem here does not lie with the UN as an institution. The ineffectiveness of these efforts is mainly to be blamed on some external and internal factors. The external one is the obdurate refusal of many arms manufacturing countries, especially the biggest ones amongst them —who also are the veto-welding members of the Security Council— to cooperate with the world body. This is due to purely economic considerations. Take the case of the United States for example. Washington is the largest single arms manufacturer in the world today. In the four years between 1996 and 1999 inclusive, the US licensed nearly US$ 2 billions worth of small arms and light weapons exports around the world.[58]Yet, at the start of the UN 2001 small arms conference, the

US Under Secretary of State for Arms Control and International Security Affairs —John Bolton, now the US ambassador to the UN— warned against negotiations leading to binding agreements with regard to applying stricter regulations in the small arms market. Commenting on the proposed UN resolution to be adopted at the end of the conference he declared: "You can see that from little acorns bad treaties grow."[59] Moreover, according to Amnesty International, by mid-2004, there were still "serious flaws in the European Union's key arms control agreements, especially the 1998 EU Code of Conduct on Arms Exports."[60]

The internal factor is the persistence of armed conflicts, especially civil wars, on the continent. While there are external factors fuelling these conflicts, the internal causes are the main factors to be blamed. Owing to the insistence of arms manufacturing nations on continuing with their business based on purely economic considerations despite the moral implications, especially when it comes to trading in conflict zones, it is unlikely that the UN alone, without much effort by African governments to immunise their countries from armed conflicts and thus arms merchants, will succeed. In any event, the efforts being made lend support to the argument that arms control is one of the sectors of conflict management that one can point to as a true UN-Africa partnership.

As regards refugee protection and care for refugees, perhaps the work of the United Nations High Commission for Refugees (UNHCR) in conflict zones needs no comment. Whenever there is an armed conflict on the continent, the UNHCR is often quick in getting its staff on the ground to care for the Internally Displaced Persons (IDPs). Where people have fled their country to seek refuge in other countries, the UN specialised agency has often worked with host countries to care for the refugees. In coordination with host countries, it sets up refugee schools and, with the assistance of other UN agencies, such as the United Nations Development Programme (UNDP), the United Nations Children Fund (UNICEF) and the like, they initiate many development projects for the refugee populations. The combined work of these agencies in the phase of Disarmament, Demobilisation and Re-integration (DDR) of former combatants in post-conflict nations is also a clear proof of UN-

Africa partnership in peace-building in the concerned countries across the continent.

Economic development and capacity building

Albeit maintaining international peace and security was the main driving force behind the formation of the United Nations, the world body was also founded "to promote social progress and better standards of life in larger freedom . . . [and] to employ international machinery for the promotion of the economic and social advancement of all peoples."[61] I have mentioned that Africa was very poorly represented at the founding San Francisco Conference of the United Nations in 1945. Most African countries were still at this time under European colonialism. By the time of the formation of the United Nations if not earlier, the rich Western countries in Western Europe and North America had founded well-established structures of the international economy and finance by whose rules and directives the newly independent states of Africa and other developing regions had to play.

In particular, they had set up the Bretton Woods system represented by two major financial institutions. These were the International Bank for Reconstruction and Development (IBRD), commonly known as the World Bank, and the International Monetary Fund (IMF), both based in the United States. While the former was to help finance the rebuilding and reconstruction efforts of war-torn European countries after the Second World War, the latter was tasked with assisting countries with short to medium-term balance-of-payments difficulties.[62] The two institutions are somehow loosely connected to the United Nations System through the Economic and Social Council but with autonomous governing boards which do not report to any United Nations body or organ.

Having regained their sovereignty and found themselves in such a world economic order, independent African states and other developing countries sought to ensure that their development would have the same priority as European reconstruction. They rather naively thought that they would readily have access to the financial assistance of the World Bank and its associated financial institutions (i.e. the International Finance Corporation (IFC) established in 1956 and the International Development Association (IDA) founded in 1960). However, as Spero and Hart contend, the developed countries that dominated the World Bank unanimously agreed that European post-war reconstruction would be the first priority of the Bank.[63] Ivor Richard, the United Kingdom's Permanent Representative to the UN between 1974 and 1979 put this more plainly when he wrote:

> The IMF and the IBRD were institutions designed to protect the flow of world trade in Western directions and to maintain currency stability between the major trading nations. The Third World, if considered at all, was perceived as a group of nations whose main economic function was as primary producers, and whose political systems would gradually and paternalistically move out of colonial era to independence and Western styles of government.[64]

It soon became clear to the newly independent African states and their other Third World allies that they had to seek either a reform of the international economic order or alternative sources of financial assistance. Given the structuralist approach (i.e. blaming their state of affairs on the structure of their economies as lacking industrial bases) that seemed to dominate their thinking at that time, and the Western countries' monopoly or the of viable alternatives, their choice fell on seeking to reform the international economic order while looking for alternative sources. There was no better venue for this than the United Nations. It thus became the tribunal *par excellence* to express their economic grievances vis-à-vis the capitalist Western countries, with the Soviet Union taking their side at times. This was the beginning of a long partnership between the United Nations and Africa (with other developing countries) in the sphere of economic and human development and international cooperation.

In April 1958, the United Nations established under the Economic and Social Council (ECOSOC) the United Nations Economic Commission for Africa (ECA). Addis Ababa, the Ethiopian capital was chosen for its continental seat. The ECA was mandated to "foster regional integration and promote international cooperation for Africa's development." It was further tasked to keep ECOSOC, which supervises it, informed of the economic situation on the African continent. Organised around six substantive programme divisions, the ECA has five sub-regional offices around Africa. The Cameroonian capital, Yaoundé, hosts the offices for Central Africa, the Rwandan capital, Kigali, the offices for East Africa, and the Moroccan city of Tangier the offices for North Africa, while the Southern African sub-regional office is based in Lusaka (Zambia) and the capital of Niger, Niamey, is home to the sub-regional office of West Africa.

It is true that when the OAU was formed in 1963, also based in the Ethiopian capital, and until the 1970s or early 1980s, there were often disagreements between the ECA and the OAU. This was to be attributed, on the one hand, to the vision and objectives that each of the two organisations set for themselves and, on the other, how they viewed each other and, consequently, how they drew up their working strategies. Concerning the objectives that each one of them set for itself, we have pondered on those of the ECA above. Interestingly, when the OAU was founded, the Pan-African organization sought to assert not only its competence but also its supremacy for coordinating, strengthening and harmonising cooperation between African peoples and their different governments in all fields, including economic and social development. In fact, one of the three specialised commissions of the OAU was —it could not be more conflicting— the "Economic and Social Commission." Like the ECA, this Commission was also tasked with promoting economic cooperation in Africa.[65]

From these conflicting views of their objectives and duties, and the OAU being a product of African leaders while the ECA was a creation of the United Nations and thus somehow foreign in origin, the former sought to confine the latter to a subordinated role —one of carrying out studies and surveys which could be used, if compatible with its vision and objectives, as a basis for its decisions and projects. Yet the ECA and its supervising ECOSOC did not find it expedient that an organ of the United Nations Department of Economic and Social Council, whose policies were defined and its projects financed by the United Nations, should be subordinated to African states.

As Kouassi notes, the prime grievance of the OAU about the ECA was that its planning and executive posts were held by non-

Africans, which to some extent implied that the Commission's economic policy towards Africa was dictated from New York and not decided in Addis Ababa.[66] Further, because it is funded directly by the United Nations and the main contributors to the world body are undoubtedly the rich Western countries, the implicit assumption was that the Commission's decisions were dictated by these countries.

Nonetheless, with the passage of time, the two institutions became more and more harmonious and began to coordinate their work more closely and draft common positions on Africa's human and social-economic development needs. There was for example their joint effort in drafting the *Lagos Plan of Action* in April 1980. Today, their coordination is even closer and their mutual understanding is easily recognised. In 2004, for example, the ECA published a very powerful and well-argued report about the state of regional economic integration in Africa. This report was to be the basis of consultations carried out by the Economic Commissioner of the African Union in 2005/2006 with a view to harmonizing the relationship between the pan-African organization and the regional economic communities (RECs) across Africa.[67]

The second phase of UN-Africa partnership in the field of economic development came in 1960 with the admission of numerous African states to the United Nations. The year 1960 was, without any dispute, the year of Africa in the UN system. Pressing for issues of African economic development was not an exception here. At the 25th Session of the General Assembly, on 15 December 1960, the Assembly voted Resolution 1515 in which it called for a "concerted action for economic development of economically less developed countries." It further recommended that technical assistance and the supply of development capital to developing countries should be increased and be of "a kind and in a form in accordance with the wishes of the recipients and should involve no unacceptable conditions for them, political, economic, military or other." The decade starting in the following year was declared the United Nations First Development Decade. It is safe to argue that Africa was the continent most concerned by these resolutions and pledges, for the bulk of developing countries was in Africa, or rather, the "developing countries" or "third world" is a category to which almost all of Africa belonged.

Notwithstanding all these efforts, not much seemed to have changed for Africa and most other developing countries. If changes were made, there clearly came a decline and more poverty, especially after the oil shocks of the early 1970s. Africa, perhaps more than any developing region, suffered the economic repercussions of this crisis more acutely. With a united Southern bloc at the UN at that time, the developing countries, backed by the Soviet Union, sought the establishment of a New International Economic Order (NIEO). Again using the platform of the United Nations, the developing countries sought and obtained the General Assembly's support. Thus, during the Sixth Special Session of the General Assembly in May 1974, to the irritation of the rich Western countries, the Assembly overwhelmingly passed a resolution calling for the adoption of the NIEO. The Assembly was then chaired by the current president of Algeria, Abdelaziz Bouteflika, who remained president for more than a year, thereby overseeing the development of the new initiative. Throughout the 1970s and until the rich developed countries were able to break their ranks by the classical policy of divide-and-rule, the developing countries used the NIEO, through the United Nations, as their vehicle for reaching a set of economic goals that had been explicitly fixed through an earlier political process by the developed countries.[68]

The fourth instance of UN-Africa partnership in the field of economic development came with the economic crises of the 1980s. In this period, the United Nations adopted two major development programmes for Africa. The first was the "United Nations Action Plan for African Economic Recovery and Development, 1986-1990 (UNAPAERD)." The UN General Assembly adopted this programme in June 1986.[69] The programme was designed to solve the acute economic, social and humanitarian problems that were prevailing in Africa since the oil crisis of the 1970s. It was based on the concept of a global compact that refers to a mutual agreement between Africa and the international community. In its Annex II, the programme required the African countries to commit themselves to the launch of both national and regional programmes of economic development. On the other hand, it urged the rest of the international community to "support and complement the African development efforts." In sum, the programme and the concept of global compact on which it was based implied collective action and shared responsibility between Africa and the rest of the international community. One could argue that it was the classical counterpart of the contemporary New Partnership for Africa's Development (NEPAD) —the main difference being that the latter is the brainchild and the product of Africans themselves while UNAPAERD was the result of a collective brainstorming, involving Africans and non-Africans.

At its 46th Session held in December 1991, a "Final Review of the Implementation" of UNAPAERD was presented to the General Assembly.[70] From this assessment, the apparent failure of the programme was clear. The report concluded that the Programme "did not quite become a focal point for economic policy or for resource mobilization on behalf of Africa." It attributed this to two main factors, one internal and another external. According to the report, the internal factor came from the fact that the concept of a global compact at the continental level in Africa was difficult to achieve, as different African states sought their economic redemption from other sources and through other arrangements that "were not always related to the goals and targets of the Programme of Action."[71] Moreover, a third of African countries declined to pursue sustained economic reform. The external factor was to be found in the unfavourable external economic environment for Africa during the period of the Programme of Action (1986-1990).

Despite this disappointment, the Assembly remained upbeat about the record of the UNAPAERD. Thus, the same session adopted yet another programme for African development. This was the "United Nations New Agenda for the Development of Africa in the 1990s (UNNADAF)." The adoption of the New Agenda was seen as another opportunity for renewing the commitment of the international community to support Africa's own efforts to achieve self-sustaining social-economic growth and development. In other words, it announced the ushering in of another phase of UN-Africa partnership in the realm of economic and social development. The priority objectives of this New Agenda were stated in paragraphs 6 and 7 of the resolution adopting the Agenda as:

> the accelerated transformation, integration, diversification and growth of the African economies, in order to strengthen them within the world economy, reduce their vulnerability to external shocks and increase their dynamism, internalize the process of development and enhance self-reliance. . . . [and to promote] rapid progress towards the achievement of human-oriented goals by the year 2000 in the areas of life expectancy, integration of women in development, child and maternal mortality, nutrition, health, water and sanitation, basic education and shelter.[72]

Given that the adoption of this New Agenda coincided with the dawn of the post-Cold War era and the wind of democratisation in Africa, the prospects of success for this Programme were quite high. However, some argue that the target year of 2000 came without much to celebrate in terms of the attainment of the objectives set for the New Agenda. One of the authors who have paid particular attention to these two programmes and sought to analyse them is Adrien Ratsimbaharison. To this author, both UNAPAERD and UNNADAF were complete failures. In trying to explain why such was the outcome, Ratsimbaharison contends that this was due, on the one hand, to the ways the two programmes were formulated, adopted, and implemented by UN member states, UN bodies, and other international organisations (e.g. the World Bank and IMF); and on the other hand, to the international economic system in which the UN actions in economic and social development take place. In other words, as the Assembly's own assessment of the first programme (UNAPAERD) concluded, the author's argument is that the failure of the two programmes was due to both internal and external factors.

Identification by Africans and those that supported them of wrong policy problems, resulting in the prescription and formulation of the wrong solutions, together with flawed processes of policy recommendation and adoption are the main internal factors that Ratsimbaharison identifies as reasons for the failure of the two programmes. With regard to these internal factors, he concludes that the two programmes also suffered from

113

inappropriate processes of implementation and evaluation on the part of both African countries and their supporters in the UN General Assembly, which was actually dominated by them. The external factors that the author identifies can be summarised in what we mentioned earlier as the unfavourable world economic system, which is dominated by the rich Western countries.[73] Obviously, the latter did not want and, one may argue, do not want any radical change in the status quo —unfair as it may be.

All this notwithstanding, the United Nations-Africa partnership on social-economic development in Africa continued and the aforementioned programmes and initiatives were replaced by another initiative. With the dawn of the third millennium, the General Assembly solemnly adopted the "United Nations Millennium Declaration" in the presence of a record 147 heads of state and government in September 2000. In this declaration, the leaders of the world committed themselves to "spare no effort to free our fellow men, women and children from the abject and dehumanizing conditions of extreme poverty, to which more than a billion of them are currently subjected."[74] This, in a way, was a solemn commitment "to making the right to development a reality for everyone and to freeing the entire race from want." It is quite obvious that Africa is not the only preoccupation of this Declaration. However, given the unfortunate big share of Africa in the conditions that are the object of the Declaration, the link is hardly disputable. In fact, Chapter VII of the Declaration entitled "Meeting the special needs of Africa" is a clear case in point. It is to meet the challenge to attain the objectives of this Declaration, especially the Millennium Development Goals (MDGs) set with 2015 as the target year, that the latest opportunity of UN-Africa partnership on development is to be found. However, as a preliminary report of the Goals shows,[75] there is much to be done in order to make this rather utopian Declaration a reality. If any lesson were to be learned from its successful partnership with the UN on the issue of decolonization to be utilised on the challenge of development, it would clearly be that the bulk of the work should be done by Africa.

Conclusion

This chapter dealt with the partnership between Africa and the United Nations on a number of issues of concern to the continent. As indicative examples for this partnership, it looked at issues such as decolonization, the fight against Apartheid and white minority regimes in Southern Africa, peace-keeping and post-conflict peace building, and economic development in Africa.

With regard to decolonization, I observed that the United Nations paradoxically played two roles that were rather conflicting. One was its implicit condoning of imperialism through its adoption of the mandates system (renamed the Trusteeship system) created by its predecessor, the League of Nations, which was dominated by colonial powers victorious in the First World War. In this, the United Nations relationship with Africa seemed imperialistic. However, with the admission of a number of African countries to the UN and the intensification of liberation struggles on the ground, the United Nations, to the irritation of the colonial powers, served, or rather was used as a real partner of liberation of African territories that were still under European occupation. The case of Algeria was used here as the most indicative example for UN-Africa partnership on African decolonization. The efforts of the United Nations, especially through the General Assembly, and attempts to dismantle the Apartheid system in Southern Africa were used to further illustrate this partnership. While Apartheid could be equated with colonialism, I justified my separating the two and putting them under two different headings by some particularities that distinguished the former from the latter: in particular, the sheer cruelty and inhumanity of the Apartheid system which, albeit found also in colonialism, were more noticeable in that system than in any other form of foreign occupation. The fact that it was also confined to only one region of the continent (i.e. Southern Africa) gave another justification for this approach.

Peace-keeping and post-conflict peace-building were chosen as contrary to the whole spectrum of conflict management mechanisms because, in my view, theUN has not done enough in the field of conflict prevention in Africa. Nor has it been successful in all its peace-keeping efforts. Thus, the United Nations Missions to

Namibia (UNTAG), the Congo (ONUC) and Côte d'Ivoire (UNOCI) were used to illustrate the UN peace-keeping missions in Africa that have so far been the most indicative of a real partnership between the world body and Africa. The cases of post-war Liberia and Sierra Leone were mentioned as examples of successful UN peace-building roles in Africa.

In the final account, the chapter analysed the partnership between Africa and the UN on issues relating to social-economic development. Five UN projects and/or initiatives were used to illustrate this. In particular, the chapter analysed the role of the United Nations Economic Commission for Africa (ECA) founded in 1958, the adoption of the United Nations Action Plan for African Economic Recovery and Development – 1986-1990 (UNAPAERD) and the adoption of the United Nations New Agenda for the development of Africa in the 1990s (UNNADAF). It noted that the adoption of these projects and initiatives by the UN General Assembly does indicate a real partnership between Africa and the United Nations. It concluded that their apparent failure is attributed to both internal and external factors and that had the African governments done their part of the work as they did with regard to decolonization, the outcome could have been quite different.

Meanwhile, the list of issues dealt with in this chapter is only indicative. There are many other areas that could also be used to illustrate this partnership between Africa and the United Nations. For example, up until 1960, Africa had little to do with the International Labour Organization (ILO), the specialised agency of the United Nations that deals with labour and employment issues. Most African countries joined the Organization between 1960 and 1964. Ever since however, the ILO has increased its presence and activities in Africa, starting by setting up a Regional Office at Addis Ababa, and providing the continent with an increasing share of its technical assistance and technical cooperation resources available to it from its regular budget as well as from the United Nations Development Programme (UNDP) and many bilateral and multilateral sources.

The technical assistance of the United Nations Educational, Scientific and Cultural Organization (UNESCO) to African states has also been very significant. The partnership between UNESCO and the OAU and now the AU is quite illustrative of this. Other UN agencies too have served as a veritable vehicle for this partnership. The activities of some of them, such as the World Health Organization (WHO), the United Nations Children Fund (UNICEF), the World Food Programme (WFP) and the Food and Agriculture Organization (FAO), are obvious. Yet others, such as the International Telecommunications Union (ITU), the United Nations Institute for Training and Research (UNITAR), and the Nairobi-based United Nations Centre for Human Settlement (HABITAT), whose work is not less significant, are less known to the general public. As will be argued in the concluding chapter, the work of all these organizations, and the UN system in general, only benefits Africa and any other region for that matter as far as Africa or that other region employs its own efforts on the ground.

Notes

1. See Edmond Kwam Kouassi, "Africa and the United Nations," in Ali A. Mazrui and C. Wondji (eds.), *General History of Africa: VIII Africa since 1935* (Oxford, Berkeley and Paris: James Currey, University Press of California and UNESCO, 1999), pp. 871-904.

2. Rosalyn Higgins, *Problems & Process: International Law and How We Use it* (Oxford: Oxford University Press, 1994), p. 112.

3. Article 3 of the Charter stated that they undertook to: "respect the right of all peoples to choose the form of government under which they will live; and they wish to see sovereign rights and self government restored to those who have been forcibly deprived of them." More explicit than this was Article 6 which stipulated that: "after the final destruction of the Nazi tyranny, they hope to see established a peace which will afford to all nations the means of dwelling in safety within their own boundaries, and which will afford assurance that all the men in all lands may live out their lives in freedom from fear and want." It must be noted however that the insistence of the Americans on the application of the Charter to all peoples, including those in Africa, was not the result of a mere sympathy for the colonial peoples, but of a desire to open up their markets for American industrial goods and products as well as to have access to raw materials

from these territories once the Europeans departed. This is so because while they called for the dismantling of European empires, they were still subjecting the black people in America to exactly what their brethren were going through at the hands of the Europeans in mother Africa.

4. Victoria Schofield, *The United Nations: People, Politics and Powers* (Hove (England): Wayland Publishers, 1979), p. 14.

5. Joseph Ki-Zerbo, *Histoire de l'Afrique Noire: D'Hier à Demain* (Paris : Hatier, 1978), p. 437.

6. See General Assembly Resolution 1514 (XV) of 14 December 1960.

7. The Times, 15 November 1954.

8. Kouassi, *Africa and the United Nations*, p. 887.

9. Ibid.

10. For a first hand account of the France's wild attempts to block Guinea's admission to the UN, including its links sometimes with fears of consolidating demands at the UN for the Algerian question, see the testimony of one of the actors, on the French side, about the issue, in a biography he wrote of the first Guinean ambassador to the UN. See André Lewin, *Diallo Telli: Le tragique destin d'un grand Africain* (Paris: Jeune Afrique Livres, 1990), pp. 45-96.

11. Quoted in Kouassi, *Africa and the United Nations*, p. 887.

12. Article 2, paragraph 7 of the UN Charter prohibits the United Nations from interfering in "matters which are essentially within the domestic jurisdiction of any state."

13. UNTAG's presence in Namibia was very instrumental in ending the South African illegal occupation of the territory. It must be noted however that there were many pressures on the South African government, especially from independent African states and the positioning of Cuban troops in Angola. Similar pressures played also their part in dismantling the Apartheid regime itself.

14. It was a dazzling irony that these people called themselves Afrikaners, i.e. Africans, and called the real Africans other names such as "Bantus."

15. Nelson Rolihlahla Mandela, *Long Walk to Freedom* (London: Little, Brown & Co., 1994), pp. 127-128.

16. David Chanaiwa, "Southern Africa since 1945," in Ali A. Mazrui and C. Wondji (eds.), *General History of Africa: VIII Africa since 1935* (Oxford,

Berkeley and Paris: James Currey, University Press of California and UNESCO, 1999), pp. 249-281.

17. See Boutros Boutros-Ghali's introduction to the United Nations' book on *Apartheid: 1948-1994* (New York: Department of Public Information, 1994), pp. 3-7.

18. The complaint resulted from the adoption, in 1946, by the South African government of what it called the Asiatic Land Tenure and Indian Representation Act, which prohibited people of Indian origin from acquiring land.

19. At the time, there were more than 100,000 Indians living in South Africa. About Ghandi, see for instance Ved Mehta, *Mahatma Ghandi and His Apostles* (New York: Penguin Books, 1976), pp. 99-130.

20. For this quote, see Mandela, *Long Walk to Freedom*, p. 147. See pp. 140-161 for a full narrative of how and why the idea of the campaign was conceived and how it was organised, as well as the oppressive reaction of the Afrikaner regime to it.

21. Letter dated 17 November 1952 from Mr. Z. K. Matthews to the Chairman of the Ad Hoc Political Committee of the UN, cited in United Nations, *UN and Apartheid*, (New York: Department of Public Information, 1994), pp. 226-7. Professor Matthew was at the time attached to the University College of Fort Hare in South Africa.

22. United Nations, *United Nations and Apartheid*, pp. 10-11, para. 32.

23. See General Assembly Resolution A/RES/616 A (VII) of 5 December 1952, and Resolution A/RES/616 B (VII) of 5 December 1952.

24. Letter dated 25 March 1960. See UN document S/4279 and Add. 1, 25 March 1960. The letter made reference to Article 35, paragraph 1 of the UN Charter, which allows any member state to bring to the attention of the Security Council any dispute or any situation which might lead to international friction and is likely to endanger the maintenance of international peace and security.

25. Final Communiqué of the Second Conference of Independent African States, Addis Ababa, 24 June 1960.

26. See General Assembly Resolution A/RES/2202 A (XXI) of 16 December 1966.

27. Margaret Thatcher, *The Downing Street Years* (London: HarperCollins, 1993), p. 513.

28. Ibid., p. 514.

29. For a recent and comprehensive report about institutional racism, as it relates to Africans and French nationals of African descent, in France, see Amnesty International, "France: The Search for Justice—effective impunity of law enforcement officers in cases of shootings, deaths in custody or torture and ill-treatment," EUR 21/001/2005 of 6 April 2005; and Issaka K. Souaré, "France: Unveiling Racism and Police Brutality in the Land of Free," *African Renaissance*, Vol. 2, no. 6, November/December (2005): 130-5.

30. See Boutros Boutros-Ghali, *An Agenda for Peace: Preventive Diplomacy, peacemaking and peace-keeping* (Report of the Secretary-General, 17 June 1992), para. 20.

31. Ibid., para. 15.

32. Kofi Annan, *Prevention of Armed Conflict* (Report of the Secretary-General to the Security Council, 7 June 2001).

33. See Johan Galtung, "Three approaches to peace: peacekeeping, peacemaking and peacebuilding," in Peace, War and Defence – Essays in Peace Research, *Christian Ejlers* (Copenhagen, 1975), Vol. 2, pp. 282 – 304.

34. Ibid., para. 57. See also Iain Atack, "Peacebuilding as conflict management or political engineering?" *Trócaire Development Review* (2003/4): 17 – 32.

35. Agostinho Zacarias, *The United Nations and International Peacekeeping* (London: I. B. Tauris Publishers, 1996), pp. 51-55.

36. For a detailed study of the Congo crisis and the UN intervention, see, for example, Kouassi, *Africa and the United Nations*, pp. 871-904 and particularly pp. 877-86; Zacarias, *UN and International Peacekeeping*, pp. 42-6; and United Nations, *The Blue Helmets: A Review of United Nations Peacekeeping* (New York: Department of Public Information, 1990), pp. 213-59.

37. The Congo, with 2, 300,000 square kilometres, is literally 75 times the size of Belgium, with only 30, 528 square kilometres.

38. United Nations, *The Blue Helmets*, p. 216. For a detailed analysis of Belgian colonial rule in the Congo and circumstances surrounding the independence which led to the crisis and the UN intervention, see Ki-Zerbo, *L'Histoire générale de l'Arique Noire*, pp. 528-34.

39. Kouassi, *Africa and the United Nations*, p. 879; and United Nations, *The Blue Helmets*, p. 217.

40. United Nations, *The Blue Helmets*, p. 218.

41. Ibid.

42. Article 99 of the UN Charter allows if not obliges the Secretary-General to "bring to the attention of the Security Council any matter which in his opinion may threaten the maintenance of international peace and security."

43. Cited in Kouassi, *Africa and the United Nations*, p. 880.

44. The resolution of 22 July 1960 was S/4405 (1960).

45. See Security Council Resolution S/169 of 24 November 1961.

46. Kouassi, *Africa and the United Nations*, p. 886.

47. United Nations, *Côte d'Ivoire: Rapport de la Commission d'enquête internationale pour la Côte d'Ivoire* [available in French only] (New York: United Nations Secretariat, 2001).

48. See UN Document S/PRST/2002/42 of 20 December 2002.

49. For the 2003 General Assembly's resolution, see A/RES/58/275-A/58/586, for the 2004 one, see A/RES/58/310-A/58/831, and A/RES/59/16A-A/59/529 for the resolution of 2005.

50. See Council Resolution S/RES/1464 (2003).

51. Council Resolution S/RES/1498 (2003).

52. Emphasis is mine.

53. See Mitsuro Donowaki, *Small Arms, Africa and the United Nations: Ten Years of Interaction between Africa and the UN* (Paper presented at the PoA National Reporting Workshop held at Nairobi on 20-21May 2004).

54. General Assembly Resolution A/RES/50/70B of 15 January 1996.

55. United Nations, "Report of the Panel of Governmental Experts on Small Arms," UN document A/52/298 (27 August 1997).

56. ECOWAS press release no. 54 (15 September 1999).

57. Issaka K. Souaré, Civil Wars and Coups d'État in West Africa: An Attempt to Understand the Roots and Prescribe Possible Solutions (Lanham, MD.: University Press of America, 2006), pp. 194-5.

58. See the online database of the Norwegian Initiative on Small Arms Transfers (NISAT) at <http://www.nisat.org/default. asp?page=/ database _ info/> (25 October 2005.)

59. Thalif Deen, "Annan pushes for weapons treaty," *West Africa*, no. 4288, 13 – 19 August (2001), p. 24.

60. Amnesty International, *Undermining Global Security: the European Union's arms exports*, Index no. ACT 30/003/2004 (14 May 2004). There is also an accompanying press release Index no. POL 30/024/2004 (14 May 2004).

61. See the Preamble to the Charter of the United Nations.

62. See Robert Gilpin, *The Political Economy of International Relations* (Princeton, NJ.: Princeton University Press, 1987), pp. 131-4; Robert Gilpin, *Global Political Economy: Understanding International Political Order* (Princeton, NJ.: Princeton University Press, 2001), pp. 234-8; and Joan E. Spero and Jeffrey A. Hart, *The Politics of International Economic Relations* (New York: St. Martin's Press, 1997), pp. 167-70.

63. Spero and Hart, *The Politics of International Economic Relations*, p. 168. See also Issaka K. Souaré, "Can the G-8 and International Financial Institutions Help Africa?" *African Renaissance*, Vol. 1, no. 2, September/October (2004): 115-20.

64. Ivor Richard, "Major Objectives and Functions of the UN: The View from Abroad," in Toby Trister Gati (ed.), *The US, the UN, and the Management of Global Change* (New York and London: New York University Press, 1983), pp. 48-63.

65. Article XX of the OAU Charter provided for the establishment of such Specialised Commissions as the Assembly of Heads of State may deem necessary, including: a) Economic and Social Commission; b) Educational, Scientific, Cultural and Health Commission; and c) Defence Commission. Albeit there is more harmony now between the African Union, which replaced the OAU in July 2002, and the ECA, the Constitutive Act of the AU is even more assertive in this regard. For one of the main organs of the AU is the Economic, Social and Cultural Council.

66. Kouassi, *Africa and the United Nations*, pp. 891-3.

67. Economic Commission for Africa, *Assessing Regional Integration in Africa* (Addis Ababa: ECA Publications, 2004); and African Union, *The Newsletter of the African Union Commission* (December 2005). See especially the interview with the Commissioner for Economic Affairs.

68. Leon Gordenker, "The UN System in Perspective: Development of the UN System," in Tobi Trister Gati (ed.), *The US, the UN, and the Management of Global Change* (New York and London: New York University Press, 1983), pp. 11-47, especially pp. 21-27.

69. See General Assembly Resolution A/RES/S-13/2 of 1 June 1986.

70. UN Document A/RES/46/151 of 18 December 1991.

71. Ibid.

72. Ibid.

73. See Adrien M. Ratsimbaharison, *The Failure of the United Nations Development Programs for Africa* (Lanham, MD.: University Press of America, 2003). See especially chapters 4 & 5 on pp. 65-100.

74. See General Assembly Document A/RES/55/2 of 18 September 2000.

75. United Nations, *The Millennium Development Goals Report 2005* (New York: Department of Public Information, 2005).

Chapter 3

Africa Disappointed by the UN

The failure of the United Nations to prevent, and subsequently, to stop the genocide in Rwanda was a failure by the United Nations system as a whole. The fundamental failure was the lack of resources and political commitment devoted to developments in Rwanda and to the United Nations presence there. There was a persistent lack of political will by Member States to act, or to act with enough assertiveness.
—Report of the Independent Inquiry into the actions of the UN during the genocide in Rwanda

The previous chapter dealt with the areas of UN-Africa relations that could be described as constituting a genuine partnership between the two entities. The most illustrative examples of this partnership were their joint efforts in achieving decolonization in Africa, their fight against Apartheid and white minority regimes in Southern Africa and attempts at socio-economic development in Africa. Of course partnership does not necessarily entail a successful outcome. In this chapter, I propose to analyze those areas of UN-Africa relations where the world body's actions are generally regarded as having failed and disappointed Africa. In particular, I propose to look at what are perceived as the UN's failed peace-keeping mission in Somalia and its alleged disastrous actions during the 1994 genocide in Rwanda. Without rushing into judgements or delivering one-sided verdicts, I shall critically look at these two projects and try to identify the failure and where the blame should lie. I shall inquire into the source of the blame: granted that the UN did actually fail Africa, was it an outright failure or is there something to do with Africa's expectations, regardless of those being justified or not? Since both Somalia and Rwanda are African countries, even if one were to conclude that the

125

outcome of the UN's engagement or disengagement in both countries was a disappointment, was there anything Africans (starting from the people of Somalia and Rwanda directly concerned) could do and did not do, and did Africans thus deserve their share of the blame or was it that they did everything they possibly could but still the UN failed them?

Somalia: When the Rambo's Became Peacekeepers

In Africa, as elsewhere in the Third World, the end of the Cold War and superpowers' rivalries led to the withdrawal of the latter's unconditional backing for many dictatorial regimes on the continent. Many of these autocratic regimes that were supported by one camp or the other during the Cold War had lost their strategic value to their respective camp leaders, the US and the Soviet Union. The political aspirations of their people that had hitherto been thwarted because of superpowers' backing came once again to the fore or were re-energized. Those leaders that were wise enough responded quite swiftly to this whirlwind of change and introduced —even if it was only theoretically— mechanisms for such a change. In particular, they offered to introduce multi-party systems and political liberalization. However, those who had an illusion of power and ignored the calls of the masses continued in their obduracy and resisted pleas for change. Such positions led often to destabilisation and civil strife. Somalia was clearly one of those states that suffered the negative repercussions of the end of the Cold War because of the lack of foresight of its ruling regime.

At the end of the Cold War, the strong man of Somalia was a certain Mohamed Siad Barre. General Siad Barre had come to power through a military coup d'état in 1969. Shortly thereafter, Siad Barre banned multi-party politics in the country and introduced an autocratic style of government. Playing the different clans and religious leaders of the country against one another, his policy of divide-and-rule and his mastering of how to play the strategic carte between the two superpowers helped him remain in power until his overthrow in January 1991. Somalia's strategic location - situated along the oil routes from the Middle East - made it an important sought-after geostrategic ally of both superpowers.

In the 1970s, Siad Barre professed socialism to win Soviet military support for his drive to annex Ethiopia's Ogaden region, whose inhabitants are predominantly Somali and some of whom clearly wanted to be part of Somalia but without emigration. As a Marxist regime came to Ethiopia, however, the Soviets found a better ally and the support shifted. However, Siad Barre did not encounter any difficulty in getting American support. The American support for Siad Barre proved to be far superior to that of the Soviets and this continued throughout the 1980s. Such was US aid to Siad Barre's Somalia that US total military aid to the country during the 1980s is estimated at some US\$ 200 millions, with hundreds of millions in economic aid.[1] As Blaton notes:

> In the fight against Communism, arms transfers were both an instrument of influence and an indicator of U.S. political support. Within the context of superpower competition, U.S. arms transfers were part of a larger effort to promote patron-client relationships in the Third World and fortify Cold War political alignments.[2]

Despite the unconditional American support to the Barre regime however, the country was never totally peaceful throughout the 1980s, as various rebel groups were operating in various parts of the country. The armed opposition to Barre's regime intensified towards the end of the decade and eventually led to the overthrow of Barre in January 1991. This led to further instability in the country. The faction of General Mohamed Farah Aidid, Chairman of the United Somali Congress, in Southern Somalia, collided with the Interim President, Ali Mahdi Mohamed in Mogadishu, while Northern Somalia proclaimed the independence of Somaliland. Many smaller factions emerged. Violence ensued between the different factions over the control of the scarce resources in their respective regions. Somalia having lost its strategic relevance to the US that was busy with the "rich man's war" in the Persian Gulf, the Americans could not very much care and the fate of the Somalis were simply left to themselves to sort out the situation.

The continued hostilities led to widespread death and destruction, forcing hundreds of thousands of civilians to flee their homes and causing a serious need for emergency humanitarian assistance. While scores of Somalis crossed the borders to seek refuge in neighbouring countries, a significant number of them became internally displaced. According to UN estimates at the end of 1992, almost 4.5 million people in Somalia or over half of the population were threatened by severe malnutrition and related diseases. While this was a general case across the country, those living in the countryside were thought to be the most affected. It was estimated that perhaps 300,000 people died since November 1991, and at least 1.5 million lives were at immediate risk.

This was the state of affairs in Somalia when the Organization of African Unity (OAU) initiated talks between the opposing factions in the country. The OAU's initiative was backed by a number of other concerned institutions. In particular, the United Nations, the League of Arab States (LAS or the Arab League) and the Organization of the Islamic Conference (OIC) deployed significant efforts —Somalia being a member of all these organizations.[3] All these institutions were involved with the political aspects of the crisis and pressing for a peaceful solution to the conflict. It appears however that with the passing of time and in view of the worsening situation in the country, all these organizations gave way to the United Nations and limited themselves to hosting peace talks and carrying out background mediation efforts whenever the UN demanded.

The first involvement of the United Nations in the Somali conflict came on 27 December 1991. This was when the outgoing Peruvian Secretary-General of the UN, Javier Pérez de Cuéllar, informed the President of the Security Council that he intended to take an initiative in an attempt to restore peace in Somalia. With his request approved, he consulted with the incoming Secretary-General Boutros Boutros-Ghali, and they agreed that a team of senior UN officials should be dispatched to Somalia for talks with the opposing factions with the aim of bringing about a cease-fire and securing access by the international relief community to civilians caught in the conflict. The Under-Secretary-General for Political Affairs at the time was James O. C. Jonah from Sierra Leone. Jonah was thus asked to lead the team on its visit to Somalia. Apparently, all the Somali factions expressed to the UN team their desire for the UN to play a leading role in the resolution of the conflict. Aidid however made no secret of his opposition to the deployment of any peace-keeping force.

Boutros-Ghali took over the Secretary-General post in January 1992 and the Somali crisis naturally became one of the very first dossiers he had to work on. In the same month (January 1992), the Security Council passed a resolution in which it urged all parties to the conflict to cease hostilities, and decided that all States should immediately implement a general and complete embargo on all deliveries of weapons and military equipment to Somalia. The Secretary-General was requested to increase humanitarian assistance to the affected population and to contact all parties involved in the conflict to seek their commitment to the cessation of hostilities, to promote a cease-fire and to assist in the process of a political settlement of the conflict.[4] Despite the signing of a cease-fire agreement between the opposing factions in March, hostilities continued in the country. Thus, following two reports of the Secretary-General on 21 and 24 April, the Council passed Resolution 751 (24 April 1992) establishing the United Nations Operation in Somalia (UNOSOM) and agreed, in principle, to establish a UN security force to be deployed in the country as soon as possible. A unit of 50 UN observers was to be deployed immediately to monitor the cease-fire in Mogadishu.

The Secretary-General was asked to continue his consultations with the Somali parties regarding the proposed UN security force. Boutros-Ghali soon appointed the veteran Algerian diplomat, Mohamed Sahnoun, as his Special Representative, but Sahnoun did not last long in the post because of disagreements between him and the headquarters in New York, as will be seen later. He was replaced in November 1992 by the Iraqi diplomat, Ismat Kittani, whose mandate also proved short-lived as it ended when the Americans took over, after only five months (November – March 1993).

Led by Brigadier-General Imtíaz Shaheen of Pakistan as the Chief Military Observer, the advance party of UNOSOM arrived in Mogadishu in early July 1992. The government of Pakistan had agreed to contribute a unit to UNOSOM. The first group of security personnel arrived in Mogadishu on 14 September 1992 after considerable delays. Whilst one should not forget the difficulties with the Somali factions on the ground, the delays can also be attributed to the fact that the UN was focusing attention on the conflict in the former Yugoslavia. By the time the UN's mission arrived, the ailing institutional structures in Somalia had further collapsed. As Zacarias notes, the delay in the UN's intervention "forfeited the opportunity to support the failing administrative structures and those Somalis trying to prevent the disintegration of the governmental system."[5]

Obviously, the delicate political and security situation in Somalia compounded with the desperate and urgent need for humanitarian assistance for the many displaced people meant that the strength of UNOSOM was insufficient for the task on the ground. Following the advice of his Special Representative, the Secretary-General realised that there was an urgent need not only to address the above issues, but also to embark on a well-planned project of institution-building in the country. Moreover, the widespread banditry and criminal activities in the country meant that the UN force not only needed to protect the Somali civilians from the gangs of thugs, but also to protect UN workers tasked with the transport and distribution of humanitarian assistance. Thus, in a report to the Security Council, the Secretary-General strongly advised that the United Nations rethink the strategy of its involvement in Somalia and that its efforts needed to be enlarged in order to bring about an effective cease-fire throughout the country, while at the same time promoting national reconciliation.

This led to the Security Council authorizing in August an increase in the strength of UNOSOM. The total strength of UNOSOM was now to be 4,219 all ranks, including the unit of 500 authorized in Mogadishu and 719 for logistic units. As always, the Secretary-General was urged to continue working in close cooperation with the OAU, the Arab League and the OIC in "his efforts to seek a comprehensive political solution to the crisis in Somalia."[6] Despite all this, it would appear that UNOSOM was without any clear strategy. This stemmed mainly from the disagreement in tactics and strategy between Ambassador Sahnoun, the Secretary-General's Special Representative, and UN headquarters. While the latter advocated, doubtless because some troop contributing countries pressed for this, a quick fix so that UN could be swiftly relieved, Sahnoun, with his vast knowledge of the terrain and the region, urged a long-term solution which certainly needed patience on the part of not only headquarters but troop contributing member states. It also needed a special kind of diplomacy, engaging not only the politicians or warlords but also their supporters amongst the ordinary people.[7] At the end of the day, Sahnoun resigned and was replaced by an Iraqi diplomat, as mentioned above.

As a result, the political aspect of the crisis, which was the main issue behind all that appeared on the surface, was neglected by UN strategists. Instead, they saw the issue first and foremost as a humanitarian issue and not necessarily a political one.[8] This was also reflected in the nature of the mandate given to UNOSOM until the involvement of the Americans. UNOSOM's mandate had always been under Chapter VI of the UN charter. This does not have the enforcement provisions of Chapter VII. That came only when the Americans offered to contribute but independently of the UN force.

In a resolution of 3 December 1992 (S/RES/749), the Security Council approved the offer of the United States to lead a coalition force to assist the UN force in its efforts in Somalia. While the overall strength of the UN force had never surpassed 5,000, this force known as the United Task Force (UNITAF) consisted of an impressive 36,000 officers, with an unprecedented American contribution of 23,000, about 63 per cent. The code name of the operation was to be "Restore Hope," and it was to work under the enforcement provisions of Chapter VII, which authorises the UN peacekeepers to be peace enforcers (i. e. use force) if necessary. UNITAF was to be independent from UNOSOM but there was to be a close coordination between the two and the overall political task in the country was to be left to the UN. Of the 24 countries that contributed to UNITAF, there were six African countries (Botswana, Egypt, Morocco, Nigeria, Tunisia and Zimbabwe) and a number of Islamic countries, including Saudi Arabia, Turkey and Pakistan. The force was however dominated by Western states, including the UK, France and Australia and spearheaded by the United States, which also had the overall military command.

131

With no clear strategy and dominated by the United States whose Rambo's and Commandos were trained for combat and not for peace-keeping,[9] UNITAF encountered an avalanche of difficulties on the ground, having started its deployment on 9 December. Soon, the force came to be regarded by a number of Somali factions, especially those of Farah Aidid, as another adversary rather than a neutral force sent to their rescue. The situation continued deteriorating —both on the ground, speaking in security terms, and between UNITAF and the Somali factions— throughout the first half of 1993. UNITAF was not well-equipped for the task of disarming the Somali factions and it lacked the appropriate coordination with the United Nations forces and civilian administrators on the ground. It was also observed that not all its forces used the same weaponry, as the American contingents used more sophisticated weapons and communications equipment than other contingents. Consequently, not all the contingents had the same combat readiness, which led to contradictory responses by the different UNITAF contingents to the different Somali factions. Yet this was one of the factors that led some of those factions whose areas were under American control to allege that they were being subjected to a force greater than what other factions were facing, and thus concluded that they were deliberately targeted.

From UNOSOM I to UNOSOM II

From the deteriorating security and humanitarian situation despite the presence of more than 30,000 soldiers and military observers, it was clear that UNOSOM and UNITAF had failed and that their overall structure needed a rethink. Thus, in March 1993, following an earlier report of the Secretary-General, the Security Council authorised the establishment of UNOSOM II, the initial United Nations force having been renamed in retrospect as UNOSOM I. The new force was to take over the task of UNITAF and was to be composed of 20,000 soldiers, 8,000 support personnel, and a civilian staff of 2,800. The tasks of the expanded UNOSOM included disarming Somali factions, assisting in the provision of humanitarian relief and economic rehabilitation of Somalia, assisting the Somali people to promote and advance national reconciliation, and assisting in the return of refugees and displaced persons to their homes. Ensuring all the Somali factions' strict respect for and adherence to the peace process and the cease-fire agreement in place was also one of the main tasks of UNOSOM II. The force operated under the same enforcement provisions of Chapter VII of the UN Charter.[10] The Secretary-General appointed the American retired Admiral, Jonathan T. Howe as his Special Representative from the date of the establishment of UNOSOM II until February 1994. He was replaced by the veteran Guinean diplomat, Lansana Kouyaté as the Acting Special Representative. Kouyaté remained in this position until June 1993, when the Ghanaian diplomat, James Victor Gbeho filled the position from July 1994 to April of the following year.

Curiously, despite the deteriorating situation in the country, perhaps because of it, the UN decided in August 1993 to reduce the number of troops to about 17,200 all ranks by the end of September 1994. The Security Council decided to end the Mission in March 1995 and to withdraw all UNOSOM II forces and assets from the country. The authorised strength of UNOSOM II was then 22,000 all ranks and the actual strength on 2 August was 18,761.

It seems that the turning point in UN involvement in the conflict in Somalia came in October 1993. This was when 18 American Rangers were killed in fierce battle with the forces of Farah Aidid. Seeing the footage of this battle and the dead body of an American soldier being dragged by the "poor Somalis" on the streets of Mogadishu was said to have greatly angered American public opinion. Many of them and those that did not like American involvement in African wars, or in any multilateral peace-keeping operation with the UN, charged the world body with all that had gone wrong. With a new Democratic president in office, in the person of Bill Clinton, cynical Republicans went on criticising the world body, saying that "these failures raise larger questions about the United Nations' competence."[11] Many such critics blamed the UN for the killing of the American soldiers and this led to the withdrawal of American troops in Somalia.

As a matter of fact, these American commentators did not know or chose to ignore two things. The first thing was that three months before this incident, in June, the Pakistani contingent lost 23 of its peacekeepers and had 60 wounded in a similar encounter with the same faction led by Aidid.[12] This did not cause any uproar. The other thing is that, contrary to these charges, the American Rangers were not under UN command. As Clarke and Herbst demonstrate, the Rangers were commanded by a US Special Forces officer who reported directly to U. S. Central Command at MacDill Air Force Base in Florida. Moreover, the searches for Aidid, including the one that led to the October fatalities, were all approved by the relevant senior American authorities in Washington.[13]

The American withdrawal dealt a big blow to the UN force in Somalia. The US had failed the UN and the people of Somalia. Contrary to their declared aims and the responsibility they were tasked with, the Americans had refused to disarm the Somali factions and even told the warlords that they could keep their weapons if they moved the arms from Mogadishu or into their respective cantonments in Mogadishu. As Boutros-Ghali later revealed, even when they came upon a major cache of weapons, "the American forces of UNITAF were under orders not to seize them."[14] This raises many questions about the real intentions of the Americans in coming to Somalia in the first place. Was it a Rambo show in the combat films of Hollywood to demonstrate American supremacy or it was a real peace-keeping mission?

The departure of the American forces did not lead to a direct and immediate withdrawal of the UN forces. This was a very courageous decision by the world body. The UN however kept to its deadline of March 1995 for complete withdrawal. Thus, by 2 February 1995, with the repatriation of the Indian, Zimbabwean and Malaysian contingents, some headquarters personnel and those of the Pakistani hospital, UNOSOM II troop strength was reduced to 7,956. With these drastic cuts in the strength of the UN force, it was no longer possible for UNOSOM II troops to extend the necessary protection even within Mogadishu. Humanitarian agencies were then advised to evacuate their international staff to Nairobi. By the end of March 1995, UNOSOM II had completed its withdrawal from Somalia. However, the conflict had not yet been resolved.

To the UN, and this is quite true also from the Secretary-General's view, only the Somalis themselves could establish a viable and acceptable peace. The international community could only help in that process. Such assistance, however, could not be sustained indefinitely. In other words, the justification advanced by the world body for the withdrawal of its forces from Somalia is that the Somalis did not create a suitable environment for their presence. Further, since their presence and indeed their success were conditioned on the cooperative efforts of the Somali parties, including respecting the different cease-fire agreements they had signed, there was no use for the continuation of the UN forces. However, if the Somali leaders had succeeded in creating and maintaining favourable security conditions, the United Nations and the international community might have taken a different approach. By this, the UN also insists on the fact that its mission did not fail as critics charge.

To those critics however, the UN is not totally innocent in the creation of this situation. The American military approach in Somalia did contribute to the antagonising of some Somali factions and the UN allowed itself, to a large extent, to be influenced by the Americans. As Clarke and Herbst note, when US officials of UNITAF gave formal control to the UN in May 1993 when UNOSOM II was created, "they had already determined the nature of the follow-up operation." A retired American officer, Admiral Jonathan Howe, was appointed UN Secretary-General's Special Representative to Somalia.[15]

The impact of the disagreement between the first Special Representative of the Secretary-General and the headquarters on the outcome of the mission has been mentioned above. Though Sahnoun resigned as early as November 1992, because his resignation was due to differences of strategies, the subsequent Special Representatives of the Secretary-General were expected to have a different policy from his. This is not to argue that his strategy was necessarily the best. However, it proved difficult for the subsequent Representatives to sell their new strategy to the Somali parties and this caused disturbance in the overall political strategy of the UN in Somalia. Moreover, a Comprehensive Report of the UN Department for Peace-keeping Operations (DPKO) about UNOSOM implicitly admits the failure of the mission. The report attributes this to three main factors: the mission's vague mandate, lack of proper planning, and poor if not total lack of coordination.[16]

As regards the Operation's mandate, the report notes that this was "vague, changed frequently during the process and was open to myriad of interpretations." One of the intriguing aspects of the mandate of the UN operation was when orders were given to capture warlords such as Farah Aidid and later to encourage negotiations with them. One explanation for this, especially the mandate's subjection to different interpretations, is that many troop contributing countries were not sufficiently consulted during the formation stage of the mandate. Consequently, they had varying perceptions and interpretations during its execution. If we add to this the full knowledge of some troop contributors of the exact meaning of the mandate and their choice to deliberately ignore it and take a different approach, as evidenced in the refusal of the Americans to disarm the Somali factions despite this being explicit in their mandate, one can see how the very mandate of the operation contributed to its failure.

Before the establishment of any peace-keeping force of this nature, a good knowledge of the terrain is necessary for the good planning of the operation and, along with this, the success of its outcome. Yet the report shows that in the establishment of the UN operation, "integrated planning was limited to [just] two short visits to Somalia by interdepartmental technical teams." This, in the view of the drafters of the report, was not sufficient. To them, and quite rightly, "a viable, integrated plan requires ample information and analysis in advance of an operation." Concerning coordination, the report criticises the lack of a coordinated overall plan in terms of command relations, rules of engagement, coordination and standard operating procedures, intelligence management, and administrative and logistics policy and procedures. It notes that the UN operation suffered from a lack of unity among its different components. After establishing how crucial the central authority of the Special Representative of the Secretary-General (SRSG) is for the success of the operation, it asks whether frequent changing of the individuals serving in this capacity contributes to, or detracts from, developing an integrated structure in the field? Yet UNOSOM I and II had a total of five SRSGs within a period of just three years (1992-1995). The report thus concludes that because of all this, "there were obvious and direct operational consequences."[17]

Rwanda: The Unforgettable Scar on the Conscience of the World

If the failure of the United Nations in Somalia can be, to some extent, attributed to local conditions and the hostility shown by some warring factions towards the UN operation, this was not the case in Rwanda. On the contrary, the people of Rwanda appealed for UN intervention and cried at its withdrawal at the time they most needed it. In Somalia, apart from the attitude of the United States, the failure of the UN's operation was mainly the result of strategic mistakes committed by the UN headquarters. In Rwanda, in addition to this, were not only serious efforts by some member states of the UN to prevent the world body from taking any meaningful action in the direction of preventing or stopping the genocide, but also the active role of some member states in helping those that committed the genocide. Here therefore, we are faced with a case of omission and commission.

It was mentioned in *Chapter 1* that the UN is an inter-governmental organization; that is an organization that works according to the wishes and commitments of its individual member states. Thus, if a number of its members acted in a way that prevented it from undertaking an action that it ought to undertake by virtue of its Charter and other members did not counter those machinations, the whole organization may be held accountable for the failure —albeit that is unfair on those members that may have advocated another course of action. The same goes for the successes. For this, we could have limited our analysis of the UN's role in the genocide in Rwanda to what the United Nations as a whole did or did not do, as some have done.[18] However, given the magnitude of the errors committed by some individual member states and the undeniable effect of these actions on the overall response of the UN to the genocide in Rwanda, I could not resist studying this issue in some detailed way, by separately analysing the role of the member states that bear the biggest responsibility in this matter. For this, I shall, in addition to the United Nations system, look at the actions of Belgium, the United States and France —the three countries that bear, in the view of many analysts, the biggest responsibility in shaping UN response and approach to the genocide in Rwanda. Also, what role did the Rwandan and African actors play in all this and what is their share of responsibility, if any? However, in order to put all this in proper historic context, I shall begin by looking at the genocide itself and the events leading up to it.

The 100 Days that Changed the History of Rwanda

According to Article 2 of the 1948 "Convention on the Prevention and Punishment of the Crime of Genocide," the concept of genocide means any acts committed with intent to destroy, in whole or in part, a national, ethnic, racial or religious group by systematically killing members of the group, causing serious bodily or mental harm to members of the group, deliberately inflicting on the group conditions of life calculated to bring about its physical destruction in whole or in part, imposing measures intended to prevent births within the group, or forcibly transferring children of the group to another group.[19]

Yet between April and June 1994, Rwanda, Africa and the world at large witnessed one of the most horrific atrocities committed against unarmed civilians in the twentieth century. In this relatively short pace of time, the small Central African state lost about one tenth of its 10 million populations —1 million according to the post-genocide government in Kigali and 800,000 according to some other sources. Regardless of the exact figures, or even considering the lower statistics, there is no denial that the 1994 events in Rwanda were purely and simply what the above cited Convention referred to as "genocide." The genocide in Rwanda was an event that never will be forgotten in contemporary history of mankind. It put Rwanda on the world map —though in a very sorrowful way. Moreover, it is now clear that the genocide had been in the planning for months if not years before its actual execution on the ground. The 6 April 1994 plane crash in which the President of Rwanda was killed is however what triggered the process and made it on the large scale that we now know.

To most outsiders, the 1994 events in Rwanda were the result of an African tribal war whereby the majority "Hutu" perpetrated the despicable violence that we all now know on the minority "Tutsi." Many engaged in profiling the two groups by providing distinctions between the two "tribes" or "ethnic groups." The former are often described as generally short and chubby while the latter are presented as generally tall with lighter skin compared to the Hutu. They can be forgiven because this is what the Belgian colonialists sought to establish and they were the ones who first wrote the history of the country. In reality however, these (now) two groups belong to one ethnic group. They speak —and this is true even today— the same language (i.e. Kinyarwanda), share the same ideals, venerate and celebrate the same national historic heroes and practice the same religions. What they constituted before the coming of the Europeans (i.e. the Germans and then the Belgians after the First World War under the League's mandate) was two distinct working classes of the same society. In contemporary parlance, one may describe them as the upper/middle class and working class.

The term "Tutsi" was originally used to describe the social status of an individual rich in cattle, and the word "Hutu" was used to describe the subordinate group. Thus, the Tutsis represented the Aristocrats, while the Hutus were thought of as being inferior in social status. The description of the pastoralist communities and power-holders as "Batutsi" and the subordinated farming communities as "Bahutu" was becoming general when the Europeans first arrived in the country. All poor men came to be known as "Hutu" while the rich were described as "Tutsi." However, people could still change rank on the basis of their achievements. Most people married within the occupational group in which they had been raised, as happens anywhere in the world. Even today, especially in conservative societies, rich people intermarry while the poor generally marry people from their same social class. Yet this practice created a shared gene pool within each group, which meant that over generations, pastoralists came to look alike and cultivators looked like other cultivators. They thus developed similar physiological features.[20]

In any case, the transformation of the social groups into veritable distinct ethnic groups came in 1933. The Belgians had decided to limit administrative posts and higher education to the Tutsis. They were thus faced with a challenge —how to distinguish between the two groups given that the differences of physical appearance were sometimes quite blurred. Against the background of their own society divided between the French-speaking Walloons and the Dutch-speaking Flemish, they decided to organise a national census of all Rwandans. Every Rwandan was counted by a team of Belgian bureaucrats and measured: the height; the length of their noses; the shape of their eyes. They were then issued with an identity card bearing all the personal details that an ID card bears plus what the Belgians thought was their "ethnic group." All Rwandans born subsequently would then be registered according to this so-called ethnic group.[21] This system became customary and remained in place and these ID cards were often used during the genocide to identify and track down the Tutsis and mercilessly kill them.[22] It was not changed until 1997.

Shortly before the country's independence, with the Hutus in power, the policy of President Gregoire Kaybanda and his *Parti du mouvement de l'emancipation hutu* (Parmehutu) led many Tutsis, including the Tutsi king, the Mwami Kigeri V, to go into exile in neighbouring countries, mainly in the Kivu province of the present-day Democratic Republic of the Congo (DRC), and in Uganda, Tanzania and Burundi.[23] The Tutsi refugees began organizing themselves to call for their return under a power-sharing government in Rwanda. They never succeeded in attaining their demands. This refugee crisis remained unabated until the end of the genocide in July 1994.

After he had been in office for nearly two decades, the power of the Rwandan Hutu leader, President Juvénal Habyarimana was being seriously challenged by a Tutsi-dominated rebel group called the Rwandan Patriotic Front (RPF). The RPF was formed in 1988 in refugee camps in neighbouring Uganda and was backed by the government in Kampala. Some of these refugees had been in exile for decades —some were even born there. They mainly spoke English and Kinyarwanda and did not speak French, which was the official language in Kigali. Their incursion into Rwanda in 1990 was the beginning of a bitter civil war which later turned into —or was rather exploited by the regime in Kigali to carry out— the genocide.

The OAU got involved in the civil war from the start. With the leadership role being played by the Tanzanian president, Ali Hassan Mwinyi, and the OAU Secretary-General, Salim A. Salim, himself from Tanzania, the Pan-African organization sent an observer mission to the country and succeeded, in 1992, in getting the Rwandan parties to agree to a ceasefire. It sent in a fifty-member Neutral Military Observer Group (NMOG) to monitor the border between Rwanda and Uganda to ensure that the latter was not supporting the RPF rebels as the former had alleged. The efforts of the OAU led, in 1993, to the triumphant signing of the Arusha Accord in Tanzania between the government of Rwanda and the RPF rebels. A comprehensive peace accord of 163 articles, the Arusha Agreement signed on 4 August 1993 in the Tanzanian city whose name it bears, provided a radical and a wide-range political, military and constitutional reform in the country. Under the terms of this Accord, Rwanda was to have a broad-based government of national unity comprising the ruling *Mouvement révolutionnaire national pour le dévoppement* (MRND) party of President Habyarimana and the RPF rebels. An international neutral force was to be deployed to monitor the implementation of the peace accord, which was to be followed by the withdrawal of the French forces in the country by the invitation of the Habyarimana government, as it will be seen later. The RPF forces were to be integrated into the Rwandan national army and the group was to be assigned some ministerial portfolios. A new Prime Minister from the *Mouvement démocratique républicain* (MDR), the largest internal political opposition party, was appointed and the transitional government was to remain in power for twenty-two months with the possibility of one extension "if warranted by exceptional circumstances." The Transitional Government was never however inaugurated.

In October 1993, exactly three years after the RPF's first incursions into Rwanda, and about two months after the signing of the Arusha Accord, the democratically-elected Hutu president of Burundi was assassinated. The murder of President Melchior Ndadaye was the work of some Burundian Tutsi soldiers. Thus, the Habyarimana regime, already reluctant to implement the Arusha Accord and the Hutu extremists, especially the movement known as "Hutu Power," used this occasion to advance their own propaganda against the minority Tutsi in their midst. Through the state-owned *Radio Télévision Libre de Mille Collines* (RTLMC), they played on past memories of Tutsi domination and maltreatment of Hutus before and during the colonial era and confirmed the fears of the moderate Rwandan Hutus that Tutsis would never tolerate a Hutu government. They portrayed the Tutsis as well as the Hutus that did not acquiesce in or approve of their plans as *Ibytso* or accomplices of the enemy —the RPF.

It was also in October 1993 that the UN Security Council, after paying tribute to the efforts and the role played by the OAU and the Tanzanian government in the conclusion of the Arusha Agreement, passed Resolution 872 (5 October) establishing the United Nations Assistance Mission for Rwanda (UNAMIR). The main objective of this mission was to serve as the international neutral force provided by the Arusha Agreement in order to oversee the implementation of the Agreement. Its mandate, as set forth by the Resolution, was to contribute to the security of the city of Kigali and its surroundings, to monitor observance of the cease-fire agreement, to monitor the security situation during the final period of the Transitional Government, to monitor the process of repatriation of Rwandan refugees from neighbouring countries, and to assist in the coordination of humanitarian assistance. Boutros-Ghali appointed the Cameroonian former Foreign Minister, Jacques-Roger Booh-Booh as his Special Representative, and the Canadian officer, Major-General Roméo A. Dallaire as the force commander. Booh-Booh was replaced in June 1994 by the Pakistani diplomat, Shaharyar M. Khan, while Dallaire's replacement was another Canadian military officer, Major-General Guy Tousignant, who began his service in August 1994 and remained so until December 1995. It took however about five months before the requested 2,548 strength of UNAMIR was found. It comprised 32 nationalities, half of which were African. Belgium provided UNAMIR with almost the best and the most experienced battalion —no doubt because Belgium had been the colonial power of the country.

Meanwhile, the regime in Kigali was surreptitiously preparing the organization and logistics to attack the Tutsis in the country. In retrospect, one could argue that all they were waiting for was a pretext. Some government loyalists engaged in recruiting civilians and young people and training them with the active assistance of the French government, as will be seen later. They were trained by former soldiers and the communal police who would direct them in how to attack "the enemy." These militia groups later became what they called the *Interhamwe* meaning "Those Who Stand Together or Those Who Attack Together."

The April 1994 plane crash gave the extremist Hutus their long awaited pretext to attack the Tutsis and start the machine of genocide. On 6 April 1994, the Rwandan president's personal jet was shot down by some unknown people. Both Habyarimana and the new Burundian president, Cyprien Ntaryamira, were killed in the crash. The two presidents were returning from Tanzania where they had been meeting with regional leaders concerning events in both Burundi and Rwanda. Habyarimana himself was pressed to implement the Arusha peace Agreement that his government had signed with the RPF a few months back and which had reached an impasse. There certainly were some extremist elements in the military as well as some government officials that were opposed to the full implementation of the Agreement. They did not see any place for themselves in a new Rwanda. No wonder then that some observers suspect them of the shooting down of the presidential plane.

Shortly after the plane crash, units of the Presidential Guard, their minds poisoned by the regime's ethnic hatred discourses, and the extremist Interahamwe militia group set up roadblocks and barricades across the city and began the organised and systematic slaughter of Tutsis and opposition Hutus. They started in the capital, Kigali, and then took it to the provinces. Their first targets were the opposition Prime Minister, a moderate Hutu, and the president of the constitutional court, opposition priests, leaders of political opposition, the Information Minister and the negotiator of the Arusha Peace Accord. In short, they targeted those that were likely to resist their genocidal plans. The ruthless machine of genocide was now working at full speed.

At first, some Hutu opponents remained away from the killings. They even helped and saved a good number of Tutsis from the killing. They were their fellow countrymen. For centuries, their ancestors, their parents and they had lived next to one another; they attended the same schools and worship areas, and worked in the same offices. Besides, they shared a single language, a common history and the same ideals and cultural values. Perhaps out of fear of being killed themselves by the Interahamwe extremist militiamen or persuaded by the regime's increasing propaganda against the Tutsis, some joined the train of genocidal killers but very reluctantly. However, a handful of them remained committed to their principles and never did co-operate with the genocidal killers, or at least never participated in the killings until the end. Some paid for it with their own lives.

The international press widely reported the events. In short, the world was warned and informed about what was going on. From the first week, as the killing intensified, Western countries sent troops to evacuate their citizens and other Western nationals. They did so and left. The international community looked on. UNAMIR's force commander, Dallaire, sought to intervene to stop the killings. The Canadian commander and his men were however ordered from New York not to intervene. In fact, on 21 April, barely two weeks after the start of the mass and horrific killings in the country, the UN withdrew all its troops but a mediocre 270 from Rwanda under heavy American and Belgian pressure. Western countries closed their embassies and left Rwanda. Rwanda was now deserted and Rwandans were thus implicitly told to care for themselves.

The French later returned but more to the rescue of their allies, the genocidal regime, from RPF advances and to keep their face than to save lives of innocent Rwandans who were being brutally massacred. In July 1994, the RPF fighters succeeded in controlling the capital and, subsequently, the whole of the highly centralized country. Tens of thousands of Hutus and Rwandan armed forces fled to neighbouring countries. On one day they created a massive exodus of people rarely seen in modern history between two countries on a single day. The RPF formed a broad-based government of national unity with as many Hutu members as Tutsi.

This notwithstanding, the damage had been done. About a million innocent people had been ruthlessly and brutally killed in the space of just three calendar months. A whole nation had been deeply traumatised. Even now, more than a decade on, some still live with the terrible psychological effects of the horrors. Many women, including some very young ones, had been gang-raped and their human dignity flagrantly violated. An already divided nation by generations of European colonial rule and indigenous oppressive and opportunistic regimes had been pushed further apart from one another. But why did the genocide happen? Or was it preventable? Who is to be blamed?

Belgium and the United States: Aidid told us not to go

We have seen above the relationship between Rwanda and Belgium under both the League of Nations' mandates system and the United Nations' Trusteeship Council. We have also seen the rather regrettable decision of the Belgian mandatory (colonial) authorities to introduce an identity card in Rwanda which specified what they thought was the bearer's ethnic group. Belgium was nonetheless one of the first countries to respond to the Security Council's appeal for troop contributions to UNAMIR. The enthusiasm of the Belgians in this matter may however be explained in their attempt to regain what they considered their rightful place in Rwanda as the former colonial power. Belgium thus provided UNAMIR with a well-equipped and experienced battalion. As we will see below, France had outdone them and by the end of the Cold War, Paris had become the first foreign partner of the regime in Rwanda and this partnership continued throughout the genocide. Did the strategists of the genocide in Rwanda know that the Belgians were not strong or determined enough to remain in the country if a number of their soldiers were killed? Or did the Belgians naively agree to contribute to a peace-keeping force to UNAMIR thinking that their soldiers were divinely protected from bullets? One cannot be sure. However, in January 1994, as it will be further elaborated later, it came to the knowledge of the UN force commander, General Dallaire, that the Hutu Power and other extremist Hutu militia groups loyal to the Habyarimana regime had, in their search for a trigger to start the genocide and have a free hand in carrying it out, drawn up a number of possible actions. One of those was to provoke the Belgians and possibly kill some of their troops. They hoped that this would lead to Brussels deciding to withdraw its troops, which could also lead to other troop contributing states following suit. By this, they would have an unobstructed hand in their mass killing campaign. Given the seriousness and dangerous nature of this plan, which was leaked to Dallaire by an insider of the strategy who did not approve of it, both UN headquarters and the

145

UNAMIR forces, including the Belgians, were informed. As the OAU's commissioned report into the genocide in Rwanda reveals, as early as 14 January 1994, Belgian military intelligence reported fears that the Interahamwe might attack the UN's Blue Helmets (UNAMIR), "particularly its Belgian soldiers."[24]

With chilling accuracy, the events that followed the 6 April presidential plane crash proved the information relayed to Dallaire absolutely true and the scenarios it contained were played out exactly as it was passed on the appropriate authorities in the UN, including the killing of ten Belgian peacekeepers. The Belgians not only decided to withdraw their troops, but also engaged in a campaign for all other contingents to be withdrawn so that they would not be blamed alone. Meeting Boutros-Ghali in Bonn, then capital of Germany, shortly afterwards, the Belgian Foreign Minister sought to convince the UN to withdraw UNAMIR altogether. In order to get his request accepted, the Belgian official claimed that he had information that the Ghanaian contingent had fled, leaving the UNAMIR with only 1,500 troops. This was however untrue. The Secretary-General informed the Security Council about the Belgian position in a letter written the following day on 13 April. Eventually, the Belgians withdrew. Henceforth, the Belgian government engaged in a high level campaign with Council members in order to get the Council to withdraw UNAMIR.[25] In this high level lobbying, they found an enthusiastic ally in the United States.

As regards the United States, it should be remembered that after the Somali incident in which 18 American soldiers were killed in October 1993, the Clinton administration introduced what it called Presidential Decision Directive or PDD 25. This document was created to govern the United States' future intervention policies in UN or any multilateral peace-keeping operation in the world. Guided by this directive, the Clinton administration, through the US Permanent Representative to the UN, Ambassador Madeline Albright, used its considerable power in the Security Council to help muzzle the call for UN intervention to halt the genocide because they were not prepared to intervene. They would be, as the Belgians thought, quite embarrassed had other nations done so or remained in Rwanda without them. The American position went further than this by even denying the existence of "genocide" so as to avoid being legally bound to intervene according to the 1948 Convention on genocide prevention. In a series of declassified US government documents, memoranda and minutes of private meetings of top US officials at the time of genocide in Rwanda made public in 2004, one sees the bewildering effort of the US government to prevent UN from intervening in Rwanda.[26]

From one of these documents, one learns that on 11 April, just five days after the shooting down of the Rwandan president's private plane, some top US officials discussed the Rwandan situation during a dinner conversation. This conversation between Under Secretary of State, Frank Wisner, the third ranking official at the Pentagon, and former Secretary of State, Henry Kissinger, shows the Pentagon's candid assessment of the situation in Rwanda. The Pentagon's Africa analyst concluded his assessment of the situation by the following words: If the peace process fails: "a massive bloodbath (hundreds of thousands of deaths) will ensue," and the "UN will likely withdraw all forces," and the US will not get involved "until peace is restored." According to Ferroggiaro, albeit Rwanda was not such an important country in US foreign policy, the concerned American governmental departments were well informed about the situation on the ground. They were able to do get information through a variety of sources. In particular, the US Embassy in Kigali, before its closure, and the ones in Kampala and Nairobi were very useful in this regard. Their frequent dispatches to the State Department in Washington kept the US policy-makers well informed about the daily developments and positions and/or reactions of the different Rwandan and regional parties to the conflict. US embassies in Paris, Brussels and Ottawa relayed valuable information about government position and public opinion in these capitals to Washington. The US Mission to the UN was also instrumental in that it provided US policy-makers with the views of the different stakeholders in the crisis, including the views of the Rwandan Permanent Representative and those of the African Group of states at the UN.[27]

Four days after this dinner conversation, on 15 April, while the UN force commander was calling for reinforcements of the UNAMIR's strength against the background of the eminent Belgian withdrawal and an increase in mass slaughter of the Tutsis by the extremist Hutus, the US Department of State sent a "confidential" telegram to the US mission to the United Nations, at the time headed by Albright. This cable was entitled: "Talking Points for UNAMIR withdrawal." In it, the State Department advised the Mission that "this withdrawal does not require a UN Security Council resolution." The Mission is further instructed that "we will oppose any effort at this time to preserve a UNAMIR presence in Rwanda." This was to anticipate a Security Council debate on a draft proposal to be submitted by other countries, especially the African Group, on Rwanda. About a week later, on 21 April, the Security Council voted to withdraw most of UNAMIR troops, reducing the force to a token 270.

A month after the genocide, as pressures from civil society organizations mounted and evidences of genocide became more and more apparent to the general public, the Clinton administration was expected to acknowledge the occurrence of genocide. However, since this would have legally obliged them to act, the Department of State instructed its officials never to use the term "genocide" but instead, use formulas such as "acts of genocide have occurred." In fact, one paper in the declassified documents, dated 1 May 1994, reveals a discussion between some US government officials who had the day-to-day responsibility for the Rwandan crisis. During one of their discussions, the term "genocide" comes up. One of them warns his colleagues: "Be careful. Legal at State was worried about this yesterday —Genocide could commit USG [US government] to do something." According to the drafters of the OAU's report, this controversial action of the US government "made them look ridiculous to the rest of the world —except, of course, to peers on the Security Council who had adopted the same shameful position."[28]

Yet this is what guided American position throughout the genocide —their public acknowledgement of the occurrence of "genocide" coming only in June, after nearly a million lives had been tragically lost. Linda Melvern for example reports a heated debate between the Nigerian Permanent Representative to the UN, Professor Ibrahim Gambari, and the American delegation during an informal Security Council meeting. The meeting was held on

Friday, 15 April, thus shortly before the withdrawal of the Belgian contingent from UNAMIR. Gambari made a plea for reinforcements arguing that however weighty the advice from Belgium may be, the ambassadors must realise that no other country had withdrawn its troops and that, in any case, the peacekeepers had a vital role to play protecting the population and promoting a ceasefire. The Americans rigorously rejected his suggestion. America, they argued, would not accept any UN resolution that fell short of calling for total withdrawal of UNAMIR from Rwanda. According to the author, who says that she has a leaked confidential report of this informal Security Council meeting and many others on Rwanda, Gambari said that the troops on the ground were at least accomplishing something, even without the Belgians. The Americans however remained adamant.[29]

According to Boutros-Ghali, when the Security Council finally, though lately, approved UNAMIR II with an increased strength of 5,500 troops and an expanded mandate,[30] the American representative "employed the requirements of PDD 25 to pressure the other Security Council members to delay the deployment of the full 5,500-man contingent to Rwanda until I could satisfy her that all of the many U.S. conditions had been met."[31] Such was the position of the American government with regard to the genocide in Rwanda, which many found intriguing. The Americans however did not lack excuses. For example, on 5 May 1994, Anthony Lake, then National Security Advisor, said during a press briefing on PDD 25: "When I wake up every morning and look at the headlines and the stories . . . of these conflicts, I want to work to end every conflict [. . .] But neither we nor the international community have the resources nor the mandate to do so. So we have to make distinctions. We have to ask the hard questions about *where* and *when* we can intervene. And the reality is that we cannot solve other people's problem. . . ."[32] Indeed, unless they are sitting over wells of oil and other natural resources in the Persian Gulf.

France: when le gendarme de l'Afrique became l'allié des génocidaires

Belgium and the United States can rightly be blamed for their omission or inaction in terms of their refusal to contribute to the UN force or, in the case of Belgium, the withdrawal of their troops from it. The French however can be held responsible for commission, as they assisted, financially, diplomatically and militarily the genocidal regime and its militias. In her relationship with Africa, France is best known for siding with and backing dictators. In Rwanda however, France's role went beyond that to something that baffles healthy logic and human ethics. The famous French political activist, F.X. Verschave, succinctly explained France's initial response to the genocide in Rwanda in the following terms:

> For a moment we were all bemused by the chain of events and the reaction of the French authorities. Their role appeared to be limited to the evacuation of French and other European nationals and the smuggling, from the country, of a group of Habyarimana's entourage to Paris and 34 unknown Rwandans under the cover of evacuating an orphanage. We soon learned that what was going on was genocide. A genocide that was carried out by an army and militia groups trained and equipped by France. And without repeating oneself, France continued its support for the genocidal camp throughout.[33]

As seen above, France never was a colonial power in Rwanda. However, with the withdrawal of Belgium from the country and exploiting the French language which is the official language of Rwanda, France came to edge-out Belgium from the 1970s onwards. There followed a very close relationship between Paris and the Habyarimana autocratic regime in Kigali. Soon, France became Rwanda's closest Western ally, its foremost creditor and arms supplier.[34] Given the situation on the ground and while waiting for the deployment of the UNAMIR II on the ground, the Security Council voted, on 17 May 2004, for an arms embargo on Rwanda. Yet in a flagrant violation of this embargo, France continued supplying arms to the Hutu Power regime. Some observers even note that French forces fought alongside the genocidal camp against the RPF advances as they had been doing since the outbreak of the civil war in October 1990.

Ambassador Khan, who was Boutros-Ghali's Special Representative to Rwanda from July 1994 to the end of the UN mission in the country in 1996, asserts that within three weeks of the start of the civil war in 1990, "the Rwandese government army, assisted by French and Zairian [Congolese] forces, repulsed the attack, pushing the RPF back towards Uganda."[35] Glaser and Smith confirm the same thing and further contend that French forces fighting shoulder to shoulder with the Rwandan forces often worked as military planners, instructors, trainers, and technicians. They commanded the heavy artillery of the Rwandan army supplied by France, as they positioned them in the battlefield against RPF targets and positions and then stepped back for the Rwandan soldiers to shoot, so as to be able in the future, as the largely discredited report of the French government into the genocide in Rwanda did, to distance themselves and suggest that everything was done by the Rwandans themselves.[36] The OAU's report found that "French troops interrogated military prisoners, engaged in counter-insurgency, and provided military intelligence." More striking is the revelation that "French soldiers were deployed, manning checkpoints and scrutinizing identity cards far from where any French citizens were known to be living, but very close to FAR [Rwandan government forces loyal to the genocidal regime] zone of control."[37]

As the killing intensified and international criticism mounted against the genocidal killers, the François Mitterrand government in Paris received a high ranking army officer of the genocidal government in Kigali. According to Verschave, Lieutenant-Colonel Ephrem Rwabalinda, the second ranking military officer in the Rwandan army, came to Paris from 9 May 1994 and stayed there for 34 days. During the visit, Verschave claims that the Rwandan officer met with many important figures of the French government and secret services, including a certain General Huchon, described by the author as a high ranking French military officer and close to the French president. According to the author, many things were discussed during this visit. The army officer had come to request more French aid. General Huchon told him that France had just sent some communications equipment to Rwanda and that "further aid could be forthcoming *if Rwanda managed to end bad publicity about the slaughter!*" It would seem the communications equipment referred to is what the author claims was a number of telephones with a secure telephone line between the Rwandan officers and their

French counterparts which would prevent a third party from eavesdropping on their conversations. France reportedly also urged Rwandan forces to establish a zone under their control where they could be delivered ammunition confidentially and in security.[38]

Towards the end of genocide and seeing the imminent victory of the RPF forces over the genocidal regime, France proposed to the UN Security Council to be allowed to send to Rwanda an independent French force under the enforcement provisions of Chapter VII with the declared aim of ensuring "the security and protection of civilians in Rwanda." The Security Council authorised this force in June 1994 despite reservations by some members (Brazil, China, New Zealand, Nigeria and Pakistan), which abstained from voting. The French named their force "Opération Turquoise," the code name of an earlier French counter-insurgency force during the Algerian liberation struggle in the late 1950s. The French force was launched on 23 June, just the day after its authorisation by the Council. It comprised some 2,500 troops. One wonders why this was not available to the first UNAMIR force. In any event, Cattier found this, as did many other observers, motivated in reality by the desire of the French government to preserve what he called "Hutuland."[39] In retrospect, the force served to help the genocidal forces and, where they were likely to be overpowered, to protect them from RPF advances. Perhaps the most comprehensive analysis of the French operation is what we find in a Human Rights Watch report prepared after a field mission in Rwanda. The report describes the activities of the French operation soon after its deployment:

> Soon after, the French government, without prior U.N. approval, declared its intention to carve out a "safe zone" in southwestern Rwanda. It was to this zone that the rump government and the majority of the Rwandan armed forces and militias retreated following the fighting in Kigali and the RPF's military advance. Under French protection, the FAR and militias were able to exert their control over the vast population that was quartered in the safe zone. The rump government moved its radio station into the zone where it continued without interference to incite Hutu to kill Tutsi in its broadcasts. For the duration of Operation Turquoise, the FAR

continued to receive weapons inside the French-controlled zone via
Goma airport [in neighbouring Zaire, now the DRC].[40]

In the French occupied zones, "Hutu Power" brigades draped
their vehicles with French flags to lure Tutsis from their hiding
places to their death. Even when French troops found survivors,
they often told them to wait for transport. Before they returned, the
people were killed by "Hutu Power" militiamen. Thus, many
African leaders, including South Africa's President Nelson Mandela
and Archbishop Desmond Tutu, openly questioned France's
motives.[41] Such was France's role in the genocide in Rwanda
operating under a mandate of the United Nations. Yet, it is puzzling
to note that more than a decade on, official France still refuses to
acknowledge this regrettable role. In fact, jumping over the Everest
of propaganda and manipulation, but making itself a laughing
stock, the French official inquiry into the genocide concluded that
France was the only country in the international community that
tried to act to keep the genocide —perhaps they meant "keeping it
going."

United Nations: it was a collective mistake

It was pointed out from the outset (see *Chapter 1*) that the failure of
some members of an inter-governmental organization like the
United Nations to do something as required by its own Charter or
principles and the inability of other members to call them to order
constitutes a failure of the whole organization. This should have
bound me to limit the analyses here to the role of the United
Nations as an institution. Indeed, it remains my opinion that the
whole UN system is somehow responsible for this failure. However,
I justify this chosen approach on the grounds of the significant role
that those individual members of the UN played in this failure. It
would be hard, if not impossible, to establish the UN's utter failure
in Rwanda without touching on the actions of Belgium, the United
States and France. But this does not mean the UN as an institution,
through its secretariat, did not commit an independent error. It did
so indeed.

In the UN's own commissioned report, the members of the
inquiry committee avoided laying blame on the shoulder of any

individual country. Instead, they attributed it to the whole UN organization. They acknowledged the failure of the UN. The report concludes that "UNAMIR, the main component of the United Nations presence in Rwanda, was not planned, dimensioned, deployed or instructed in a way which provided for a proactive and assertive role in dealing with a peace process in serious trouble." The report further notes that "the mission was smaller than original recommendations from the field suggested. It lacked well-trained troops and functioning material." With regard to the mission's mandate, the report found this inadequate and criticised the failure of the Security Council to correct this "despite the significant warning signs that the original mandate had become inadequate."[42]

The OAU's report found the UN's failure in four main areas, which is almost in line with the findings of the UN's report that was published a year earlier. The first observation of the OAU's report is what its drafters considered the failure of the world body to treat UNAMIR, once established, as a particularly difficult mission and thus equip it accordingly. The report notes that the Security Council approved a force "substantially weaker than the one the Arusha negotiators deemed necessary." Secondly, the report blames the UN for not providing an adequate mandate for the force sent. Thus, in the view of the drafters of the report, this denied the force the capacity to function effectively. Clearly, given that the French operation was allowed a Chapter VII mandate lends even more credit to this charge. The third point observed by the OAU's report on the UN is that despite the wealth of information available to the Security Council from press reports about the situation on the ground in Rwanda, the Council never found it expedient to expand the mandate or troop strength until five weeks after the start of genocide. And even then, the report notes that "not one of the new soldiers assigned had arrived" in the country by the end of genocide. And finally, the report blames the UN for its "insistence and utterly wrong-headed neutrality regarding the génocidaires [genocidal killers] and the RPF." This, according to the drafters of the report, "compromised its integrity" and led it to view the conflict as a mere civil war rather than genocide.[43]

One may be tempted to try to explain the latter point by the fact that Rwanda was sitting on the Security Council at this moment as a non-permanent member. Thus, since the loyalty of its representative was to the genocidal government in Kigali, he was bound to do what he did, mislead the Council and the whole UN system that what was going on was a mere civil war and not genocide. Melvern notes that the Rwandan ambassador to the UN, Jean-Damascène Bizimana, became an essential element in the interim government's propaganda campaign. He used his advantageous position as member of the Security Council to peddle the genocidal government's line that the killings in Rwanda were part of the civil war.[44] And this misleading message being compatible with the sort of argument the obstructionists (e. g. Belgium and the US) wanted, there was little effort to discredit his thesis. But this cannot in any case be an excuse, as the Council, and more so the big powers, knew all too well that the reality on the ground was different from what he was making out.[45]

To Boutros-Ghali, the blame should be attributed to the Security Council. He found the behaviour of the Council quite "shocking." To him, the Council "meekly followed the United States' lead in denying the reality of the genocide." In effect, one could argue that Boutros-Ghali's argument is directed to the United States more than to the whole of the Security Council since he acknowledges the good effort of many members of the Council and lengthily deals with the many obstructionist efforts of Washington.[46]

Not everyone however agrees with this straightforward sentencing of the UN and this apparent unanimous "guilty" verdict levied on the world body. In his thought-provoking analysis of the genocide in Rwanda, Michael Barnett acknowledges that the Security Council, by refusing to call the events by their proper name —*genocide*— for fear of being compelled to act, can be, in its entirety, "credited for failing Rwanda."[47] He also acknowledges that "the UN bears some moral responsibility for the genocide," but contends that this responsibility "derives from its actions in April 1994, not during the period leading up to the genocide."[48] He further posits that:

> Institutions must constantly choose among various responsibilities; responsibilities that have immediate consequences for various constituencies. Fulfilling one set of responsibilities may lead to the

neglect of another. It is in this way that the act of indifference can have an ethical basis. The UN had responsibilities not only to Rwandans but also to UN personnel who were at risk in the field and to the integrity of an institution that might be severely damaged by another Somalia-like failure in the field.[49]

Thus, to Barnett, the UN's inaction in Rwanda can or should be excused for it having many other commitments and not only Rwanda. The author provides another excuse for the UN, which is that the UN knew little about the nature of the events until it was quite late. Perhaps this is why he postulated above that the UN cannot be blamed for anything prior to April 1994. Barnett's views about the responsibility or non-responsibility of the UN seem to be a bit contradictory and not consistent as he acknowledges the process of the formation of these views was. As a Political Officer at the U.S. Mission to the UN at the time, the author finds himself at times defending or at least finding excuses for inaction, but while enjoying this and the many philosophical concepts he employs to explain it, he suddenly remembers the wealth of evidence suggesting otherwise. And while turning round to admit this, he remembers half-way that he is an American and was a member of the US mission to the UN at this critical moment. He thus turns back to finding excuses for the UN, and directs any blame to the Secretary-General who was at odds with the United States.

Clearly, the ignorance thesis cannot help the UN in any way, especially for actions or inactions after receiving the famous January cable of General Dallaire. This Cable that is mentioned by almost all those that have dealt with the UN's actions or inactions in the Rwandan genocide was sent by the Canadian UN force commander on 11 January 1994 —almost three months before the start of the genocide. On 11 January 1994, General Dallaire sent a Cable to the Military Advisor to the Secretary-General, Major-General Maurice Baril entitled: "Request for Protection for Informant." The Secretary-General was away in Europe for most of January and he claims that he did not learn about the cable until very late. The telegram stated that a confidential and reliable piece of information had been conveyed to General Dallaire by a senior Rwandan government official, only known as "Jean-Pierre." The informant was not a likely victim, who was likely to exaggerate, but was from within the inner circle of genocide planners. It is obvious that Jean-Pierre did not approve of what was going on and what he was tasked with by the government against his fellow Tutsi countrymen.

The information conveyed to the UN force commander revealed the Hutu plan to provoke and then kill some Belgian peacekeepers so that they would withdraw from Rwanda and this would encourage others to follow suite, as stated above. The informant also said that the Interahamwe had trained 1,700 men in the government camps, scattered in groups of 40 throughout Kigali. He had been ordered to register all Tutsis in the city, and suspected it was for their extermination once the campaign of genocide had begun. He said that his personnel were able to kill up to 1,000 Tutsis in 20 minutes. Finally, Jean-Pierre told Dallaire that he knew about a major weapon cache with at least 135 weapons (i.e. G 3 and AK 47s). He promised that he was prepared to take a small contingent of the UN mission to seize the weapons provided his family was given protection.

This is what Dallaire's telegram to the UN headquarters contained asking for authorisation to protect the informant's family and evacuate him from the country. He informed the Secretariat that it was UNAMIR's intention to take action within the next 36 hours pending that authorisation. Though the telegram was addressed only to General Baril, the latter shared it with other senior officials within the Department of Peace-keeping Operations, including the then head of this department, Kofi Annan. The Secretariat declined to authorise Dallaire's request and urged for more prudence towards the information. Yet the information was confirmed by the Rwandan Prime Minister designated by the Arusha Agreement who expressed "confidence in the veracity and true [intentions] of the informant." In any case, nothing happened and the chain of events later proved the informant and the instincts of General Dallaire chillingly true.

During the genocide, a similar scenario was played out. The role of the government-controlled RTLMC radio station in encouraging Tutsi hatred and inciting extremist Hutus to kill them and moderate Hutus was no secret to anyone, except those that shared its message. Disgusted by the hate message that was being broadcast by this station, including instructions about how to kill, Dallaire pleaded with the Secretariat for permission to neutralise the station. Again in vain.[50] Such were the actions or rather inactions of the United Nations in Rwanda, albeit influenced or restrained by the three countries mentioned, which makes it, in my view, guilty of the utter failure of its mission in Rwanda and thus, morally responsible to a large extent for what everyone knows about what happened in Rwanda.

Conclusion

This chapter looked at areas of Africa-UN relations where it can be argued that the actions or inactions of the world body failed or disappointed Africa. The two incidents most illustrative of this are arguably UN's involvement and then failure in the conflict in Somalia and its inaction during the 1994 genocide in Rwanda. In Somalia, the failure of the UN mission is mainly attributed to the lack of adequate planning and mandate for the mission as well as differences of view and strategy between the UN mission on the ground and officials at the headquarters. The aggressive attitude of the UN authorised multilateral force of UNITAF under the leadership of the Unites States contributed also to the failure of the UN mission. Finally, the sheer lack of coordination between UNOSOM and UNITAF was a major strategic and policy failure that had its consequences for the UN mission. Of course, the unscrupulous Somali warlords cannot be exonerated. By the unhelpful attitude of some of them, they too can be held responsible for the failure of the UN mission.

In Rwanda, the undisputed failure of the United Nations to prevent and, subsequently, to stop and minimise the effect of the genocide was an accumulation of failures by a number of powerful member states who deliberately chose not to take effective action and/or worked hard to prevent others from doing so. Belgium, the United States and France shoulder the biggest responsibility. While the first two worked against the UN taking any active role in Rwanda, France threw its full political, diplomatic and military weight behind the Rwandan government officials responsible for the genocide. In my view, of all the outside actors in the Rwandan genocide, France shoulders the biggest responsibility. And if the responsibility attributable to Belgium and the UN may only be described as "moral," France can actually be held responsible for directly or indirectly participating in the killings of innocent Rwandans. But because none of the other members of the UN managed to call them to order or to take action where they failed, in addition to the Secretariat's own omissions, the UN as an institution can also be held responsible. And this leads us to another question —the role of the Africans.

The tremendous effort made by the OAU in the Rwandan crisis from its very first day is not a secret to anyone. The world also acknowledges the Pan-African organization's role in negotiating the Arusha Peace Accord. In fact, it is safe to note that the triumphant signing of the Arusha Accord was one of the very brightest moments of OAU's history, in terms of conflict resolution in Africa. Even the UN Security Council itself could not afford to ignore this in any of its many resolutions with regard to Rwanda. These efforts continued up until the start of genocide. At the UN, too, the African Group, spearheaded by Nigeria, was very active in urging the Security Council to take urgent action to protect the lives of civilians and reinforce UNAMIR. In her account of what she calls the "secret meetings of the Security Council," Melvern tells us of the many lobbying efforts of Nigeria's ambassador to the UN, Ibrahim Gambari, in trying to persuade other members of the Council to take effective action to protect the civilians in Rwanda. She also tells us how opposed the African Group, and Kofi Annan, either as an African or a responsible international civil servant, were to the withdrawal of UNAMIR.[51]

This notwithstanding, in my view, the African Group at the UN and indeed the OAU should have done more than contenting themselves with calls on the UN and the international community to take action. I mean here military action. After all, those who were being killed were Africans killed by Africans in Africa. For example, as the Security Council was preparing in April 1994 to vote a decision to reduce UNAMIR's strength in Rwanda, Ambassador Gambari met with the Secretary-General and asked him to counter moves in the Council to withdraw UNAMIR. According to the UN's report, perhaps out of frustration by the attitude of the big powers,

Boutros-Ghali pressed Gambari to encourage African heads of state to rally behind his position and write letters against the withdrawal.[52] There is however no indication in the report or anywhere else that such letters by African heads of state were sent. Again, when Resolution 918 was adopted by the Security Council in May 1994 authorising an increase in the strength of UN force or the establishment of UNAMIR II, the Secretariat held a number of meetings with potential troop contributors. The Special Representative of the Secretary-General in Rwanda travelled to a number of African countries to seek contributions to UNAMIR II. Boutros-Ghali himself contacted a number of African Heads of State and enlisted the help of the Secretary-General of the OAU in an effort to mobilise African offers of troops. The response was however very meagre. The few African countries that signalled some willingness to contribute conditioned their offer on their receiving financial and logistical assistance.[53]

In the light of this, it is safe to argue that, as an African, the Secretary-General did his best to deal with the situation in Rwanda. The African Group at the UN, led by Nigeria's ambassador, made a very good effort but perhaps could have done better. Perhaps they did. They were only representatives and their leaders back home knew very well what was going on. The OAU did a marvellous job in the Rwandan crisis up until the start of genocide. The inability of the African Heads of State to take over the military task, despite their meagre resources, and the limitation of their efforts to mere calls on the international community to take action instead constituted a failure on their part and this makes them liable to a share of the blame in this international fiasco. In my view, having seen the actions and inactions of the different actors of the international community, the OAU should have not only taken military action but taken over the whole operation from the UN, as they had marvellously done during the negotiation of the Arusha Accord. The so-called *"Opération Turquoise"* should have been *"Opération Africaine."* This was yet another illustration that Africa's relationship with the UN only works to the advantage of the continent when, and only when, it sees its partnership with the world body as complementary to its own efforts, rather than something to depend on.

Notes

1. See Gregory S. Sanjian, "Promoting Stability or Instability? Arms Transfers and Regional Rivalries, 1950-1991," *International Studies Quarterly*, Vol. 43, no. 4 (1999): 641-70; Emira Woods, "Somalia: Problems with Current US Policy," *Foreign Policy in Focus*, Vol. 2, no. 19 (February 1997); Peter J. Schraider, *United States foreign policy toward Africa: Incrementalism, Crisis, and Change* (Cambridge: Cambridge University Press, 1994), p. 160; and George B. N. Ayittey, "The Somali Crisis: Time for an Africa Solution," *Cato Policy Analysis*, no. 205 (28 March 1994).

2. Shannon Lindsey Blaton, "Foreign Policy in Transition? Human Rights, Democracy, and U.S. Arms Exports," *International Studies Quarterly*, Vol. 49, no. 4 (December 2005): 647-668.

3. See Christopher Clapham, "The United Nations and Peacekeeping in Africa," in Mark Malan (ed.), *Whiter Peacekeeping in Africa?* Monograph no. 36 (Pretoria, Institute for Security Studies, April 1999).

4. See Security Council Resolution S/RES/733 (1992) of 23 January 1992.

5. Agostinho Zacarias, *The United Nations and International Peacekeeping* (London: I. B. Tauris Publishers, 1996), pp. 67-8.

6. See Security Council Resolution S/RES/775 (1992) of 28 August 1992.

7. Clapham, The United Nations and Peacekeeping in Africa.

8. Zacarias, The UN and International Peacekeeping, p. 69.

9 Ibid., p. 70.

10. See Security Council Resolution S/RES/814 (1993) of 26 March 1993.

11. This is for example the thrust of the article of John R. Bolton, "Wrong Turn in Somalia," *Foreign Affairs*, Vol. 73, no. 1 (January/February 1994).

12. Woods, *Somalia*.

13. See Walter Clarke and Jeffrey Herbst, "Somalia and the Future of Humanitarian Intervention," *Foreign Affairs*, Vol. 75, no. 2 (March/April 1996).

14. Ibid.; and Boutros Boutros-Ghali, *Unvanquished: A US-UN Saga* (London & New York: I. B. Tauris Publishers, 1999), p. 60.

15. Clarke and Herbst, *Somalia*.

16. United Nations Department for Peacekeeping Operations, *The Comprehensive Report on Lessons Learned from United Nations Operation in Somalia (UNOSOM), April 1992 – March 1995* (New York: Department of Public Information, 1995).

17. Ibid.

18. This is for example the case of the United Nations' commissioned *Report of the Independent Inquiry into the Actions of the United Nations during the 1994 Genocide in Rwanda*, UN document S/1999/1257 of 16 December 1999. This is not a surprise as diplomatic practice would encourage paying heed to some sensibilities between the member states, especially given that some powerful member states were involved in this.

19. The Convention was signed in 1948 and adopted by UN General Assembly's Resolution A/260 (III) of 9 December 1949 and it comprises 19 articles.

20. See Joseph Ki-Zerbo, *L'Histoire de l'Afrique Noire: D'Hier à Demain* (Paris: Hatier, 1978), pp. 310-11 ; and Human Rights Watch, *Leave None to Tell the Story : Genocide in Rwanda* (New York : HRW, 1999).

21. See Linda R. Melvern, *A People Betrayed: The role of the West in Rwanda's genocide* (Cape Town, London & New York: NAEP & Zed Books, 2000), pp. 10-11.

22. Jim Fussell, *Group Classification on National ID Cards as a Factor in Genocide and Ethnic Cleansing* (Paper presented to the Seminar Series of the Yale University Genocide Studies Program, November 2001).

23. Melvern, *A People Betrayed*, p. 15.

24. Organization of African Unity, *Rwanda: The Preventable Genocide* (International Panel of Eminent Personalities, 2000), Ch. 9, para. 13. This report was commissioned by the OAU and prepared by a seven-member International Panel of Eminent Personalities, comprising both Africans and non Africans. It was chaired by Sir Ketumile Masire (former President of Botswana) with Amadou Toumani Touré (then a former President of Mali, before coming back to power in June 2002), as the vice-chairman, the other members of the Panel coming from India, France, Liberia, Canada and Sweden.

25. United Nations, "Report of the Independent Inquiry into the Actions of the United Nations during the 1994 Genocide in Rwanda" UN Document S/1999/1257 of 15 December 1999, p. 19; and Boutros-Ghali, *Unvanquished*, p. 132.

26. For a detailed analysis of these documents and a link to the different pieces, see William Ferroggiaro, *The U.S. and the Genocide in Rwanda 1994: Information, Intelligence and the U.S. Response* (published on 24 March 2004) at <http://www.gwu.edu/~nsarchiv/NSAEBB/NSAEBB117/#3.> (27 February 2006.)

27. Ibid.

28. OAU, *Rwanda: The Preventable Genocide*, Ch. 12, para. 45.

29. Melvern, *A People Betrayed*, pp. 161-3.

30. See Security Council Resolution S/RES/918 (1994) of 17 May 1994.

31. Boutros-Ghali, *Unvanquished*, p. 136.

32. Ferroggiaro, *US and the Genocide in Rwanda*. Emphasis in *italics* is mine.

33. François-Xavier Verschave, *La Françafrique: Le plus long scandale de la République* (Paris: Éditions Stock, 1998), p. 76.

34. See Linda R. Melvern, *Conspiracy to Murder: The Rwandan Genocide* (London: Verso Publishers, 2004), pp. 56-7; and Nelson Alusala, "The Arming of Rwanda, and the Genocide," *African Security Review*, Vol. 13, no. 2 (2004): 139-40.

35. Shaharyar M. Khan, *The Shallow Graves of Rwanda* (London & New York: I. B. Tauris Publishers, 2001), p. 6.

36. Antoine Glaser and Stephen Smith, *Comment la France a perdu l'Afrique?* (Paris: Calmann-lévy, 2005), p. 142.

37. OAU, *Rwanda: The Preventable Genocide*, Ch. 12, para. 26.

38. François-Xavier Verschave, "Continuation, après le 7 avril 1994 de l'alliance militaire antérieure," in Laure Coret and François-Xavier Verschave (eds.), *L'horreur qui nous prend au visage : l'État français et le génocide au Rwanda* (Paris : Rapport de la Commission d'enquête citoyenne & Éditions Karthala, 2005), pp. 56-60.

39. Emmanuel Cattier, "Les intentions réelles de Turquoise," in Laure Coret and François-Xavier Verschave (eds.), *L'horreur qui nous prend au visage*, pp. 381-87.

40. Human Rights Watch, "Rwanda/Zaire: Rearming with Impunity — International Support for the Perpetrators of the Rwandan Genocide," *Human Rights Watch Arms Project*, Vol. 7, no. 4 (May 1995). Available at <http://www.hrw.org/reports/1995/Rwanda1.htm.> (27 February 2006.)

41. Human Rights Watch, *Leave None to Tell the Story*.

42. United Nations, *Report of the Independent Inquiry*, p. 30.

43. OAU, *Rwanda: The Preventable Genocide*, Ch. 13, para. 11.

44. Melvern, *A People Betrayed*, p. 159.

45. See Khan, *The Shallow Graves*, p. 2.

46. Boutros-Ghali, *Unvanquished*, pp. 135-8.

47. Michael Barnett, *Eyewitness to a Genocide: The United Nations and Rwanda* (Ithaca & London: Cornell University Press, 2002), pp. 2-3.

48. Ibid., p. 20.

49. Ibid., p. 6.

50. Melvern, *A People Betrayed*, p. 156.

51. Ibid., pp. 158-64.

52. United Nations, *Report of the Independent Inquiry*, p. 22.

53. Ibid., p. 25.

Chapter 4

Africans in the UN System

I had been elected as Africa's candidate to take "Africa's turn" in the job of UN Secretary-General. Because of my decades of involvement with the economic, political, and diplomatic problems of Africa, I committed myself to try to advance the cause of the continent throughout my term in office. As time went by, I became increasingly frustrated yet reinforced in my determination as I saw my worst fears coming true.
—Boutros Boutros-Ghali, *Unvanquished*, p. 157

It has been repeatedly said in this book that the United Nations Organization (UN) is an inter-governmental organization (IGO). IGOs are generally structured in a way that it is difficult for a single person, and this includes their heads, to control the decision-making process in a personal way. Likewise, the loyalty of the staff members of an IGO is expected to be to the organization and not to their home governments. It is however true that depending on the support the head of an IGO gets from other staff members and, most importantly, from the different stakeholders of the organization (i. e. state members of the organization), he or she may be able, to a large extent, to influence the attention given by the concerned organization to its different priority issues or to make a particular issue a priority one. It is also true that most staff members, while carrying out their duties as international civil servants, strive as much as possible not to hurt the interests of their home nations or allow those to be hurt by other staff members. As it will be seen below, their success or failure in this regard depends to a large extent on how assertive and/or supportive their home nations are.

These twin issues —public loyalty to the employer and conscious or hidden loyalty to home nation— are clearly, though indirectly, acknowledged by the provisions of the UN Charter related to the recruitment criteria for its staff members. Article 101 (3) of the UN Charter stipulates that "the paramount consideration in the employment of the staff and in the determination of the conditions of service shall be the necessity of securing the highest standards of efficiency, competence, and integrity." However, the same paragraph maintains that in so doing, "due regard shall be paid to the importance of recruiting the staff on as wide a geographical basis as possible." In effect, the geographical distribution or balance in employment within an IGO will have no significant meaning if it is not aimed at ensuring that the interests of all the stakeholders are given due regard. The United Nations as a universal IGO acknowledges that only by this will its member states have confidence in it.[1] Yet if this is the case, which it is, those who are expected to ensure this balance of views are no one else but the recruited staff members. They are thus actually told, albeit implicitly, that in addition to ensuring a higher standard of efficiency in their work for the United Nations, they are also the ones responsible for looking after the interests of their respective geographical regions. Perhaps this is why many countries, especially the big powers, insist on the right to control certain high-ranking UN posts and to name their nationals to hold those posts.

It is in recognition of this fact or these facts that I thought it useful to look at Africans in the UN system —their itineraries, their achievements or failures, and their representation of Africa and its interests. As it will be observed later that Africans do not seem to be adequately represented in the UN system, I will also try to explain why this is the case. Moreover, because the UN consists not only of its six main organs based at Headquarters —with the exception of the International Court of Justice (ICJ) — but also of its specialised agencies scattered around the world, I propose to look at the itineraries of a selection of prominent Africans that have held or hold (as this book was completed) high professional positions within the UN system. This will serve to complete the study of Africa-UN relations. Before we start however, an important point must be highlighted. This is that diplomats posted at the UN are not considered amongst the UN staff members. They represent and work for their governments, not for the UN. All member states maintain permanent missions in New York, which are, in effect, their countries' embassies to the UN. These diplomats, unlike the staff members, except for a few, enjoy the legal privileges and immunities allowed under international law for diplomats everywhere. An individual may however change from being a representative of his or her home country to the UN to being a UN staff member. In fact, most of the UN high officials, especially from developing countries, which include Africa, passed through this route. The converse scenario is not very frequent. In this chapter therefore, the focus will be on those Africans that fall in the category of UN staff members.

Africans at the United Nations Secretariat

It has been mentioned earlier (see *Chapter 1*) that the UN at headquarters is composed of six main organs. These are the General Assembly, the Security Council, the Economic and Social Council, the Trusteeship Council, the Secretariat and the International Court of Justice (ICJ). It has also been noted that of the sixty elected presidents of the General Assembly between 1946 and 2005, ten came from Africa. Likewise, of the fifteen judges that composed the ICJ at the end of 2005, three were Africans. As is obvious, apart from the ICJ and the Secretariat, those Africans or nationals of any other regions that are elected to any of the other organs are in essence representatives of their home nations. They take their decisions from their capitals and refer to them whenever needed. Their loyalty is therefore directly to their national governments and it is the interests and the views of these governments that they represent and defend.

The cases of the ICJ and the Secretariat are different. Judges of the ICJ are elected by member states. They do not however represent these member states (i. e. their national governments) but act as independent magistrates. At the Secretariat, albeit the Secretary-General is initially proposed and supported by his or her home country, once elected, his or her loyalty is not however to that country but to the organization as an independent international civil servant. There are also appointments in the Secretariat that do not concern member states, but are made directly by the Secretary-

General or the UN Human Resources department. It is with these staff members that are Africans, and not those whose direct loyalty is to their national governments, that this chapter deals.

It should be noted from the outset that the current employment system of the United Nations is more in favour of the rich developed countries than the relatively poor developing countries. The rich countries are naturally the biggest contributors to the UN budgets —both assessed and voluntary. For example, at the end of 2001, nearly 47.5 per cent of UN posts in the professional category were held by nationals of developed countries, while the developing countries held only 41.6 per cent. The remaining posts were held by those countries that are described as Emerging countries or countries in transition. Among all staff, 50.6 per cent were from developing countries, 43 per cent from developed countries, and 6.4 per cent from countries in transition. This is despite the fact that developing countries represent about 78 per cent (149 out of a total of 191 member states) of the UN membership and 82 per cent of the world's population.[2] Though this disproportionate representation of the rich developed countries seems unfair, the theorisation provided in *Chapter 1* of the motives and expectations of the different stakeholders of the UN when they decided to join the world body should help, at least in part, to explain this.

It would seem that, looking quite closely at the share of the developing countries in the UN's top professional posts, Africa is the least represented region, while it is the single largest regional group at the UN. For example, at the end of 2005, of the sixteen or so Under-Secretaries-General (USG) of the UN or Directors-General (DG) with the rank of USG, only one was from Africa. That was Ibrahim Gambari of Nigeria, who was the USG for Political Affairs as from July 2005, having served, from the middle of 2003, as USG and Special Adviser on Africa, a position established by Kofi Annan in that year. Even the Director-General of the United Nations Office in Nairobi was a European national from Germany and not an African. Yet both the UN Office at Geneva (UNOG) and the UN Office at Vienna (UNOV), the other two regional UN offices headed by DGs, had two Europeans (a Russian for the former and an Italian for the latter) as their heads. In the early 1990s, however, there were at one time two African USGs when James Jonah of Sierra Leone and Kofi Annan of Ghana served respectively as USGs for Political Affairs and Peace-keeping Operations.

Moreover, the UN recently created a post of Special Envoy of the Secretary-General (SESG) for HIV/AIDS in four geographical regions: Africa, Asia, Caribbean and Eastern Europe. Nonetheless, while, by the fall of 2005, the SESGs to all these regions were from their respective regions, the SESG to Africa was Stephen Lewis, a Canadian national and not an African. This said, however, it should be acknowledged that some Africans have held high professional positions within the UN Secretariat. It is to a selection of these Africans and their itineraries at the UN that we now turn.

Boutros Boutros-Ghali: I got caught in American politics

Boutros-Ghali of Egypt became the sixth Secretary-General of the United Nations and the very first African to be elected to this prestigious post in world diplomacy and public administration. Appointed by the General Assembly on 3 December 1991 after the approval of the Security Council, according to the provisions of the UN Charter in this regard, he began his five-year term in January 1992. A diplomat, academic, jurist and widely published author, Boutros-Ghali had served in many academic positions, having obtained his PhD in International Law in 1949, and from 1977 to 1991 served as Egyptian Minister of State for Foreign Affairs. In 1987, he became a member of the Egyptian parliament representing the ruling National Democratic Party of President Hosni Mubarak, a position he held until his appointment for the UN top job. Boutros-Ghali had just been promoted in May 1991 to the post of Deputy Prime Minister for Foreign Affairs with the portfolio of Minister for Emigration. In Egyptian administration, the holder of the latter portfolio is responsible for more than three million Egyptian emigrants scattered around the world in the different Arab countries, Europe, Japan, Australia and North America.

While Boutros-Ghali, in that capacity, was representing Egypt at the June 1991 summit of the Organization of African Unity (OAU) in Abuja, the possibility of filling the post of UN Secretary-General was raised by the African Heads of State. Of the many candidates suggested from across the continent, his candidacy seemed to win the support of the majority of the African leaders gathered at Abuja. This does not however mean that he was the only African candidate for the UN's top job. Of all his rivals, the former Finance and Economic Planning Minister of Zimbabwe, Bernard Chidzero, who had the backing of Britain amongst the big five of the Security Council, was the closest. It was generally agreed that it was Africa's turn to produce the UN Secretary-General that time round. All the continents had produced one or more Secretaries-General. Europe had produced three; U Thant from Myanmar had represented Asia-Pacific; the Americas had produced the immediate predecessor of Boutros-Ghali, the Peruvian Pérez de Cuéllar.[3]

The coming of Boutros-Ghali to the UN Secretariat coincided with the end of the Cold War. He was thus the first post-Cold War Secretary-General. Though the end of the Cold War had ushered in a new era of successful multilateralism and one was right to be optimistic about the bright future of the United Nations, his job was not a light one. The UN needed some radical structural and administrative changes. The budget of the UN was in crisis. Many countries had, for one reason or the other, failed to pay their dues in full or in part. Unpaid assessments were close to US\$ 1 billion, with the United States, the biggest contributor and the world's richest nation, being the biggest debtor nation in the UN family. Only 67 of the then 159 member states had paid their regular assessments in full. In order therefore to get the UN's finances back on track, the new Secretary-General needed some creative diplomatic and managerial engineering with a tough language in order to get the debtor nations to pay their dues. Failure to do this would be synonymous with failure in his mission, as the UN was now faced with more tasks than ever before. None of these responsibilities could have been properly discharged without adequate funding. The first African Secretary-General was now faced with this mammoth task. Even in terms of modern administrative equipment, the UN Secretariat was lagging behind, as Boutros-Ghali recalls:

> In 1992, the United Nations had barely begun to acquire information technology that by then was taken for granted by government agencies, businesses, and academic institutions involved in world affairs. The staff, which included many

dedicated, intelligent, and well-educated people, was nevertheless bloated, slack, and out of touch, partly because the United Nations had been marginalized by the superpowers during the Cold War.[4]

In the face of the magnitude of the task, albeit he had no authority to transform the system on his own, he found himself obliged to "launch some drastic reform" in the system so as to make it compatible with his vision of the world body. As always with reformers, he made some friends and many enemies, including among the staff members at the Secretariat. Since these often turned to their national governments, he also made enemies in some capitals.

As the UN chief administrator, the Secretary-General is required by the Charter to bring to the attention of the Security Council any matter which, in his opinion, may threaten international peace and security. The main purpose of the UN itself is "to save succeeding generations from the scourge of war." Safeguarding international peace and security is therefore the main task of any Secretary-General, and Boutros-Ghali had his hands full with that task. Of the many armed conflicts that he had to work on with a direct involvement of the United Nations, one may count Somalia, Bosnia-Herzegovina, Rwanda, Iraq, Apartheid South Africa, Angola, Cambodia, and Haiti, to mention only these. Although the UN got involved in Liberia, its involvement there was nowhere to be compared with the contribution and the efforts of the regional organization, the Economic Community of West African States (ECOWAS). The UN's involvement in Sierra Leone came much later, after Boutros-Ghali had left, but even when it happened, it was nowhere near the contribution of ECOWAS. In effect, the UN's efforts in these two countries were mainly complementary to those of the regional organization.

As regards Boutros-Ghali's achievements for Africa or, rather, his relationship with the continent, one could argue that this was characterized by two things. On the one hand, there was his determination to bring Africa's issues and concerns to the UN's attention and get the world body and the international community more interested in issues relating to Africa. He knew he owed his election and indeed his backing and support to Africa. It was a reflection of this feeling or determination that he set to appoint Africans to high positions within the UN. As he later revealed, commenting on his appointment as his Special Representative to Rwanda of Jacques-Roger Booh-Booh, the former Cameroonian Foreign Minister:

> As a West African, Booh-Booh would be objective about the situation in Rwanda. In addition, I wanted to reinforce the African presence in the United Nations. With this appointment, there would be two Special Representatives helping a Secretary-General from Africa deal with issues of war and peace in Africa, the other being Alioune blondin Beye of Mali, whom I had appointed as Special Representative for Angola[5]

On the other hand, he seemed ready to push forward African initiatives within the UN but, quite rightly, he expected the support of Africa, for all he could do was to propose and the rest was for Africa to argue and/or support his initiatives. This was the case for instance when he urged the Nigerian ambassador to the Security Council during the Rwandan crisis in 1994 to encourage African states to argue against the withdrawal of UNAMIR, and also when he wrote to a number of African Heads of State asking them to contribute troops to the proposed enlarged UNAMIR II in Rwanda (see *Chapter 3*).

Meanwhile, leading the UN in all the aforementioned hot spots was not a light undertaking for Boutros-Ghali. At times, he collided with some major actors who criticised his leadership. Perhaps the most noticeable of these criticisms were those by the United States after their Somali debacle in 1993. As pointed out in the previous chapter, many Americans erroneously but unfairly criticised the UN and, consequently, its Secretary-General for the killing of their peace-keeping soldiers by the militiamen of General Farah Aidid in Mogadishu in October 1993. The American opposition to Boutros-Ghali that resulted in this, combined with other issues, haunted him at the approach of the end of his term of office and developed into open hostility towards him by the world's only superpower. The American Secretary of State, Warren Christopher, and the Permanent Representative to the UN, Madeline Albright, became the two flag-bearers of this campaign of hostility.

In addition to this unfounded charge, the Americans thought of him as an "arrogant" Secretary-General who wanted more power and emphasised more the independence of his position. There was an argument that he was the most outspoken Secretary-General after Dag Hammarskjöld, as he would repeatedly criticise the Security Council's neglect of the famine in Somalia while focusing all its attention on Bosnia.[6] Boutros-Ghali himself acknowledges that a lecture he gave at Oxford University in January 1996 in which he emphasised the need to give more independence to the Secretary-General of the UN was not received well in Washington. Perhaps Washington found the language of this lecture unacceptable, especially that Boutros-Ghali also stressed the urgent need to find new ways to finance UN operations, since the United States refused to pay its contributions.[7] From a realist point of view, the US had come to regard Boutros-Ghali as a threat to its hegemonic position in the UN. Perhaps there were other factors behind the American hysteria.

At the time, some tried to explain the American opposition to Boutros-Ghali as a manifestation of what they called the xenophobic delusion of the Republican-dominated Congress towards him and the organization he headed, and suggested that the Clinton Administration was bowing to these sentiments which were out of its control. Albeit one may not rule this out completely, looking at the history of the UN and the relationship between its Secretaries-General and the big powers, it may be hard to convincingly explain this in any term other than a mere conflict of interests. For example, the USSR tried to deny Trygve Lie, the Norwegian first Secretary-General of the UN a second term upon his condemnation of the invasion of South Korea by the pro-Soviet communist North Korea in the early 1950s. It was in fact the fear of a Soviet veto of the proposed UN-backed multilateral force there that led the Western powers spearheaded by the United States to take the matter to the General Assembly. This resulted in the famous "Uniting for Peace" resolution of the Assembly in 1950, which authorised the proposed force headed by the United States. Moscow even refused to cooperate with Lie when his mandate was extended for two years. The Swedish successor of Lie, Dag Hammarskjöld had a very cool relationship with France and Britain when he condemned their triangular (with Israel) invasion of Egypt in 1956. And in 1981, China, the quietest of all the big powers and the least veto using nation of all the veto bearers, threatened to use its veto to block the third re-election attempt of the Austrian Secretary-General, Kurt Waldheim.

To Boutros-Ghali himself, "the reason was to be found in the political dynamics of the 1996 American presidential campaign, combined with the remarkable events of the previous five years."[8] In any event, the Americans went out of their way to block his re-election bid and succeeded. By this, Boutros-Ghali became not only the first African Secretary-General of the UN, but also the first and the only (by the time this book was completed) UN Secretary-General to have been denied a second term. He had been caught in the American political campaign. In an unprecedented setting of isolation, the United States used its veto against him and all the remaining fourteen members of the Security Council, including Britain, the US's closest ally. It was clear that America did not want a Secretary-General that fell short of being a poodle.

Kofi Annan: Beware the Neo-Cons!

In the colonial history of the West African state of Ghana, two great ethnic groups, the Asante and the Fante peoples, often fought with one another for control of the coastal trade with the Europeans. This was before the Europeans turned into invaders and colonialists. Because the Fante are great traders, the Asante areas, endowed with gold and other natural riches, often attracted a good number of them. With a growing Fante community in the kingdom of the Asante (or Ashanti), and following a classical African diplomatic practice, the Fante elected a chief among them to be their representative and liaison officer to the Asante king. In contemporary parlance, the Fante chief in the Asante capital was actually the Fante ambassador. He was the contact point for any Fante trader with a complaint against an Asante man or a need for something from the Asante authorities. It was also the tradition of the latter to pass through him in their dealings with any Fante merchant. This practice continued well into the colonial period. One such Fante ambassador to the Asantehene (the king of Asante), was a certain Henry Reginald Annan, the father of Kofi Annan. Thus, when Kofi was born in April 1938, he was born into a diplomatic family. In fact, his father later became a District Manager of the most important British company in colonial West Africa, the United Africa Company, and after independence he became for a time the Regional Minister for the Ashanti Region.[9]

Kofi Annan, the second African UN Secretary-General was elected the seventh Secretary-General of the UN in December 1996 for a five-year term which began on 1 January 1997. Interestingly, he was the first UN Secretary-General to be elected from amongst the UN staff members. All the previous ones, including Boutros-Ghali, were outsiders. For an organization that badly needs reform, the general and often desirable practice is to elect someone from outside the institution to bring new ideas and lead the institution to a fresh start. Electing someone therefore from within the organization is a remarkable recognition of one's personal character, competence and achievements. It was in recognition of the same achievements — and, of course, of his not having attracted the hostility of any big power, which would have been blind to any achievement as we saw in the case of Boutros-Ghali— that he was unanimously appointed by acclamation to a second five-year term in 2001, beginning on 1 January 2002.

Apart from a two-year managerial position at the state-owned Ghana Tourist Development Company in Accra (1974-76), almost the entire professional career of Kofi Annan has been within the UN system. Starting off as an administrative and budget officer with the World Health Organization (WHO) in Geneva in 1962, he climbed the UN professional ladder until he became, in 1987, the Assistant Secretary-General for Human Resources Management and Security Coordinator for the UN System —a position he held at the UN headquarters in New York until 1990. He was then appointed Assistant Secretary-General for Programme Planning, Budget and Finance, and Control (1990-92). In March 1992, Boutros-Ghali appointed him the Assistant Secretary-General for Peace-keeping Operations. He held this position for a year, before being appointed as Under-Secretary-General for the same department, in effect heading the department.

On becoming the seventh Secretary-General of the UN, Annan inherited the reform programme of the world body that had been set in motion by his predecessor. He also inherited from him the many UN peace-keeping operations and oversaw the establishment of new ones. Like Boutros-Ghali, he made the renewal or reform of the UN his first priority and chose "Renewing the United Nations" as the title of his first report to the Security Council, published in July 1997. With Africa plagued with many armed conflicts, he could not afford to take his mind and attention off this delicate issue. He thus devoted his second report to the Security Council to the study of the causes of armed conflicts in Africa. In this report, he attributed the frequent occurrence of armed conflicts in Africa to the nature of political power together with the real and perceived consequences of capturing and maintaining power. In other words, he saw the root causes of these conflicts in bad governance and lack of political freedom and transparency. After analysing the nature of power struggles of the political elite in most African countries as "winner-takes-all," he summarised the role of bad governance in causing violent conflicts on the continent. He argued:

> Where there is insufficient accountability of leaders, lack of transparency in regimes, inadequate checks and balances, non-adherence to the rule of law, absence of peaceful means to change or replace leadership, or lack of respect for human rights, political control becomes excessively important, and the stakes become dangerously high.[10]

From this time on, Kofi Annan demonstrated his excellent diplomatic skills in conflict management across the world to the acclamation of all observers. For example, in collaboration with South Africa's Nelson Mandela and the Saudi government, he used his good offices in 1999 to resolve the stalemate between Libya and the Security Council by persuading Colonel Muammar Kaddafi to hand over the two Libyan nationals suspected of involvement in the Lockerbie aircraft sabotage of 1988. He was instrumental in the same year in securing a UN peace-keeping force to Sierra Leone in support of ECOWAS peace-keeping forces (ECOMOG) there. He also strove to establish UN peace-keeping operations in many other parts of the world. Perhaps one of his most impressive diplomatic successes during his first term was the delicate one-man mission he undertook to Saddam Hussein's Iraq in 1998.

Iraq had been under a variety of sanctions after what has become known as the first Gulf War (1991). One obligation enforced through sanctions was renunciation of nuclear, chemical and biological weapons. On the basis of American information that the Saddam regime was working on the production of some illegal weapons, Iraq was obliged to accept UN arms inspectors. The Iraqi authorities however decided for some reason to ask the international inspectors out of the country. The Clinton administration thus took Iraq to the Security Council and Saddam was asked to readmit the inspectors. He had to sign a document to this effect in order to allow the inspectors to resume their work unobstructed. The Americans never believed he would. Thus, their taking him to the Security Council was regarded by many analysts as just a way to wrap their already cooked plans to bomb the country in some sort of international legitimacy. And this hidden plan was not lost on Kofi Annan and his staff at the UN. As the chief negotiator of the UN, he asked the Americans and their allies to allow him to try and get Saddam to sign the documents so as to spare the Iraqi people further suffering as a natural result of what the Americans intended to do. Thus, with the Americans and their allies praying for the failure of his mission, but with at least the moral support of all peace-loving nations, the UN Secretary-General returned from Iraq with the document in his pocket duly signed by Saddam, to the applause of all the UN staff members who had gathered in an unprecedented manner in the main entrance hall of the headquarters to welcome their smiling and certainly vindicated chief. Though the Americans later in the year executed their bombing plans, Kofi Annan's mission had nonetheless helped delay it for nearly a year.[11]

Annan's efforts in urging the UN and the international community to take effective measures and action to combat inequality and reduce the gap between poor and rich and address the HIV/AIDS endemic —which he describes as his "personal priority"— are well recognised. His April 2000 report to the Security Council served as the basis for the Millennium Declaration adopted at the Millennium Summit held at the UN headquarters in New York in September of the same year. The Millennium Development Goals (MDGs) are contained in this Declaration.

Apart from his re-election for a second five-year term in 2001, the testimonies of the world's recognition of Annan's efforts are abundant. For example, with generous German financial and logistical support, and later the assistance of many other Western countries, a Kofi Annan International Peace-keeping Training Centre (KAIPTC) was established in his home country in 1998. This centre that aims at providing mission-oriented training to military officers and civilian officials in the West African sub-region in peace-keeping techniques formally began its operations in 2002. In addition, a former Finance Minister in Guinea set up, in 1999, a *Université Kofi Annan de Guinée* in Conakry. All these appreciable gestures were crowned, in 2001, by the prestigious Nobel Peace Prize that was bestowed on him, jointly with the organization he leads. By this, Kofi Annan became one of the few African Nobel Peace laureates and the first UN Secretary-General to be honoured by the prestigious prize.

Apart from the natural frustration that a senior manager like him is expected to have at the head of such an elephantine organization, everything seemed to be working fine for Annan. However, it would appear that this was until he angered the right-wing New Conservatives of Washington. By criticising —though belatedly and in very carefully worded language— the American invasion of Iraq in 2003, and invasion launched without the UN's approval and on the basis of arguments that turned out to be untrue and ungrounded, which was a flagrant violation of international law, he aroused right-wing politicians to re-sharpen against him the knives they had used to kill Boutros-Ghali in 1996. After their "successful" invasion of Iraq and overthrow of its regime, the Americans had pushed, and the UN had found it compatible with its own reform agenda, for an independent committee to look into allegations of mismanagement in the handling of the UN "Oil-for-Food" programme. This programme was adopted by the UN to ensure that ordinary Iraqis received food and essential medicine during the time of sanctions against Iraq between 1996 and 2003.

With his criticism of the American invasion of Iraq, while the investigation committee, led by a former US Federal Reserve Bank Chairman, Paul Volcker, was still to submit its report, some hawks in Washington jumped to the conclusion that Annan's son, Kojo, was and remained for four years after the programme on the payroll of a Swiss auditing firm hired by the UN to monitor the programme; that this was corruption; that this was not possible without the knowledge if not the complicity of his father; and therefore that his father had to resign.[12] Yet the first interim Volcker report cleared Kofi Annan of any wrongdoing. But this did not seem to silence powerful far-right American political group called the "neo-conservatives" or "neo-cons." For in reaction to Annan's assertion that he had been cleared of wrongdoing, the Deputy Assistant Secretary of State in the Bush administration, Mark Lagon, was quoted as countering this and insisting that the report did not exonerate the Secretary-General.[13] Fortunately, not all Americans agreed with this misleading and prejudiced reading of the report. While the far right politicians continued insisting on their imaginary involvement of Annan, the liberals strove to explain the facts behind the report, which confirmed that the Secretary-General was not implicated.[14] Kofi Annan was also consoled by almost the entire African continent.[15]

Despite the publication of the fifth and final Volcker report, which was submitted to the Security Council in October 2005, and its reiteration of more or less the same conclusion about Annan's alleged implication in the programme, the neo-cons did not seem satisfied, as some of them did not want anything short of Annan's resignation. However, with less than a year (by the completion date of this book) to go to the end of his term and the strong support he has, not only from Africa but also from the rest of the world, it is unlikely that the Bush administration will be able to do to him what the Clinton administration did to his predecessor.

Africans in the UN System

As noted in *Chapter 1*, the United Nations system consists of the six main organs based at headquarters in New York, with the exception of the ICJ, and the many programmes, funds and specialised agencies linked to it through one or more of these main organs. While the programmes and funds are almost bodies created by the UN and overseen by the General Assembly (e.g. UNHCR, UNICEF, WFP), the specialised agencies are more or less

179

autonomous bodies working with the United Nations through the Economic and Social Council (ECOSOC). It is through these programmes, funds and specialised agencies that UN's wider relationship with the different geographical regions, including Africa, is conducted.

Issues of food production and security, as well as soil improvement for agricultural production, which are of a high priority to Africa are dealt with by the UN agency specialised in this, the Food and Agricultural Organization (FAO). This organization has been very active in Africa in addressing, with African states, these issues. The International Labour Organization (ILO) works with African governments and trade unions to promote the fundamental principles and rights in the workplace and the ratification of labour standards. In addition to this, the Geneva-based UN specialised agency devotes also a fair share of its attention and resources to combating child labour in Africa, as well as giving support to African countries on labour market information systems, human resources development and training.

Safety in air travel is of a paramount importance to all nations. The global monitoring body of this is the International Civil Aviation Agency (ICAO), with headquarters in the Canadian city of Montreal. The work of this agency in promoting the safe and orderly growth of international civil aviation in Africa is directed from two regional offices in Africa based in Dakar (Senegal) and the Kenyan capital, Nairobi. While the activities of organizations such as the World Health Organization (WHO) and UNESCO are fairly known in Africa by their many activities related to the continent, many do not think, for example, of the International Atomic Energy Agency (IAEA), the International Telecommunication Union (ITU), the World Meteorological Organization (WMO), and the World Intellectual Property Organization (WIPO) as bodies to have many dealings with Africa. Yet while it is true that some of those specialized agencies have more dealings with Africa than others, the activities of some are less known because they are taken nowadays for granted.

The fact is that many people, and this is not just in Africa, wake up in the morning and go to their boxes and take their mail sent from the other corner of the world with no hindrance, or take their bags to the airport and travel easily from Bamako to Tokyo and from Canberra to Conakry, oblivious of the superb behind-the-scenes work done by bodies such as the Universal Postal Union (UPU) and the ICAO. And because they can sit in their rooms and press their telephone keypads to talk to their relatives and pals on other continents of the world, many take for granted the magnificent work done in facilitating this by the ITU. Only when something goes dramatically wrong in one of these sectors and the concerned UN specialized agency intervenes will many people realise their utility or even their existence. For example, apart from a few specialists, only a few people in West Africa knew the UNHCR prior to 1990, when the civil wars broke out in Liberia and Sierra Leone, yet its activities were quite known in some Southern African countries because of the civil strife in these areas at this time.

With our concern about the relationship between the UN and Africa through these specialized institutions, and our focus on African professionals in these institutions, it should be noted that there have been a good number of Africans who have occupied or occupy (as this book was completed) high positions in some of these organizations. In addition to the UN Secretariat, one can argue that nationals of Egypt and Senegal have been the most African high flyers in these organizations. With Boutros-Ghali as the first African Secretary-General of the UN, Egypt's Mohamed El Baradei was the first African to be elected Director-General of the UN atomic energy agency (IAEA). Senegal produced the very first African high-level professional when Amadou-Mahtar M'Bow was elected Director-General of UNESCO in 1974. The Senegalese Jacques Diouf, who was still heading the Food and Agricultural Organization (FAO) as this book was completed, was also the first African to reach that position in that specialized agency of the UN. Those apart, at the end of 2005, a number of other specialised agencies were headed by Africans, who were the first from their continent to head them. These included Kandeh Yumkella of Sierra Leone, who assumed the position of Director-General of UNIDO in December 2005, Taïeb Chérif of Algeria, who was the first African Secretary-General of ICAO as of August 2003, and Kamil Idris of Sudan, who was re-elected for a second term as Director-General of the World Intellectual Property Organization (WIPO) in May 2003.

At a relatively lower level but prestigious in their own right, Cyril Enweze of Nigeria was serving at the end of 2005 as the Vice-President of the Rome-based International Fund for Agricultural Development (IFAD), while Hamadoun I. Touré worked as the Director of Telecommunication Development Bureau (BDT), one of the three main sectors of the ITU, a position second only to that of the Secretary-General of the Union. At the World Health Organization (WHO), there were also two African Assistant Directors-General. These were Anarfi Asamoa-Baah of Ghana, in charge of HIV/AIDS, TB and Malaria, and Joy Phumaphi of Botswana, who worked as Assistant Director-General for Family and Community Health. Let us now succinctly look at the itineraries of a few of these people.

Amadou-Mahtar M'Bow (UNESCO)

As noted above, on becoming Director-General of the United Nations Educational, Scientific and Cultural Organization (UNESCO) in 1974, Amadou-Mahtar M'Bow of Senegal was the first African to have reached such a high level not only in the hierarchy of the Paris-based institution, but in the whole United Nations system. M'Bow remained at the head of UNESCO for two six-year full terms, leaving office in 1987. This was before the duration of the tenure of office at the organization was reduced to four years.

Born in Senegal in 1921, M'Bow held several ministerial positions in the fields of education, youth and cultural development in his home country before joining UNESCO. He also held a parliamentary position in the Senegalese National Assembly. Elected to UNESCO's Executive Board in 1966, he became Assistant Director-General for Education in 1970, from which he moved on to be elected Director-General four years later.

During his time in office, he further strengthened the healthy cooperation that was becoming quite solid between UNESCO and the different African countries through the OAU. Likewise, he was very instrumental in supporting the publication of the eight-volume *General History of Africa*, which is arguably the most comprehensive written history of Africa. Each of its eight volumes, in its unabridged edition and published in many languages, contains more than 900 pages of expert first class research. The editorial board of its eight volumes included such outstanding African historians as Ali A. Mazrui of Kenya, Joseph Ki-Zerbo of Burkina Faso, A. Adu Boahen of Ghana, Djibril Tamsir Niane of Guinea, and G. Mokhtar of Egypt. In his preface to the volumes, M'Bow regretted the myths and prejudices that had for so long concealed the true history of Africa and contended:

> Although the *Iliad* and *Odyssey* were rightly regarded as essential sources for the history of ancient Greece, African oral tradition . . . was rejected as worthless. In writing the history of a large part of Africa, the only sources used were from outside the continent, and the final product gave a picture not so much of the paths actually taken by the African peoples as of those that the authors thought they must have taken. Since the European Middle Ages were often used as a yardstick, modes of production, social relations and political institutions were visualised only by reference to the European past. [. . .] In this context, the importance of the eight-volume *General History of Africa*, which Unesco is publishing, speaks for itself.

In the middle of his second term however, the Reagan administration in the US and many other Western countries grew in hostility towards him and the institution he was leading. Looking at the history of Boutros-Ghali with the Clinton administration and of Kofi Annan with the Bush administration since the middle of 2004, one can see clearly that it is only history repeating itself with always the same arguments or rather allegations. They accused him and UNESCO of poor management and bias against Western capitalist values in favour of the communist bloc. The Reagan administration eventually withdrew the US from the institution in December 1984. Referring to the American withdrawal from the institution and the allegations charged against him and UNESCO, a reporter of the Australian newspaper, *The Australian*, wrote in January 1985:

> Critics have claimed Dr. M'Bow allowed UNESCO to become an Iron Curtain spy base. Of 47 Soviets expelled from France in 1983, 12 were on the UNESCO's payroll and three were on Dr. M'Bow's top staff. The US has just left UNESCO, Britain has served notice it will leave this year unless management standards improve, while West Germany, the Netherlands, Belgium and Denmark have also

183

warned they may reconsider membership unless changes are made[16]

As the reporter announced, in December 1985, Margaret Thatcher followed in the footsteps of her friend, Reagan, and pulled Britain out of the institution. It is hard to explain this. But perhaps M'Bow himself provided the best analysis of it when he denounced the Western actions as "campaigns of denigration and attempts at destabilisation."[17] With the coming to power of the Labour Party in Britain, the Tony Blair government brought the United Kingdom back to the institution in July 1997. It was the events of 11 September 2001 and the American need for support, especially from the developing countries, in their so-called war on terror that led the Bush administration to ask for the return of the United States to UNESCO, and in October 2003, Laura Bush led the American delegation to the inauguration to mark the official return of the United States to the fold of the UN cultural organization.

Jacques Diouf (FAO)

Dr Jacques Diouf, also from Senegal, became the seventh Director-General of the UN Food and Agriculture Organization (FAO) in November 1993 and assumed his office in January the following year. He was the first and the only African national to occupy this post within that UN specialised agency. At the expiry of his first six-year term in 1999, he was re-elected to a second term which began in January 2000, and a third term at the beginning of January 2006. With a doctorate degree in Social Sciences of the Rural Sector (Agricultural Economics), Dr Diouf began his international career in 1963 becoming the Executive Secretary of the Lagos-based African Groundnut Council (AGC) between 1965 and 1971. Still in the agricultural development sector, he assumed the post of Executive Secretary of the West African Rice Development Association (WARDA), based in the Liberian capital, Monrovia, from 1971. He remained in this position for six years. It was in recognition of his efforts in this post that the late Liberian president, William Tolbert, decided in 1977 to decorate him with the "Grand Commander in the Order of the Star of Africa," arguably the highest national honour in Liberia.

On his return home at the end of 1977, the late President Léopold Sédar Senghor of Senegal appointed him Secretary of State for Science and Technology, a post he kept even after the departure of Senghor from power. After a brief period (1983-84) as a member of the Senegalese parliament, he joined the Canadian International Development Research Centre as Adviser to the President and Regional Director of the Centre, where he served until his appointment, in 1985, as Secretary-General of the Dakar-based CFA franc-zone Central Bank of West African States (BCEAO —*Banque Centrale des États d'Afrique de l'Ouest*), where he remained until his election as FAO's Director-General.

To measure the recognition of his service to Africa in the field of agricultural development and poverty reduction, it suffices to take a glance at the many national honours he has been decorated with by an array of African states. These apart, Dr Diouf has been awarded by a good number of other states as diverse as France, Canada, Peru, Guatemala, Venezuela, Cuba, Panama, the Philippines, Uruguay and Monaco, not to mention but these.[18]

With the FAO's mandate being to raise levels of nutrition, improve agricultural productivity, better the lives of rural populations and contribute to the growth of the world economy, it may be curious to look at the seemingly food crisis and agricultural decline throughout the African continent and yet have an African as the Director-General of this organization. One may be tempted to ask what he has done, is doing or can do in respect of this situation. Frankly put, very little apart from bringing the situation to the attention of the institution he leads, the wider UN family and the international community. He would also be expected to provide expert advice to the different African countries as to how best they can manage their resources —human and material resources included— and utilize them to raise their agricultural production and ensure food security and sustain it in the long run. Looking at his many public pronouncements on the issue of food security and agricultural development and the multitude of opinion pieces that he writes now and again in the different international papers, one may argue quite confidently that he is doing his best for Africa. The problem seems to be what Africa had done or does to complement his efforts and those of his institution.

In an op-ed in the famous French paper, *Le Monde Diplomatique*, in late 2004, he began by appealing to the international community for help in combating hunger and undernourishment in the developing world and Africa in particular. "The fight against hunger," he argued, "is not just a moral and ethical duty." In a rather accusatory language about the reaction of the international community to such appeals, he continued: "But arguments pointing out the economic benefits of wiping out hunger often meet with total indifference, even though these benefits are not just real, but vital and badly needed." But careful not to put accusations on one side, he observed with satisfaction that following the 1996 World Food Summit in Rome, many developing countries honoured their commitment by introducing major national food programmes, and then regretted: "Others, sadly, made no such progress, and in some places food shortages have grown more severe." Do we take the "others" for Africa? Almost certainly yes. For, he observes in the same article that "Africa is the only continent where agricultural production per inhabitant has fallen over the past 25 years."[19]

At present, more than half of the population in Africa works in agriculture, which accounts, according to Diouf, for 17 per cent of GDP and 11 per cent of export revenues. Yet the agricultural sector is greatly neglected in the national budgets and development planning of most African governments. While up to 17 per cent of water is used to irrigate some 40 per cent of arable land in Asia, the equivalent ratio in Africa is 4-7 per cent —that is using only 4 per cent of water to irrigate just 7 per cent of arable land. Strikingly, this figure goes down to a mediocre 1.6 per cent in some parts of the continent.[20] While there are a number of natural factors affecting the ability of some African governments to bring the agricultural production in their countries to the necessary level, lack of political will and misguided policies are the ones to be blamed for the most part. The solution is quite clear. As Clover rightly emphasised, "greater recognition must be given to agriculture as a priority sector in Africa, including the allocation of increased funding in national budgets."[21] Only by this will the superb work being done by high flying African nationals in the UN system such as Dr Diouf bear fruit for Africa and make their work recognisable.

Mohamed ElBaradei (IAEA)

The International Atomic Energy Agency (IAEA) was set up within the UN family in 1957 to promote safe, secure and peaceful nuclear technologies around the world. In December 1997, the Egyptian Mohamed ElBaradei became its fourth and first African Director-General. After his first four-year term, he was reappointed for a second term in 2001 and a third term in September 2005. Like Kofi Annan at the head of the UN wider family, Dr ElBaradei was awarded the Nobel Peace Prize jointly with the institution he leads, in his case in October 2005. In the words of the members of the award committee, this was in recognition of their efforts "to prevent nuclear energy from being used for military purposes and to ensure that nuclear energy for peaceful purposes is used in the safest possible way."

In the context of Africa, the work of the IAEA is focused on promoting safe and orderly growth of international civil aviation in the continent by working hand in hand with the International Civil Aviation Organization (ICAO) to promote the latter's policies and standards.

Contrary to what one may expect for the head of such a scientific organization, Dr El Baradei is a lawyer by training and profession. With a doctorate in International Law, he worked for four years from 1974 as Special Assistant to the Foreign Minister of Egypt. Having served in the Egyptian diplomatic service, including a period as a member of the Egyptian Permanent Mission to the United Nations in New York and Geneva, he joined the UN proper in 1980, thereby beginning an international diplomatic career full of successes. He joined the IAEA Secretariat in 1984. Climbing on the hierarchical ladder of the agency's administration, holding a number of high-level policy positions, he had become Assistant Director-General for External Relations when he was appointed Director-General in 1997.

It would seem that the biggest challenge of El Baradei's third term is how to successfully steer the controversial issue of Western powers' frenzy, led by the US, about Iran's nuclear programme. While Iran insists its nuclear programme is solely for civilian energy needs, which it has the right to supply as any other country has, the

Western countries suspect it has a hidden agenda in the programme —a long term ambition for acquiring nuclear bomb. Without an iota of doubt, the world would be safer without this weapon of mass destruction. However, granted that this is the parallel ambition of the Iranians, the Western position towards Iran does seem very hypocritical given the fact that not only they have it and have —in the case of the US in Japan 1945— callously used it against unarmed civilians, but also Israel, which is a neighbour of Iran, has it. Yet no one takes the pain to remind the West of these fallacies. If they argue that Israel has a right to have it because it is threatened by its Arab neighbours, which is to some extent debatable nowadays, so is Iran threatened, not only by Israel but also by the United States under whose economic sanctions Iran has lived since the Islamic Revolution in 1979.

Conclusion

This chapter looked at the employment structure of the United Nations and focused on the itineraries of a number of Africans who have held or hold (as this book was completed) high-level policy positions in the UN system. It began by remarking that albeit developing countries of Africa, Asia, Latin America and the Caribbean constitute the bulk of the UN membership, the employment structure in the word body is not reflective of this reality, contrary to the provision of the Charter that maintains that in recruiting for UN vacancies, "due regard shall be paid to the importance of recruiting the staff on as wide a geographical basis as possible." Perhaps it is the first clause of the same article of the Charter —which stresses the need of "securing the highest standards of efficiency, competence, and integrity"— that holds sway. While "integrity" is not an orange fruit cut at the size of the mouth of Northerners (i.e. nationals of the developed rich countries of the North) alone, objectively looking, it is regrettable, from an African and Southern standpoint, to note that if the "highest standard of efficiency and competence" is mainly acquired through quality education, training and appropriate professional working experience, Northern nationals do have a clear advantage in this regard given the many opportunities that they have compared to

Southern nationals. This has nothing to do with the different individuals, but with what their respective governments have done or achieved for them in terms of providing them with the means for quality education and early professional opportunities.

It is indeed striking to observe that almost all the high-flying Africans in the UN system did either all or a significant part of their higher education in the educational institutions of the different Northern countries —the US, the UK, France and Canada attracting the majority of them. It is there too that most of them started their professional experience. Yet few African people can afford this luxury given the exorbitant costs involved. But is it good after all for Africa and other developing countries that unless you pass through a Western educational institution, you cannot secure a prestigious international post? It is this practice of neglect of the educational system of many African and developing countries that contributes partly to the consolidation of the trend of making the acquisition of a Western degree an important yardstick in UN employment. No wonder then that the ratio of employment statistics goes in their favour and this is likely to continue unless changes are made in the developing world.

This said, it can equally be argued that the inequality in UN employment may have come with the formation of the world body and its different funds, programmes and specialised agencies. This is because the headquarters of almost all of them are based in Northern developed countries —Europe taking the lion's share of those. Hosting the headquarters of such international organizations is not only beneficial for the local economy and tourism. It also provides tremendous professional training opportunities through the various volunteering and internship programmes, which almost all international organizations have from time to time. Given that most of these internship programmes —often lasting for six months— are far from African and other developing countries' nationals and require —being unpaid for the most part— a great financial outlay from the interested individuals, from travel arrangements to accommodation and other essential expenditures, such training opportunities tend to be limited to nationals of the rich Northern countries that host these organizations or whose nationals can afford the costs. Yet such training experience is quite useful for those who benefit from them as regards their chances for recruitment by international organizations.

In any event, there have been a number of Africans who have made it to the high-level policy positions of the United Nations and its specialised agencies. Africa has produced two Secretaries-General for the UN Secretariat, and a number of Directors-General for its different specialised agencies, not to mention hundreds of other Africans serving at lower but equally prestigious positions. While the loyalty of these Africans, and all other international civil servants for that matter, is primarily to the institutions they serve, Africa has not been lost in their consciousness and calculations. They have, in their different ways and depending on their different capacities, striven to bring Africa's problems and concerns to the attention of their different institutions. The level of their success in this depends however almost entirely on the cooperation of the different African countries concerned.

In carrying out their duties, the United States has been of all UN member countries the country that has most colluded with African top UN officials. But American hostility towards these African officials is not to do with their Africanness. This should rather be seen in terms of America's disagreement with the institutions they lead. It is the American hostility toward this institution that is often directed towards them as scapegoats. Nationals of any other regions would most likely be treated the same way should their time at the head of a UN institution coincide with a period of rift between the US, the world's single superpower, and that institution on a specific issue. It is in the light of this that we can see American hostility towards Boutros-Ghali, Amadou-Mahtar M'Bow and, since 2004 though to a lesser extent, Kofi Annan. Mohamed El Baradei may invite their curse should IAEA's position on Iran's nuclear programme differ from that of Washington and its allies.

Notes

1. See United Nations, Image & Reality (New York: UN Department of Public Information, 2002), Ch. 6. This document is also available at <http://www.un.org/geninfo/ir/ref-frame.htm.> (2 March 2006).

2. Ibid.

3. See Boutros Boutros-Ghali, *Unvanquished: A US—UN Saga* (London & New York: I. B. Tauris Publishers, 1999), pp. 7-13.

4. Ibid., p. 15.

5. Ibid., p. 130.

6. See for example Dimitris Bourantonis and Jarrod Wiener, (eds.), *The United Nations in the New World Order: The World Organization at Fifty* (New York: Palgrave Macmillan, 1995), p. 96.

7. Boutros-Ghali, *Unvanquished*, pp. 3-4.

8. Ibid., p. 7.

9. See Cameron Duodu, "Like father, like son," *West Africa*, no. 4298, 22-28 October (2001), pp. 13-4.

10. See Kofi Annan, The Causes of Conflict and the Promotion of Durable Peace and Sustainable Development in Africa (Report of the Secretary General, April 1998).

11. For a report on the delicacy of this mission and the applaud Annan received from his colleagues at the UN, see for example Duodu, *Like father, like son*, op. cit.

12. See for example the *Wall Street Journal*, 30 November 2004; and Nile Gardiner, "The Volcker Investigation into the UN Oil-for-Food Scandal: Why It Lacks Credibility," *Backgrounder*, no. 1819, 1 February 2005. It should be noted that the Heritage Foundation that publishes this paper is a right-wing research foundation which defines its mission as to "formulate and promote conservative public policies."

13. Quoted in Mark Turner, "Volcker report 'did not' exonerate Annan," *Financial Times*, 21 April 2005.

14. See for example, Joy Gordon, "The United Nations and Oil-for-Food: The Facts Behind the Volcker Commission's Interim Report," *UNA-USA Policy Briefing*, no. 5, 10 February 2005. UNA-USA stands for the United Nations Association of the United States of America. The Centre defines its mission as to educate the Americans about the UN.

15. Jim Lobe, "Right-wingers gunning for Annan," *Africa Week*, Special Print Edition, December (2004), pp. 10-11.

16. See *The Australian*, 2 January 1985.

17. For this, See *The New York Times*, 9 October 1985

18. For a detailed professional biography of Dr. Diouf, see FAO's website at <http://www.fao.org/ english/dg/dioufcv.htm.> (1 March 2006).

19. Jacques Diouf, "Africa needs a Marshall Plan," *Le Monde Diplomatique*, English Edition, December 2004.

20. Ibid.

21. See Jenny Clover, "Food Security in Sub-Saharan Africa," *African Security Review*, Vol. 12, no 1 (2003).

Chapter 5

The Future of Africa-UN Relations: Towards a More Fruitful Partnership

The question for the future is whether the African states can stay united enough to repay the two primary debts that they owe to the world body. Just as the United Nations once served as an ally in Africa's liberation, can Africa now be counted as an ally in the liberation of the UN? Just as the world organization and its agencies continue to be partners in Africa's development, will African states become effective partners in the development of the world body in return?
—Edmond Kwam Kouassi

In this concluding chapter I propose to look at the superb service the United Nations has rendered the world and thus the need of the world —small and large, poor and rich countries alike— for its continuous existence and work. Acknowledging that the world body does need reform, and badly indeed, I shall look at the main arguments for this reform. In particular, I shall look at the different proposals for the reform of the Security Council, which seems to be the main concern of Africa in all the areas of reform. The chapter will then touch on the crucial issue of Africa-UN relations in the twenty-first century, suggesting a more realistic approach by Africa to this relationship so as to maximise Africa's chances to benefit from the partnership.

The World's Need for the UN

In 1991, when Iraq invaded Kuwait in a flagrant breach of International Law and the Charter of the United Nations, the United States asked the UN to authorise use of force to drive Saddam Hussein's invading troops out of Kuwait. The Security Council promptly passed a resolution authorising "Operation Desert Storm" under the enforcement provisions of Chapter VII of the UN Charter. This allowed the United States to lead a coalition of states to liberate Kuwait. While some of these states may have needed more convincing of their public opinion that perceived it —rightly or wrongly— as an American war, the invocation of the UN and its authorisation certainly helped them convince their citizens of the legitimacy and morality of their enterprise. By leading this multilateral force, given the strategic importance of the region to the US and the good relations between Washington and Kuwait, the US not only defended the UN Charter but also advanced its own foreign policy interests with UN blessing. The war was swiftly won and the US was hailed by many peace-lovers the world over. Anyone who still had some doubt about the New World Order led by Washington revised his thoughts.

A decade later, in 2003, when the United States invaded Iraq without UN sanction, it encountered a mountain of difficulties and was still encountering more difficulties as this book was completed. It first had a tough job convincing other countries to join its crusade, ending with a few countries headed by like-minded leaders or won over by the carrot of American diplomacy, but who nevertheless faced an array of difficulties in their respective countries. Some, like Spain, withdrew from the coalition when their leaders changed. With this "Coalition of the Willing," together with its unmatched military might and financial capacity, the United States may have found it relatively easy to win the war. But winning the peace has proven a different story altogether.

Both these two American interventions happened in Iraq with Saddam Hussein as its leader each time it happened. Both were carried out by an American president named George Bush —the former being the work of the father and the latter the work of the son. But what made the difference between the two American interventions is what this section is about —the utility of the United Nations and the need for it felt even by the world's only superpower.

A person's need for something he has acquired or created depends on the ability of that thing to respond to his expectations when deciding to acquire or create it. As noted earlier (see *Chapter*

1), when the independent nations of the world decided to create or agreed with the idea of creating the United Nations in 1945, they had their different motives and expectations. The common motive —albeit this was only partial for the big powers, especially the US— was their determination to preserve international peace and security and make respect for national sovereignty sacrosanct. This was true for both the big powers and other nations with less power or economic clout. Looking at the United Nations today, one can observe that these concerns are still as valid as they were in 1945. Likewise, the calculations that led the big powers to its formation then are still standing today and will almost certainly remain so tomorrow.

For the big and middle powers —that is the permanent members of the Security Council and the US in particular— the UN is still useful to them in a number of ways. The two examples above in relation to two US military interventions in Iraq with two different outcomes and/or perceptions in world public opinion illustrate the need of big powers for UN's stamp of legitimacy. This is very useful for the big powers where their national or foreign policy interests converge with those of the UN family or can be, even manipulatively, argued on that basis. As the most universal and representative international organization, the United Nations incarnates world public opinion and acceptance. As Tharoor noted, when the United Nations passes a resolution, it is seen as speaking for and defending the interests of the whole humanity. Thus, its favourable pronouncement on a particular issue confers a legitimacy that is respected by the world's governments and most of its peoples.[1]

Of the five permanent members of the Security Council, the United States and France have been the two powers that have most used or benefited from UN's stamp of legitimacy in advancing or protecting their own interests. The First Gulf War (1991) is illustrative of this for the Americans, and before it, the historic General Assembly's "Uniting for Peace" resolution of 1950. This resolution authorised the US to lead a multilateral force to drive the communist North Korean forces from South Korea. The latter was an American and Western ally. In a US Congress commissioned report about UN reform from the perspective of American interests, the drafters of the report acknowledge this crucial point. Albeit the report tends to be more in favour of American unilateralism outside the UN framework if the latter declines to acquiesce to American requests regardless of their justification or not, the drafters nevertheless admit that in certain instances a decision by the UN may be more acceptable to other governments than pressure from any single nation or group of nations.[2]

For France, for example, the strong ties between the government of François Mitterrand and the Habyarimana regime in Rwanda were well-known. It has also been proven (see *Chapter 3*) that the real motives of France's *Opération Turquoise* authorised by the UN Security Council in June 1994 were for her to be able to rescue the remnants of the genocidal regime in Kigali, which were regarded by the French, and truly so, as their allies. Yet it was the UN's legitimacy stamp that painted this ill-wired operation in the colour of a UN peace-keeping force.

Likewise, after the outbreak of civil war in Côte d'Ivoire in September 2002, and with France's vested interests in the country, Paris strove for the UN not only to authorise its forces stationed in Côte d'Ivoire since independence to become part of a UN-blessed and established multilateral peace-keeping force while remaining independent of it, but also for the world body to consider the French-brokered peace conference at Linas-Marcoussis as the main reference in efforts of peace negotiations in Côte d'Ivoire. In reality however, there was more of France's neo-colonial interests at stake here than any bona fide concern about peace and stability in the West African state. By making Marcoussis the main reference of the international community when talking about peace mediation efforts in Côte d'Ivoire, which had been well initiated by the regional Economic Community of West African States (ECOWAS) and were making good progress, France sought to advance its own foreign policy goals in the region and assert her relevance to the so-called "francophone family."[3] Again, it was in the UN's jacket of legitimacy that the French dressed their operation that might have otherwise been regarded as a pure foreign intrusion.

Added to the benefit to big powers of gaining legitimacy in operating under the United Nations umbrella or, at least, with its sanction is the equally important benefit of cost or burden-sharing or what the American report calls "diplomatic offices." As the American report acknowledges, "where an outcome is perceived to have received the endorsement of the United Nations, governments and international organizations may be more willing to lend support to that outcome, whether in the form of money, troops or humanitarian support."[4] For this, Tharoor cites the example of the overwhelming support the UN lent to United States' war on terror after the attacks of 11 September 2001. Visibly shocked and traumatised, the Bush administration appealed to the international community through the UN for help. The Security Council promptly passed a resolution under the enforcement provisions of Chapter VII of the UN Charter. In this resolution, after condemning the attacks, the Council, *inter alia*, obliged all states to criminalise assistance for terrorist activities, deny financial support and safe haven to terrorists and share information about people suspected of planning terrorist attacks.[5] As if this was not sufficient, the Council established under itself a 15-member Counter-Terrorism Committee (CTC) to monitor the implementation of this resolution.[6]

Tharoor looked at this and observed, quite rightly, that "without the legal authority of a binding Security Council resolution, Washington would have been hard-pressed to obtain such cooperation 'retail' from 191 individual states." And given the formidable diplomatic venue that the UN provides for negotiations without the need for the concerned states to travel thousands of miles to the different capitals of the world, he concluded that "it would have taken decades to negotiate and ratify separate treaties and conventions imposing the same standards on all countries."[7]

From this, it is clear that the arguments of some critics of the UN that it has become obsolete do not stand. If their aim is to leave it aside for ad hoc "coalitions of the willing" or *"multilateralism à la carte"* as opposed to *"multilateralism à la Charte"* (the Charter) that is supported by the UN, they cannot escape the fact that even in this case, they would need to create a structured club with its rules and the same issues that irritate them about the UN would pose themselves. NATO, for example, cannot be a substitute for the UN, for the North Atlantic Treaty Organization does not have the universal legitimacy of the UN for the simple reason that its membership is not universal. No-one has argued yet to scrap the

UN altogether, but as Boutros-Ghali once said, if this were to be happen, the world would need to replace it with another one. Yet, the anarchical society and the primitive jungle world that would characterise the hiatus between its scrapping and the creation of its replacement would not do service to anyone — poor or rich, weak or powerful states. It is also hard to see the 1945 big powers-cum-2005-middle powers benefiting from this. As Berridge argues, this would cause much justified anxiety to those big powers of yesteryear over whom a question mark has appeared concerning their real international weight.[8] A researcher from the [British] Royal Institute of International Affairs noted in the mid-1990s that if the UN was to be formed in 1995 for example, neither France nor Britain would be given permanent status. The two countries' permanent status in the Security Council and their veto right are now said to add to their power rather than to reflect it.[9]

Despite its apparent bias towards, and instrumentalisation by, the big powers, Africa and other developing countries have an interest in the United Nations. Its importance to them can be observed in a number of areas. It gives them the opportunity to sit side by side with the big powers and discuss with them on a more or less equal footing in the General Assembly and other UN organs. Indeed, if they are able to join their voices, as they often did in the 1970s, they can use the UN to press the big powers to pay more attention to their needs than they might otherwise be prepared to do. Perhaps the UN's endorsement of the New International Economic Order (NIEO) inspired by the developing countries in the 1970s is one of the most remarkable examples of this. Africa's alliance with the world body in its efforts on the issue of decolonization and the fight against Apartheid and white minority rule in Southern Africa (see *Chapter 2*) is another example of this.[10] Moreover, the United Nations is very cost-effective for developing countries' diplomacy. Not all of them can afford to open an embassy in every capital of the world. Indeed only the United States seems so far to have been able to do this amongst all countries of the world. Yet New York and Geneva enable them to meet the representatives of almost all sovereign states in the world at no special cost. This list of the ways in which the UN is useful to developing countries could be extended but the aim was to provide some illustrative examples.

This said however, there can be no denying that the United Nations has faults or needs reform. It does have faults and does need, badly indeed, reform. At times, some big powers have — though wrongly in most cases— found some of its work frustrating. Some developing countries, too, have on occasions been very disappointed by its work. What people —especially from an African or developing county standpoint— should however understand is that the UN is both a producer and a product of international law and international relations. Its 111-article Charter is the Qur'an and Bible of International Law. Its unique multilateral setting and universal membership provide the venue *par excellence* of International Relations and world diplomacy. Where and when International Law is invoked, its noble ideals of justice and fairness, peace and security prevail. However, when it turns, or rather when its powerful members turn it to international relations and power politics —and how often they do— this is when the cemeteries of Florence release the ghosts of Machiavelli to overshadow the work of the world body. This is where the hegemonic aspirations of the different superpowers and middle powers come to the fore. This is where nearly one million innocent civilians could be crudely massacred in Rwanda while the world body did nothing. This is where thousands of Bosnian Muslims could be mercilessly killed by Serb extremists in Srebrenica under the ears and eyes of the Dutch UN peace-keeping troops.

But discovering a shortcoming or even an outrageous mistake by one's government does not warrant nor does it make it wise to advocate becoming a stateless society. Imagine a world without the United Nations and its specialised agencies or another body with universal membership carrying out what they are doing now. Imagine international air traffic without the ICAO; international sea traffic without the IMO; international communications without the ITU; postage service without UPU; an international health or humanitarian catastrophe without the WHO, UNICEF, FAO or UNHCR. This is why reform is the best way forward.

Africa and UN Reform[11]

The current rules and procedures governing the United Nations were adopted way back at the time of its founding six decades ago. The world it represents has however changed dramatically since then. One such area where these "anachronistic" rules are more noticeable is undoubtedly within the Security Council: its structure and how it has been made to function. It has earlier been observed (see *Chapter 1*) how the interests of the great powers —especially the United States— dominated their thinking, their motives and, consequently, the structure of the United Nations when it was founded in October 1945. The great powers insisted on having some privileges, including the power to stop any action of the world body that might —really or as perceived— jeopardise their direct or indirect interests. The most controversial of these privileges was for them to be allowed to have a permanent seat in the key body of the UN —the Security Council; and to have the power to stop any action unilaterally —the veto power. On this basis, China, France, the UK, the USA and the USSR (Russian Federation since 1991) became permanent members with "veto" power to oppose any proposed action that may not be to their liking. This "autocratic" provision was then enshrined in Article 27 of the UN Charter, which remained unchanged as this book was completed. But now there seems to be a near consensus on the need to review these rules and reform the UN in general and the Security Council in particular.

The imperatives for these calls for change are quite plausible. As argued above, the world has dramatically changed from the one that saw the founding of the UN. Virtually all of continental Africa —save Liberia and Ethiopia— were still European colonies, protectorates or mandated territories when delegates gathered at San Francisco. They have now all regained their independence and are equal to any other country as far as international law is concerned. Likewise, while Germany and Japan had been defeated and were thus excluded from any deliberation leading to the formation of the UN, they now have an economic clout that undisputedly outweighs that of many of the then great powers. Moreover, India, Brazil and South Africa are becoming more and more middle powers to reckon with, while Russia, Britain and France are now said to be gaining more influence from their permanent member status than from any real power they may have compared to when they were accorded this status.

But the way in which the P-5 have used or rather "misused" these oligarchic and undemocratic privileges is what has made reform of the Security Council badly needed. There is a real sense that the often selfish and irresponsible use or threat of use of the veto privilege by some of its five bearers has done more harm to the UN than is acceptable. Its use has been driven more by the different bearers' selfish interests than by any bona fide concern for international peace and security. Only a minority of vetoes has been cast in cases where vital international security issues were at stake.[12]

By the end of 2005, there had been 257 vetoes cast, including the double ones. The first veto cast was on the "Syrian-Lebanese Question" by the Soviet Union on 16 February 1946. The last one as of the completion date of this book was used by the United States on 5 October 2004 to block a proposed resolution calling on Israel to "halt all military operations in northern Gaza and withdraw from the area." The first veto involving an African state was cast by the USSR on 16 September 1952 to stop Libya's application for membership, while the last one was a simultaneous veto (double veto in UN jargon) cast by France, UK and US on 11 January 1989 against Libya again for a complaint it had lodged "against US Downing of [a Libyan] Aircraft."

Looking more closely at some of the draft resolutions that have been vetoed, one can clearly see why people are calling for reform, with some even advocating an outright abolition of the veto right. For example, the United States was responsible for eighty of the 257 vetoes cast in this period (1945-2005). Of those, 40 (precisely 50 per cent) were used to oppose any condemnation of actions and activities of Israel in the Palestinian Occupied Territories. Perhaps this is why some jokingly argue that Israel is the hidden sixth veto bearer in the Security Council. With regard to the UK, whose vetoes have more concerned Africa,, it is unfortunate to note that of the 32 or so vetoes cast by London in this period, nine (five with the US and four with the US and France) were used to back the Apartheid regime in South Africa. A further nine (twice with the US) were used to back the minority white racist regime in southern Rhodesia (now Zimbabwe), while, worse still, it used a further seven (six with the US and France) to support the minority white regime in Namibia.[13] Of all the veto-bearers, China was the least veto user with only 4 or 5 if one counts the one used by Formosa (the pro-Western Taiwan that was occupying China's seat at the time) on 13 December 1955 to block Mongolia's application for membership.

Thus, on the basis of these observations and well-founded criticisms, there have since the early 1990s been many strong voices, including some from within the UN, calling for UN reform, especially reform of the "undemocratic" Security Council. In March 1993, the General Assembly passed resolution 48/26 establishing an "Open-ended Working Group" to consider all aspects of UN reform. On 21 March 2005, UN Secretary-General, Kofi Annan, presented his Report to the 59th session of the General Assembly.[14] His 62-page report dealt with many issues of concern to the world body and the wider world but the parts related to UN reform were the ones that unsurprisingly attracted more attention than any else. In it, Annan gave his backing to the idea of expanding the Security Council from 15 to 24. Responding to a request addressed to him by world leaders gathered for the World Summit in September 2005, he submitted to the General Assembly in March 2006 another report of 43 pages calling for urgent reforms.[15]

In mid-2005, the US-based GlobScan and the Program on International Policy Attitudes (Pipa) at the University of Maryland conducted an opinion poll in a number of mainly Western countries. The results showed that an overwhelming majority of people were in favour of UN reform, including the enlargement of the Security Council. As for Africa which has been marginalised in all these processes all along, such a survey would very likely wield the same results.

However, while people seem consensual about the need for reform, one does not find the same momentum when it comes to questions such as: How many members should the enlarged Council be? What should be the status of the newcomers? How many, if any, of those should have permanent seats? Should they have the right to veto power? Who should get the slots among all the aspirants?[16] On which criteria should their admittance be based?

If it is on their current real or potential status of influence in the world or in their respective regions, what will happen when this power balance changes and they or some of them lose this status in, say, twenty or thirty years' time, as is the case now with France, Russia and Britain? What should happen to the current veto bearers? Will enlarging the Council guarantee more democracy and representation? Will it make the Council more effective or rather make it more bureaucratic and slow to reach decisions if it ever does? Given the selfishness and intransigence of the current veto bearers, will they agree to this change and if not, what will be the consequences on the UN? Could we, in this case, avoid the fate of the UN's predecessor, the League of Nations?

With regard to the last question, given the world's need for the United Nations as shown above, this scenario is very unlikely. Since the formation of the UN, with the exception of China, all the five permanent members have taken their turns in temporarily abandoning one organ or agency of the United Nations on a particular issue and signalling their preparedness to leave the world body altogether. Over its disapproval of the Western-led UN intervention in Korea in 1950-53 and its disagreement with the then UN Secretary-General, Dag Hammarskjöld from Sweden, and his successor, Trygve Lie of Norway, the Soviet Union stayed away from the United Nations for sometime and then returned. During the Algerian liberation struggle from the mid-1950s, France, protesting against the world body's consideration of the Algerian question, arguing that it was an internal issue, and boycotted the General Assembly for sometime before returning while the UN went ahead with its consideration of the issue, until Algeria's independence after seven years of war (see *Chapter 2*). It has also been mentioned how both the United States and Britain left the United Nations Educational, Cultural and Scientific Organization (UNESCO) in the mid-1980s over their opposition to what they perceived as the organization's increasing communist bent. They both returned later —Britain in 1997 and the US in 2003 (see *Chapter 4*). The scenario of one or more of them leaving the UN altogether as some did to the League of Nations is therefore highly unlikely. But this does not mean that it is totally impossible, for people do not always follow what is in their best interest, though when they do otherwise they may regret it later.

In fact, the American Secretary of State, Cordell Hull, let it be known in 1944 that "the United States would not remain one day in the United Nations without retaining the veto power." The Soviet representative to the UN in 1950, Andrei Y. Vishinsky, declared that "the veto power is the paramount principle, which constitutes the cornerstone of the United Nations."[17]

The undemocratic and unaccountable nature of the Security Council has made it very profitable for its permanent members. Thus, one can see how unlikely it will be for them to easily agree to anything that will dramatically change the *status quo* —unjust and undemocratic as it is. Yet ironically, their consensual agreement is needed for any radical change such as Council enlargement and who should be admitted. Already, China has made it clear that it would veto any proposal to grant Japan a permanent seat. In the aforementioned Congress commissioned report on American interests in UN reform, the drafters oddly argue that "any [UN] reforms should extend to Israel."[18] Do they mean giving a permanent seat to Israel? They do not elaborate on this. In any case, those who drafted this report know all too well that they are not going to get anywhere with this controversial point. But these are points that could well be used, should it be necessary, to frustrate the whole issue of Council reform.

Because of this, one may reasonably argue that instead of Africa devoting disproportionate energy and resources to have the Council enlarged or have permanent seats, the focus should be on other key areas that are equally important to Africa. These include the big powers' self-proclaimed privileges that seem more readily negotiable than Council membership. For example, the big powers insist on the right to control certain high-ranking UN posts and to name the holders of those posts. They intervene regularly in the workings of the Secretariat and disproportionately influence the wording of reports and the shaping of initiatives. They insist on the right to have one of their nationals sit as a judge in the International Court of Justice (ICJ), so that their selfish interests will be represented there, and many other unorthodox privileges. These are the areas where the African current debate on UN reform should be based, unless Africans are calling for permanent Council seats as a strategy to at least get other reforms —aiming high in order to get at least close. Otherwise, the focus should be on other areas as stated above.

The March 2006 report of Secretary-General Annan offered a golden opportunity to Africa in terms of fighting for a fair share in the United Nations' fortunes and privileges. Chapter IV of this report deals with suggestions about the need for, and how to find, new and alternative ways of delivering UN services. Having recognized the opportunities created by the advancement of information technology, Annan proposed to the General Assembly that it should consider the option of moving certain administrative functions being currently carried out at headquarters in New York to other locations, contracting out to external providers a range of services currently performed in New York at huge cost, and making more effective use of facilities already established around the world. The considerations that led Annan to suggest these reforms are clear and he found no difficulty —no one could indeed— in explaining it in no uncertain terms:

> By so doing, [the United Nations] will disperse the economic and employment benefits of these activities more equitably among [UN] Member States, while at the same time making it more effective and efficient. In particular, it will redistribute some of the very large share of those benefits that currently flows to the richest Member State of the United Nations because it hosts a large United Nations presence. Redistributing and relocating the Headquarters' workload to other parts of the world will benefit more countries and economies; allow the United Nations to widen and deepen the skills pool from which it recruits; and enable it to reduce the overall costs of its operations.[19]

Africa could not find a better ground for argument: New York, Geneva, Paris and London are all more than ten times more expensive than Bamako, Gaborone, Dar es Salaam, Algiers and Malabo. Thanks to the advancement of information technology, services such as printing and publishing functions, translation and editing services, medical insurance plan administration, information technology support services, and staff benefits administration, could all be carried out effectively in many African and other developing capitals on a more or less an equal footing with many places where they are currently being performed. In the report, Annan asked the Assembly to undertake "systematic and detailed cost-benefit analyses" of relocation and outsourcing of some of these services by March 2007. Africa should take the lead in pressing for this and for Africa to be the prime beneficiary of many of these new opportunities. At the same time, and most importantly, African countries should strive to avoid any unwarranted contention about the locations of such new services, which could be exploited by those who do not want it, allowing them to argue that there is no agreement among the different African states after all. Without doubt, some African leaders will be approached, should the opportunities materialise and there seems to be a united African voice, to break unity and propose their capitals for it. The aim of such demarches will be nothing else but to divide Africa and thus deny it the opportunity or reduce its chances. Such moves should be resisted by all means and the African Union should play a central role in coordinating the African position on this.

These are the areas on which Africa should focus its calls for UN reform. With regard to the Security Council permanent seat issue, one can even argue that Africa does not need a permanent seat or veto power if the only reason is to have its voice heard in the world community or its interests protected. Having a permanent seat and/or veto power alone does not even guarantee this. To gain respectability in the world community, African leaders should rather focus on the home side: strengthening the African Union. They should make it an organization whose mere threat to suspend a member will frighten such a member state, not the other way round. Certainly, if African leaders really take the initiative with a genuine political will, including the timely and full payment of their contributions to the AU budget and full and effective implementation of AU treaties they adopt and sign, the AU will be able to solve any African issue without ever needing the United Nations as such. Moreover, should this be the case, no UN member, not even the big powers, will dare to oppose any action of the pan-African organization about an issue that is African, such as sending peace-keeping troops to an African country. Switzerland had international respectability even when it was not a UN member, which it only became in 2002.

Likewise, Africa does not need the UN even to condemn, say, a big power for an irresponsible act in or against an African state. This is because if Africa is united, no big power, no matter how strong and powerful it is, will ever dare to put itself in a situation whereby it will be at loggerheads with a whole continent about an issue that is purely African. Being able to solve its own problems will make the continent a real power to reckon with. And even to have a direct voice within the UN can easily be achieved given that its 53 members already constitute an impressive 27 per cent of current UN membership of 191 countries. With the addition of the potential voice of what this author calls the Sovereign Diasporian African States (SDAS) in the Caribbean islands, voting with one voice or largely so, Africa should even be able to enlist other Southern regional blocs, such as the Asians and Latin Americans, for any cause it deems important, as was the case in the mid-1960s to early 1970s, when the Afro-Asian bloc held sway, especially in the General Assembly. By this means, the veto or even permanent status may largely become ceremonial.

Future Africa-UN Relations: complementary partnership not dependency

After decolonization and the effective dismantling of the system of Apartheid and the white minority regimes in Southern Africa, the main areas of Africa-UN relations are now conflict management and peace-keeping/peace-building, economic development, and technical assistance in various social, economic and technological sectors. The United Nations' partnership with Africa on decolonization and the fight against the Apartheid system and white minority regimes in Southern Africa was a success because the bulk of the work was done by Africa —that is the efforts of the different African governments individually or through the OAU, and those of the liberation movements on the ground. The role played by the United Nations in this regard was only complementary to the efforts of Africa and those of the liberation movements or political parties in the various African territories. With the position of the European colonial powers sitting on the Security Council known, had Africa left the liberation struggle solely or largely to the UN, perhaps many countries would still be under European colonialism.

Contrary to the success of the partnership on these issues however is the apparent failure of Africa-UN partnership in the field of conflict management and economic development. In the field of conflict management, we have seen this acutely in Somalia and Rwanda (see *Chapter 3*). Economic development, too, has not been a success. Is this because Africa has changed the strategy it used during decolonization —counting the UN as a complementary partner rather than depending on it— and adopted another one — dependency and questionable victimization— when it comes to economic development? Or is it that the strategy has not changed but the UN is to blame? It is to the answer to these questions that we now turn and to consider how best to make Africa's partnership with the United Nations in these domains a success as it was with regard to decolonization.

Conflict management and conflict resolution

As far as the safeguarding or restoration of international peace and security are concerned, the United Nations Security Council is the prime responsible body for this. This is in fact the main purpose of setting up the United Nations. It is the one that the international community has entrusted with this task through approval of the UN Charter. This is so especially when it comes to peace enforcement, which may necessitate economic sanctions, arms embargoes and actual use of force. Moreover, the United Nations has such enormous resources and such a wealth of expertise in the field that no one can question it being the best body to deal effectively with conflict issues around the world. Two main points are worth pointing out here however.

First, as a global institution, the United Nations has a global constituency. It thus has to be ready to serve all its constituents. Yet despite its enormous resources, when the needs of many of these constituents arise at more or less the same time, it finds it difficult to deal with all effectively. Whenever this is the case, *Realpolitik* comes into play. This entails choosing between the different constituents and giving priority to some over others. Yet reading through the history of UN engagements and the responses and reactions of the international community to armed conflict situations around the world, one observes that these have been below expectations as far as Africa is concerned. Critical observation shows that these responses have been largely different when such conflicts occurred elsewhere in the world than Africa. Look for instance at the slow and poor response of the UN and the international community to the civil wars in Liberia, Sierra Leone and the Democratic Republic of the Congo or, most tellingly, the 1994 genocide in Rwanda. Contrast this with the more sophisticated and robust forces sent to Kuwait in 1991, Bosnia and Herzegovina in 1995 and East Timor four years later. Clearly, it may be justified here to assume that there is a tendency of discrimination against Africa, which is in a way telling Africans to care for and help themselves.

The other point is that even if the UN were to intervene in an armed conflict situation, the process of agreeing to this is slow, cumbersome and lengthy —of course depending on the location of the conflict.[20] First, the proposal to establish a UN peace-keeping operation is transmitted to the Security Council either by the Secretary-General personally or by a member state through the Secretary-General or directly to the Council. The latter looks at the proposal and decides on its conformity or non-conformity with the requirements of UN peace-keeping operations. A proposal may thus be authorized or refused. This requires active diplomatic shuttling by the Secretary-General or the sponsoring member state or group of states of the proposal. Such activities generally precede the formal submission of the proposal to the Council, for it is common practice in diplomatic circles to make sure of one's chances before committing oneself to something.

If the Council approves the operation and sets its mandate — again this depends on where the armed conflict occurred— in a resolution it passes, it refers the matter to various Secretariat departments in order to prepare the operation and implement the mandate in consultation with the Council and the General Assembly. The mandate takes into account the views of the Military

Staff Committee, which is directly under the Council and comprises the Chiefs of Staff of the Council's five permanent members. The matter is then referred to the Department of Peace-keeping Operations (DPKO), whose head at Under-Secretary-General level reports directly to the Secretary-General. The DPKO tries to secure offers of military contingents from a number of member states. The Secretariat then prepares a mission budget and submits it to the Advisory Committee on Administrative and Budgetary Questions (ACABQ). Set up in February 1946, this committee is a subsidiary organ of the General Assembly, consisting of 16 members appointed for three-year renewable terms by the Assembly in their individual capacity, observing the principle of broad geographical representation, personal qualifications and experience. With the approval of the mission budget by the ACABQ, the matter goes to the General Assembly's Fifth Committee before going to the plenary session of the Assembly for formal approval of the operation.

But this is not the end of the story, for a substantial chunk of the necessary funding for the mission comes from voluntary contributions of some rich member states. The commitment of the different rich countries to this voluntary budget depends largely on that country's real or potential geopolitical interests in the region or country where the peace-keeping operation is going. The funds pledged may never be delivered fully. It could also take several weeks, if not months, before those who do deliver do so. This excludes any realistic chance of early conflict prevention activity. In fact, depending on the location, many countries do not tend to consider a looming conflict a threat to international peace and security —which is the main requirement for UN intervention— until hostilities begin. Yet this is the most effective period of preventive diplomacy and conflict prevention that Boutros-Ghali rightly stressed in his *An Agenda for Peace.*

This state of affairs has led to an animated debate about the best way forward in conflict management in Africa: Should Africans continue to rely on the UN despite the increasing reluctance of the Security Council to commit itself to establishing effective peace-keeping operations in Africa because the Western countries do not want to commit their soldiers or resources to it? If so, what will be the consequences for peace and security in Africa? On the other hand, should Africa cease to be a "Prisoner of Expectations," to start being in charge of its own security independently of the UN? In that case, where will it get the necessary resources? And what will be the consequences of a poorly equipped peace-keeping operation?

Here emerge three main schools of thought, which are in fact two. One school argues that despite all the issues enumerated above related to UN peace-keeping operations in Africa, given that the continent lacks the appropriate and adequate institutional structures, managerial capacity and resources to properly manage peace-keeping operations, the task should still be left to the United Nations which has the comparative advantage in this regard. The role of Africa, according to this school of thought, should be limited to providing troops to the UN operations which should be under the command of UN force commanders. Another school argues that Africa should take the lead in preliminary negotiations, securing a cease-fire and committing itself to provide the troops. It should then ask the international community to provide the logistic, technical, transport and other support facilities. This could be through the UN or even through bilateral arrangements between Africa and the different Western countries. This school of thought credits itself with guaranteeing African ownership of the process to a large extent while avoiding the financial hassles that may hinder the operation should everything be left to the poor Africans.[21]

There does not seem to be much difference between these two schools of thought. True, advocates of the second school may claim that their formula guarantees African ownership of the process and avoids the cumbersome process of securing a direct and full-fledged UN peace-keeping operation. However, the argument of seeking to secure logistical and other support facilities from the international community —if necessary through the UN— makes it no different from the first school of thought. To start with, it is clear and indeed understandable that the UN does not fund any peace-keeping operation which it did not create and/or set its mandate. On the other hand, putting the so-called bilateral arrangements under serious scrutiny reveals their risks, inadequacy and unreliability.

The reason behind this observation is clear and simple to grasp —not all outside actors have a bona fide interest in ending these conflicts. The so-called bilateral partners may never commit their resources if they do not have any significant geopolitical interest in the region or country concerned and thus have a stake —not of a humanitarian nature in most cases— in the outcome of the conflict. In any case, they will want to make sure of publicity and public relations opportunities in their engagement and will thus be more focused on scoring diplomatic goals than on caring for the people they are being called upon to save. Yet, this will have its impact on the quality and the timing of the delivery of any assistance they may commit themselves to offer, and that will lead many of them to seek a prominent public role in the whole process. Yet there are some actors who somehow benefit from these unstable situations or like fishing in troubled waters, so to speak.

More often, whenever one mentions the fact that the West may not be as sincere about its proclaimed interest in finding just and lasting solutions to many of the conflicts in the Third World in general and in Africa in particular as it pretends, the question one usually gets is something like this: "What interest does the West have in seeing these nations suffer?" We could find the answer to such questions more eloquently in the analysis made by Joseph Ki-Zerbo, the renowned Burkinabè historian, of the situation. According to Professor Ki-Zerbo, the situation is sometimes like that in the so-called slave trade era of the sixteenth century. That was when the Europeans coming to Africa for people to be taken and enslaved wished that Africans would go to war between themselves as the resulting prisoners of war would facilitate their business. Would one not be justified in making a comparison between the twenty-first century arms dealers and these sixteenth-century human traffickers?[22] At times, some foreign mediators offer their services, when they do not actually force their way into the peace process, to better control the situation and fashion the peace process to their liking. Some may actually engage in selling arms to all parties while peace negotiations are prolonged.

As for the argument that Africa does not have the adequate institutional structures, this is at best no longer valid. Both the African Union —inheriting the OAU— and a good number of regional organizations in Africa have developed effective conflict management mechanisms and structures. Perhaps the example of the Economic Community of West African States (ECOWAS) is the most illustrative amongst all the regional organizations in the continent. Only a few people may question the thoroughness of the *Protocol Relating to the Mechanism for Conflict Prevention, Management, Resolution, Peace-keeping, and Security* adopted by ECOWAS in Lomé in 1999.

It is these observations that lead to the third school of thought. Some may perceive this as rather radical, but it is nevertheless the most reliable and realistic one and one which this author adopts. That is that Africans should be in the driver's seat not only in mediation, but also in the whole process of peace-keeping and peace-building. Because there are countries always looking for a way to feel good, some will offer their assistance, be it logistical or financial, when they see Africans doing it alone and making good progress. Such assistance should be welcomed and duly credited should the donors ask for that as they are very likely to. However, this should in no way allow that external "donor" to ask for it to be in charge of the operations or set up a parallel operation. In addition to the observations made above, this approach may be further explained, substantiated and justified by the following two considerations.

First, the AU or the regional organization to which it chooses to delegate the task of conflict management in a given African country is considered as an "insider", closely connected to the conflict at hand, with an intimate and profound knowledge of local conditions. It also shares norms and experiences with the parties involved and may even have personal links with some of them, which certainly facilitates their task.[23] This is at the diplomatic level, and it is also true even if a military campaign turns out to be necessary. The local actors have the unrivalled advantage of knowing the terrain. For example, after the horrific attacks of 11 September 2001 in the US, the Bush administration thought that the country had been attacked by terrorist groups based, at least in part, in Afghanistan and in the care of its then Taliban regime. Thus, the defeat of the Taliban, from this perspective, was in America's national interest. In such a military campaign, one would have expected the Americans —with their unmatched military and intelligence capacities— to achieve their goals swiftly and at a very minimal financial and human cost. Yet the Americans had to rely on local opponents of the Taliban, the so-called Northern Alliance, even to start their bombing campaign. Even then, they encountered a mountain of difficulties due chiefly to their lack of knowledge of the terrain and the people they were dealing with. One can therefore see why the Americans swiftly withdrew from Somalia after the incident of October 1993 and the Belgians from Rwanda in April 1994 (see *Chapter 3*).

Secondly, the conflits in question are African wars and those dying are Africans. Armed conflicts cause the death of thousands of people. They also lead to massive refugee flows to neighbouring countries. These refugee populations in six figure numbers become somehow a burden on host countries. Refugee camps tend also to be a breeding ground for rebel movements, as fleeing rebels may infiltrate the refugee populations and regroup their forces from there. This is to say that neighbouring countries have more at stake in the outcome of the conflict than any other actors. They are thus the only ones that can commit the necessary resources and make the necessary sacrifices to put an end to the conflict.[24] The role played by Tanzania in the Arusha negotiations is illustrative of this. The performance of the African contingents of UNAMIR during the 1994 genocide, especially the Ghanaian contingent in comparison with that of the Western contingents that were pulled out from the country following the path of the Belgians as the situation deteriorated is also illustrative of this.

Another example illustrating this in West Africa occurred in Liberia in late 2003. There was intense fighting between the rebel group called Liberians United for Reconciliation and Democracy (LURD) and troops loyal to the government of Charles Taylor. In Monrovia, the Liberian capital where the heavy fighting had reached, people, mainly women and children, were dying or being maimed on a daily basis by gunfire. There was a real risk of famine and the spread of killer diseases in the country. The rebels were demanding as a *sine qua non* for their stopping fighting the departure of Charles Taylor without conditions. On the other hand, Taylor was adamant against conceding especially because the UN Special Court for Sierra Leone had indicted him for involvement in the civil war in that country. Meanwhile, Liberians called for the international community and the United States in particular to intervene to stop the violence and killing. They invoked their so-called "shared history" with Washington in a desperate attempt to persuade the White House to act. ECOWAS and other African leaders urged Washington and the rest of the international community to at least help financially, saying that they would be ready to send troops. But both the Americans and the international community proved unwilling. The fighting was only ended by the intervention of ECOWAS thanks to the good offices of President Olusegun Obasanjo of Nigeria and President Thabo Mbeki of South Africa, then the Chairman of the African Union. This is not to blame the outsiders for their inaction. It is just not their problem and they have many of their own anyway.

Thirdly, African leaders should recognise —indeed many fortunately do nowadays— that Africa's saviour is no one but themselves, especially through the African Union. In order for the latter to carry out this task, it has to have credibility not only in the eyes of the international community, but first and foremost in the eyes of the African peoples. To have this, it needs to be seen in the driver's seat rushing to their rescue in conflict situations. Negotiating cease-fire agreements just to retreat to the background leaving the UN or the like of *Operation Restore Hope* or *Opération Turquoise* to take over does not augur well for this confidence-building between the AU, and thus the African governments, and the African peoples. It does not even help the image of Africa in the world community. Yet it is this confidence of the African peoples that constitutes the sole winning asset of the African Union and African governments. This is why it is the view of this author that the debates about UN intervention in the Darfur region of Sudan should not have started in the first place. This is the very first peace-keeping operation of the African Union after it replaced the OAU in 2002. Everything should be done to make this operation a successful *African* operation. There is more ground to be suspicious of the apparent sudden enthusiasm of some Western states concerning Sudan. But the killings must stop and the AU has to review the mandate of its force and the Sudanese government must fully cooperate. Khartoum has an obligation to protect all its citizens without discrimination.

For the arguments about weak and poor military and financial capabilities of African states, two observations can be made. First, the military issue does not arise since African troops serve on equal footing with all other contingents in UN peace-keeping operations, be they in Africa or elsewhere. The problem is solely that of logistics and financial resources. And here again, the assumption that Africa does not have the necessary resources is questionable. In effect, what seems to be lacking in Africa is genuine political will; nothing more. It may be interesting to note here that never has an African country refrained from going to war because it lacks resources. Whenever there is war or a threat of war, either the government or the so-called bilateral partners will strive to come up with the necessary resources. So why not when it comes to peace-keeping or conflict prevention? Granted that Africans do not have the *necessary* resources to carry out *ideal* peace-keeping operations, should Africans fold their arms and watch their brethren die as happened in Rwanda just because they are waiting for a reluctant international community to come forward with millions of dollars? On what moral justification would they base such an action? Clearly, fighting with one's old sword may be better than waiting for a gun from someone of whom you know from experience that he may not give it to you or may not give it on time.

My conclusion therefore from this discussion is that Africans should take the lead role in conflict management and conflict resolution activities on the continent, as Europeans do in Europe. It should begin by insisting on good governance and economic development which are the most effective conflict prevention instruments there are. This is not a call to abandon or even sideline the United Nations. Quite far from it. For the African Union to undertake mediation efforts and, if necessary, military action and inform the Security Council about its actions is not only in conformity with the UN Charter, but encouraged by it. Article 52 (1) makes it clear that nothing in the Charter "precludes the existence of regional arrangements or agencies for dealing with such matters relating to the maintenance of international peace and security as are appropriate for regional action" so long as the activities of these regional agencies or organizations are "consistent with the Purposes and Principles of the United Nations."

Economic development

We have seen (see *Chapter 2*) how the many social and economic development initiatives or programmes that have so far been adopted by Africa with a significant United Nations input, if not under UN impetus, have apparently failed. The latest one in date (as of the time of completion of this book) is the Millennium Development Declaration which contains the Millennium Development Goals (MDGs), targeting the year 2015 for halving illiteracy and abject poverty rates in the world. Africa is not the only developing region concerned by this Declaration, but it does concern it in a significant way. With just ten years to go from 2005 and without any tangible results recorded as yet, one may not need a multiple dose of pessimism to doubt its success, at least by the set deadline.

The apparent failure of all these initiatives is generally explained, at least in part, by the fact that neither Africa nor the rich Northern states fulfilled their commitments under these initiatives. The argument is that when the UN General Assembly adopted the United Nations Action Plan for African Economic Recovery and Development, 1986-1990 (UNAPAERD) in June 1986, and subsequently the United Nations New Agenda for the Development of Africa in the 1990s (UNNADAF), what was implied was collective action and shared responsibility between Africa and the rich developed countries. Africa was to commit itself to the launch of both national and regional programmes of economic development, while the rich countries were urged to "support and complement the African development efforts." Thus, the programmes ultimately ended in failure when most African states failed to fulfil their obligations under these programmes and the rich countries did not live up to their promises.

One can understand from this that the United Nations, not being a financial institution in its own right, can only provide a venue for discussion between rich and poor countries. If the agreement sought is about financing development projects in the developing world, experience shows that the rich countries tend to prefer other ways and other venues for this rather than the United Nations. In fact, to many of them, the United Nations is a place for debate and rarely for negotiation. Many developed countries are reluctant to accept that what they consider as important decisions affecting the world's trading or monetary system, the distribution of international investment, or significant transfers of resources to developing countries should be decided at the United Nations.[25] They prefer their various capitals (for bilateral arrangements) and other bodies (e.g. the G-8 or the Bretton Woods institutions) where they are in full control of the process.

It would seem therefore that when we talk about United Nations' development conferences, they are in actual fact forums where developing countries lay down a list of their demands and the world body passes it onto the developed world in its own envelop. Perhaps the best description of the role played by the UN in this process is that of a dating agency —but an agency where only one party is interested and offers himself or herself to the other while the agency tries to persuade the latter. Thus, in order to properly deal with this issue, one should instead look at the preferred venues of the rich Northern countries —that is, the bilateral arrangements, the Bretton Woods institutions and the G-8.

Perhaps one example may be used to summarise the whole process when it comes to bilateral arrangements and the myriad public relations declarations by Northern countries in favour of Africa in this regard. In October 2001, in his Labour Annual Conference speech at the southern English town of Brighton, the British Prime Minister, Tony Blair, claimed that "Africa is a scar on the conscience of the world." He even followed this by a week long trip to West Africa. In February 2003, he set up what he called "The Commission for Africa," supposedly aimed at helping the continent out of poverty. It is however instructive to note that while Tony Blair felt the need to establish a commission for Africa, Britain has so far refused to co-operate with the Nigerian authorities in recovering part of the loot the late Nigerian dictator, General Sani Abacha, stashed in various British banks before his sudden death in 1998. This is despite the fact that the Nigerian authorities have provided them with undisputed documents about the loot. By the end of 2005 London was still adamant claiming that the Nigerian authorities could not prove that the funds in question were public money, as if they had known Abacha to be a successful entrepreneur before he took over power in his country.

Likewise, at the end of each of their annual summits since it began in 1975, the G-8 countries thrive in their promises to help Africa. However, while their final communiqués always have such clauses in favour of Africa, the amount of pillaged funds by corrupt African leaders deposited in their banks and possibly with their complicity was estimated at the end of 2001 at some US$ 140 billion.[26] There can be no plausible argument that these funds cannot be located since the so-called terrorist funds were located after the events of 11 September 2001 in the US. So, if Tony Blair and his colleagues in the other G-8 countries are serious about their readiness to helping Africa, they should first help return these stolen funds to Africa, as they are obviously Africa's. That would be helping Africa though only by returning Africa's own money to Africa.[27] But if they do not do this, and all signs indicate that they will not, then, what can one expect from them with regard to helping Africa if one is not fooling oneself?

From this, it is quite clear that it is unrealistic for Africans to rely on outsiders for their economic recovery or redemption. Neither the G-8 countries nor their protégé international financial institutions are capable of providing the answer to the economic problems of Africa. But is it their responsibility anyway? True, besides the obvious negative impact of European colonialism that lasted for over seven decades, the neo-colonial policies that have been in place over the last half a century or since African countries regained their sovereignty are also having very unpalatable effects on the continent. But does this justify the West being held solely responsible for all the current woes of Africa? For example, the aforementioned US$ 140 billion "pillaged" funds from Africa deposited in various Western banks may have been facilitated by the complicity of some Western actors. But who were their accomplices? In fact, it was the corrupt African leaders who stole these funds and stashed them in these foreign accounts. Africans should therefore take their part of the blame and face their responsibilities, especially when we consider the fact that neo-colonialism always relies on local partners in any region.

The most reliable strategy therefore for economic redemption in Africa is without doubt "self-help." Foreign assistance should be welcomed if and when it comes. However, given its unreliable nature and at times the unacceptable conditions attached to it, the solution should be sought from within the continent. To do this, in addition to political good governance motivated by the realisation that it is the best way forward and not just to please the international community, at least three other things can be recommended. These are a rigorous fight against the miasma of corruption, development of local economic production capacities especially in the agricultural sector, and more regional economic integration in the framework of the New Partnership for Africa's Development and the different Regional Economic Communities (RECs).

It is generally accepted that corruption or graft is the main obstacle to economic development in Africa. Corruption refers mainly to the misuse of entrusted power for personal gain. The African Union Convention on Preventing and Combating Corruption, singed at the second Ordinary Session of its Assembly at Maputo in July 2003, identifies nine sorts of acts which can be considered as corruption.[28] The phenomenon of corruption has had a profound impact on the different developmental projects in the continent. The AU Convention acknowledges these negative effects of the phenomenon. In the Preamble to this Convention, the Assembly expressed its concerns "about the negative effects of corruption and impunity on the political, economic, social and cultural stability of African States and its devastating effects on the economic and social development on the African peoples."[29] The responsibility for implementing the recommendations of this Convention lies however on the shoulders of the different national governments, the AU Commission having done its job and superbly.

These are the policies that Africa should take and the different specialised agencies of the United Nations may be asked for technical expertise and assistance. By this, Africa can ensure its economic development in a partnership with the United Nations that is based on complementarity and not dependency. With an economically prosperous Africa and Africa's preference for multilateralism as opposed to unilateralism being clear, African states can become effective partners in the development of the world body in return. As diplomatic weight always comes with economic clout, a prosperous Africa can also contribute more to the different United Nations funds and programmes that will ensure Africa's position within the world body and thus allow it to play a leading role in the UN in particular and in world affairs in the twenty-first century in general.

Conclusion

This concluding chapter looked at the future of Africa's relationship with the United Nations in the twenty-first century. It began by highlighting the world's need for the UN in stabilising the world and facilitating international relations. It noted that preserving the United Nations and working towards making it more effective is in the interest of all the regions and states of the world —poor and rich, weak and powerful alike. It however acknowledged that despite this, the United Nations is not perfect. It has many faults and some of its actions have at times tended to undermine its credibility. But this does not warrant calls for its abandonment. Rather, it only needs to be reformed to make it more effective and allow it to correct those mistakes.

Turning therefore to UN reform, it was observed that Africa should play an active role in this. This role however must be based on realistic aims and some core and selected attainable points. A particular target should be the unfair balance of wealth distribution of the UN system in terms of employment and other economic opportunities. Africa and other developing regions are largely denied many of these opportunities because of the concentration of UN headquarters —both the Secretariat and the seats of its funds, programmes and specialised agencies— in Northern developed countries. While it is true that a number of the specialised agencies existed and had already been located in their current locations well before the formation of the United Nations in 1945, as some were part of the League of Nations or even existed before that (e.g. the ILO and ITU), the location of almost all the newly created ones in the same areas is grossly unfair and should be addressed. This may not require relocating whole agencies as some may think. Rather, some services within these institutions, especially at UN headquarters in New York, should be relocated and outsourced. Africa should actively campaign to be one of the prime beneficiaries of such relocation and outsourcing opportunities. These are the aspects of UN reform that should concern Africa more than the expansion of the Security Council, which is not necessary for Africa to have its voice heard in world affairs, as some may assume.

Finally, in order for Africa's relations with the United Nations in the twenty-first century to be more fruitful for the continent, Africa should look at its partnership with the world body in areas of economic development in terms of complementarity rather than dependency. In other words, Africa should not sit and wait for the UN to come up with development initiatives on its behalf or insist that it may not put in place such initiatives without a significant UN input. Perhaps NEPAD represents the best way forward. However, even with NEPAD, Africans should strive to ensure African ownership of it. It would seem that Articles 150-154 of NEPAD are not in this direction and they thus need revision. As argued above, while foreign assistance may be welcome if and when it comes, it really should not be something on which the implementation of such African initiatives should be based. Experience shows that this is not workable. While emphasis on attracting foreign investment, as in those parts of NEPAD, may be a good policy, more emphasis should be on creating internal or local investment. Local entrepreneurship should be encouraged and African governments still have a significant role to play in this. In this, as with foreign investment, the main preoccupation of the different African governments should be job creation and not necessarily the direct taxes that could be levied on new companies. Yet this is largely absent in development prescriptions on the continent. It is by this that Africa can well achieve economic development and prosperity, starting with self-sufficiency. It is also by this, and only this, that Africa can ensure its respectful and rightful place in world community.

Notes

1. See Shashi Tharoor, "Why America Still Needs the United Nations," *Foreign Affairs*, September/October (2003).

2. Task Force on the United Nations, *American Interests and UN Reform: Report of the Task Force on the United Nations* (Washington, DC.: United States Institute of Peace, 2005), p. 3.

3. See Issaka K. Souaré, Civil Wars and Coups d'État in West Africa: An Attempt to Understand the Roots and Prescribe Possible Solutions (Lanham, MD.: University Press of America, 2006), pp. 64-6.

4. Task Force on the UN, American Interests and the UN Reform, p. 3.

5. See Security Council Resolution S/RES/1373 (2001) of 28 September 2001.

6. For information about the establishment, composition, mandate and activities of the CTC, see <http://www.un.org/sc/etc/.> (8 March 2006.)

7. Tharoor, Why America Still Needs the UN, op. cit.

8. G. R. Berridge, *Diplomacy: Theory and Practice*, 2nd ed. (New York: Palgrave, 2002), p.151.

9. Emma Matanle, *The UN Security Council* (London: Royal Institute of International Affairs, 1995), p. 30.

10. See Ivor Richard, "Major Objectives and Functions of the UN: The View from Abroad," in Toby Trister Gati (ed.), *The US, the UN, and the Management of Global Change* (New York & London: New York University Press, 1983), pp. 48-63.

11. In addition to an earlier unpublished work, this section draws quite heavily on Issaka K. Souaré, "The Debate on the UN Reform: Near Consensus on the Need for Reform but Rifts on how to go about it," *African Renaissance*, Vol. 2, no. 5, September/October (2005): 10-14.

12. James Paul and Céline Nahory, "Theses Towards a Democratic Reform of the UN Security Council," *Global Policy Forum*, 13 July 2005 at <http://www.globalpolicy.org.> (25 July 2005.)

13. For an up-to-date table of all vetoes cast in the Security Council and the subject of draft resolutions vetoed since 1945, see the Global Policy Forum website at <http://www.globalpolicy.org.> (9 March 2006.)

14. See Kofi Annan, *In Larger Freedom: Towards development, security and human rights for all* (Report of the Secretary-General, March 2005).

15. Kofi Annan, *Investing in the United Nations: for a stronger Organization worldwide* (Report of the Secretary-General, March 2006).

16. For an overview of the array of African states that have expressed their ambition or aspiration to this opportunity, see Wafula Okumu, "Africa and the UN Security Council Permanent Seats," *African Renaissance*, Vol. 2, no. 5, September/October (2005): 16-22.

17. Stephen Ryan, The United Nations and International Politics: Studies in Contemporary History (New York: Palgrave Macmillan, 2000), p. 44; John G. Stoessinger, The United Nations & the Superpowers: China, Russia & America (New York: Random House, 1977), p. 1; and Anjali V. Patil, The UN Veto in World Affairs, 1946-1990: A Complete Record and Case History of Security Council's veto (Mansell, UK.: Continuum International Publishing Group, 1992), p. 13.

18. Task Force on the UN, American Interests and the UN Reform, p. 7.

19. Annan, *Investing in the United Nations*, Ch. IV, paras. 57-63.

20. For a detailed analysis of the decision-making structure of UN peacekeeping operations, see Agostinho Zacarias, *The United Nations and International Peacekeeping* (London & New York: I. B. Tauris Publishers, 1996), pp. 26-37.

21. For a discussion of these schools, see Margaret Aderinsola Vogt, "Co-Operation Between the UN and the OAU in the Management of African Conflicts," in Mark Malan (ed.), *Whither Peacekeeping in Africa?* Monograph no. 36 (Cape Town: Institute of Security Studies, April 1999).

22. Joseph Ki-Zerbo, *A Quand l'Afrique?* (Paris: Éditions de l'Aube, 2003), pp. 57 – 58 and p. 61.

23. See Ole Elgström, Jacob Bercovitch, and Carl Skau, "Regional Organisations and International Mediation: The Effectiveness of Insider Mediators," *African Journal on Conflict Resolution*, Vol. 3, no. 1 (2003): 13.

24. Amitai Etzioni, "A self-restrained approach to nation-building by foreign powers," *International Affairs*, Vol. 80, no. 1 (January 2004): 1 – 18.

25. See for example Sidney Weintraub, "US Participation in International Organizations: Looking Ahead," in Toby Trister Gati (ed.), *The US, the UN, and the Management of Global Change* (New York & London: New York University Press, 1983), pp. 184-209, particularly p. 185.

26. Desmond Davies, "What about other foreign bank accounts?" *West Africa*, 5 – 11 (August 2001).

27. See Issaka K. Souaré, "Can the G-8 and International Financial Institutions Help Africa?", *African Renaissance*, Vol. 1, no. 2, September/October (2004): 115 – 120. It should in fact be pointed out that when the G-7 (it became G-8 only in 2002 with the admission of Russia), comprising Britain, Canada, France, Germany, Italy, Japan and the United States, was formed following the oil crises and the ensuing financial disturbances of the early 1970s, the main purpose was, as it still remains, to discuss the world's financial situation and how to regulate it and control it according to their interests.

28. African Union, *African Union Convention on Preventing and Combating Corruption*, Maputo (11 July 2003), Article 4, pp. 7 – 8.

29. Ibid, p. 2.

AFTERWORD

ISSAKA K. SOUARÉ has written a well-informed and timely book on an important subject. He has rightly set his exploration of the contemporary UN-Africa relationship in its historical context, something that Europeans, for understandable reasons, are often reluctant to do.

Historically, European activities in Africa were rather distinctive by comparison with their operations either in the Americas or in East, South and South East Asia. In all cases there was the drive to destroy existing state structures. In the Americas this was combined with a redrawing of state boundaries and the crushing of native cultures and languages, replacing the existing ruling groups with European settler elites who imposed dominant European cultures and languages. Sometimes, as in the United States and Argentina, this was done by the physical liquidation of the native populations. In other cases, the native populations as well as the African slaves and their heirs became an underclass. In East Asia on the other hand, and partially in South and South East Asia, the Europeans were too weak to destroy local populations or even to subordinate their cultures to a colonizing dominant class. Even state boundaries were in many cases little altered and some of the states were not even formally colonized.

In Africa too, the old political systems were destroyed by the European colonizers and new state boundaries were established at the diplomatic dinner tables of Europe. But despite local genocides, there was not the wholesale liquidation of local populations. Instead, in large parts of Africa, white settlement was combined with turning the local population into a labour resource. This was the pattern in Southern Africa: South Africa, Namibia, Zimbabwe, Angola and Mozambique, as well as Kenya. In other parts of sub-Saharan Africa, where white settlement was minimal, the European policy involved using hand-picked local elite elements as colonial stooges while exploiting territories for raw materials. But everywhere African colonial state boundaries paid no regard to local, African realities, whether political, cultural or linguistic.

This historical experience created uniquely unfavourable conditions in Africa for the building of integrated, modern capitalist societies. One precondition for such societies is an integrated capitalist class with a common state-building project. Yet in much of post-colonial Africa the bulk of the business class has been made up of ethnic minorities: the white settlers in South Africa, Zimbabwe and Namibia, for example, and other ethnically distinct economically dominant minorities in many other parts of Africa. Another precondition for modern capitalism is that the social and economic polarization between a rich capitalist minority and a mass of market-dependent labourers is counter-balanced by an effort to construct national entities in which the labouring classes are integrated into a social system in which they can believe that there is an identity of some sort between leaders and led. This too is extremely difficult within state boundaries which do not respect real patterns of language and culture amongst populations.

And, of course, these state and nation-building efforts depend upon access to material resources. State budgets and foreign currency earnings must be sufficient for states to be able to establish the necessary social infrastructure for integrated societies and economies. And these requirements in turn depend upon the ways in which African states are integrated into the world economy. In much of post-colonial Africa the form of insertion has been raw material and mineral production for Europe. And the terms of trade for raw material producers have turned remorselessly and catastrophically against Africa in most cases.

As Issaka Souaré indicates there was a period in which there were to some extent positive international conditions for African development, conditions which were also reflected in the UN. This was the period of the Cold War, the turn to independence, the rise of the Non-Aligned Movement (NAM) and the campaign for a New International Economic Order (NIEO). This gave the newly independent African states allies in the UN General Assembly, while at the same time the European powers and the US were to some extent inhibited from predatory intervention by the existence of the Soviet Bloc, checking them in the UN Security Council. Thanks to these factors, bodies like the United Nations Conference on Trade and Development (UNCTAD) and the UN Centre on Transnational Corporations were established and the UN became a source of some flexibility and room for manoeuvre for African governments seeking a strong insertion in the world economy.

But this "golden age" should not be exaggerated. Predatory intervention by the European powers and the US still took place: the devastating intervention in the Congo in the early 1960s is one dramatic and appalling example, in which the officials of the UN Secretariat were complicit in the overthrow of the government of Patrice Lumumba. And atrocious wars were orchestrated by the US and Apartheid South Africa in Mozambique, Angola and Namibia. Only Cuban military aid ensured the failure of these US-South African efforts in Angola and Namibia. And at the same time, much of sub-Saharan Africa remained firmly in the neo-colonial grip of *Françafrique*.[1] Meanwhile the ACP arrangements of Africa's key market —the European Union— were geared to facilitating the continuance of Africa's role as raw material suppliers rather than moving up the value chain into textiles and industrial processing.

But with the oil price rises and debt crises, the Atlantic powers were able to seize the initiative to destroy the push for a NIEO and to undermine the influence of the NAM. And the Soviet Bloc collapse completed the collapse of a supportive framework for African development within the UN General Assembly. As a result, the UN's earlier role as a support for a stronger insertion of Africa in the world economy has ended. All such matters to do with the international political economy have been transferred to the IMF, the World Bank and the WTO where the Atlantic powers have effective control. The result has been predictable: a new problem definition of Africa's relation to the world economy. Instead of adapting the world economy to the needs of African development the problem definition has been changed to the internal imperfections of African political economies and the need for stronger market compulsions on Africa's working populations. And this new emphasis has had predictable results —a mounting economic crisis in much of Africa. And not just an economic crisis.

The IMF-World Bank drive to impose market compulsions has generated or exacerbated social and political tensions which many African states have been too weak to cope with. The result has been acute political crises in much of Africa.

The Western powers, now more than ever in command of the UN apparatus and its resources, have, since the early 1990s, increasingly turned that apparatus towards what is called "peace-keeping": preventive diplomacy, peace-enforcement and peace-building, in the jargon. Yet the discourse of "peace" has legitimated an effort which can more properly be described as diplomacy of regime change backed by coercive military intervention. The rationale for this seems to be that since African states are in many cases too weak to build capitalist societies external intervention is required to force through this project. This new role for the UN in Africa was heralded by the so-called *An Agenda for Peace* in 1992. It produced the aggressive intervention in Somalia —a debacle for all concerned. It then produced the UN military intervention in Rwanda which, combined with the military attack by predominantly-Tutsi RPF forces in Uganda, was supposed to produce regime change, removing the authoritarian Hutu government in Kigali. The result of this UN regime change effort was the Rwandan genocide. This has been followed by a plethora of tragic crises and conflicts in Southern and West Africa in which UN Security Council-backed forces of one kind or another have sought to impose solutions on local populations, or more minimally to contain the international consequences of the conflicts.

Issaka Souaré's book provides a valuable account of many of the important issues of the UN relationship with Africa. It is hard to believe that the Western powers currently dominant in the UN have the answer. Their problematic is a very traditional one: the old imperial *"mission civilisatrice"* for the continent under the sign of liberal individualist capitalism. We are led to believe that if only Africa had free markets, democracy and "good governance" all would be well.

This simply does not address many of the fundamental issues, far less solve them. And throwing in the need for more aid is also superficial. A classic example of this superficiality has been Zimbabwe's crisis. Any dispassionate observer could long have seen that Zimbabwe could not become an integrated, stable social system when the white settlers continued to control the economy and sought to use their wealth to control the political system. From the moment of independence this was a crisis waiting to happen. Yet instead of planning for a solution to this impossible situation, the British sought to freeze the status quo, exerting pressure for two decades to prevent the Zimbabwean government from delivering on its independence promise on the land question. And as economic crisis mounted and IMF programmes generated internal tensions, the white farmers constructed and funded their black political party to shore up their social position. The stage was set for a devastating crisis. Mantras about free markets, democracy and good governance are beside the point in cases like this.

A new start would involve a single benchmark for external influence on the continent: is it making the lives of ordinary Africans more economically and socially secure or more insecure? By that test the league table for good governance and Africa would probably be headed by the Chinese while many of the Western governments who are current masters of the UN would remain at the bottom of the list.

Peter Gowan
Professor of International Relations
Dept. of Law, Government and International Relations
London Metropolitan University

Note

1. A term coined to denote the network of political, military and business relations between France and generally corrupt leaders of some mainly French-speaking African countries.

BIBLIOGRAPHY

African Union, *African Union Convention on Preventing and Combating Corruption*, Maputo (11 July 2003).

― ―, The Newsletter of the African Union Commission (December 2005).

Akpan, M. B., "Liberia and Ethiopia, 1881 – 1914: the survival of two African states," in A. Adu Boahen (ed.), *General History of Africa–VII: Africa under colonial domination 1880–1935* (Paris and Berkeley: Unesco and University of California Press, 1985).

Akpan, M. B. and R. Pankhurst, "Ethiopia and Liberia, 1914-1935: Two Independent African States in the Colonial Era," in A. Adu Boahen (ed.), *General History of Africa–VII: Africa under colonial domination 1880–1935* (Paris and Berkeley: Unesco and University of California Press, 1985).

Alusala, Nelson, "The Arming of Rwanda, and the Genocide," *African Security Review*, Vol. 13, no. 2 (2004): 139-40.

Amnesty International, *Undermining Global Security: the European Union's arms exports*, Index no. ACT 30/003/2004 (14 May 2004).

― ―, "France: The Search for Justice —effective impunity of law enforcement officers in cases of shootings, deaths in custody or torture and ill-treatment," EUR 21/001/2005 of 6 April 2005.

Annan, Kofi, The Causes of Conflict and the Promotion of Durable Peace and Sustainable Development in Africa (Report of the Secretary General, April 1998).

― ―, *Prevention of Armed Conflict* (Report of the Secretary-General to the Security Council, June 2001).

― ―, In Larger Freedom: Towards development, security and human rights for all (Report of the Secretary-General, March 2005).

― ―, *Investing in the United Nations: for a stronger Organization worldwide* (Report of the Secretary-General, March 2006).

Atack, Iain, "Peacebuilding as conflict management or political engineering?" *Trócaire Development Review* (2003/4).

Ayittey, George B. N., "The Somali Crisis: Time for an African Solution," *Cato Policy Analysis*, no. 205 (28 March 1994).

Baehr, Peter R. and Leon Gordenker, *The United Nations: Reality and Ideal* (New York: Palgrave Macmillan, 2005).

Barnett, Michael, *Eyewitness to a Genocide: The United Nations and Rwanda* (Ithaca & London: Cornell University Press, 2002).

Bebbé-Njoh, Étienne, "Mentalité africaine" et problématique du développement (Paris: l'Harmattan, 2002).

Berridge, G. R., *Diplomacy: Theory and Practice*, 2nd ed. (New York: Palgrave, 2002).

Blaton, Shannon Lindsey, "Foreign Policy in Transition? Human Rights, Democracy, and U.S. Arms Exports," *International Studies Quarterly*, Vol. 49, no. 4 (December 2005): 647-668.

Bolton, John R., "Wrong Turn in Somalia," *Foreign Affairs*, Vol. 73, no. 1, January/February (1994).

Bourantonis, Dimitris and Jarrod Wiener, (eds.), *The United Nations in the New World Order: The World Organization at Fifty* (New York: Palgrave Macmillan, 1995).

Boutros-Ghali, Boutros, *An Agenda for Peace: Preventive Diplomacy, peace-making and peace-keeping* (Report of the Secretary-General, June 1992).

— —, *Unvanquished: A US-UN Saga* (London & New York: I. B. Tauris Publishers, 1999).

Brahm, Eric, "International Regimes," *Beyond Intractability*, Guy Burgess and Heidi Burgess (eds.), Conflict Research Consortium, University of Colorado, Boulder <http://www.beyondintracatability.org/m/international_regimes.jsp> (September 2005).

Bull, Hedley, *The Anarchical Society: A Study of Order in World Politics*, 2nd ed. with a new foreword by Stanley Hoffmann (London: Macmillan Press, 1977).

Callahan, Michael D., *A Sacred Trust: The League of Nations and Africa, 1929-1946* (Brighton: Sussex Academic Press, 2004).

Cattier, Emmanuel "Les intentions réelles de Turquoise," in Laure Coret and François-Xavier Verschave (eds.), *L'horreur qui nous prend au visage : l'État français et le génocide au Rwanda* (Paris : Rapport de la Commission d'enquête citoyenne & Éditions Karthala, 2005).

Chanaiwa, David "Southern Africa since 1945," in Ali A. Mazrui and C. Wondji (eds.), *General History of Africa: VIII Africa since 1935* (Oxford, Berkeley and Paris: James Curry, University Press of California and UNESCO, 1999).

Clapham, Christopher, "The United Nations and Peace-keeping in Africa," in Mark Malan (ed.), *Whiter Peace-keeping in Africa?* Monograph no. 36 (Cape Town: Institute for Security Studies, April 1999).

Clarke, Walter and Jeffrey Herbst, "Somalia and the Future of Humanitarian Intervention," *Foreign Affairs*, Vol. 75, no. 2, March/ April (1996).

Clavin, Patricia, *The Great Depression in Europe, 1929-1939* (New York: Palgrave Macmillan, 2000).

Clover, Jenny, "Food Security in Sub-Saharan Africa," *African Security Review*, Vol. 12, no 1 (2003).

Coogan, John W., "Wilsonian Diplomacy in War and Peace," in Gordon Marten (ed.), *American Foreign Relations Reconsidered 1890-1993* (London & New York: Routledge, 1994).

Cronin, Bruce, "The Paradox of Hegemony: America's Ambiguous Relationship with the United Nations," *European Journal of International Relations*, Vol. 7, no. 1 (2001):103-130.

Danticat, Edwidge, "Ghosts of the 1915 US Invasion Still Haunt Haiti's People," *Miami Herald*, 25 July 2005.

Davidson, Basil, *Modern Africa: A social and political history* (London: Penguin Books, 1978).

Davies, Desmond, "What about other foreign bank accounts?" *West Africa*, 5–11 August (2001).

Deen, Thalif, "Annan pushes for weapons treaty," *West Africa*, no. 4288. 13–19 August (2001).

[United Nations] Department for Peace-keeping Operations, *The Comprehensive Report on Lessons Learned from United Nations Operation in Somalia (UNOSOM), April 1992 – March 1995* (New York: UN Department of Public Information, 1995).

Diouf, Jacques, "Africa needs a Marshall Plan," *Le Monde Diplomatique*, English Edition, December (2004).

Donowaki, Mitsuro, *Small Arms, Africa and the United Nations: Ten Years of Interaction between Africa and the UN* (Paper presented at the PoA National Reporting Workshop held at Nairobi on 20-21 May 2004).

Duodu, Cameron, "Like father, like son," *West Africa*, no. 4298, 22-28 October (200).

Economic Commission for Africa, *Assessing Regional Integration in Africa* (Addis Ababa: ECA Publications, 2004).

Economic Community of West African States, press release no. 54 (15 September 1999).

Elgström, Ole, Jacob Bercovitch, and Carl Skau, "Regional Organisations and International Mediation: The Effectiveness of Insider Mediators," *African Journal on Conflict Resolution*, Vol. 3, no. 1 (2003).

Ellis, Stephen, The Mask of Anarchy: The Destruction of Liberia and the Religious Dimension of an African Civil War (London: C. Hurst & Co., 2001).

Etzioni, Amitai, "A self-restrained approach to nation-building by foreign powers", *International Affairs*, Vol. 80, no. 1 (January 2004): 1 – 18.

Fassbender, Bardo, "The Better Peoples of the United Nations? Europe's Practice and the United Nations," *European Journal of International Law*, Vol. 15, no. 5 (2004): 857-84.

Fasulo, Linda, *An Insider's Guide to the UN* (New Haven: Yale University Press, 2005).

Ferroggiaro, William, *The U.S. and the Genocide in Rwanda 1994: Information, Intelligence and the U.S. Response* (published on 24 March 2004) at <http://www.gwu.edu/~nsarchiv/NSAEBB/ NSAEBB117/#3 > (27 February 2006.)

Freund, Bill, The Making of Contemporary Africa: The Development of African Society since 1800 (London: Macmillan Press, 1998).

Fussell, Jim, *Group Classification on National ID Cards as a Factor in Genocide and Ethnic Cleansing* (Paper presented to the Seminar Series of the Yale University Genocide Studies Program, November 2001).

Galtung, Johan, "Three approaches to peace: peace-keeping, peace-making and peacebuilding," in Peace, War and Defence – Essays in Peace Research, *Christian Ejlers*, Vol. 2 (Copenhagen, 1975).

Gardiner, Nile, "The Volcker Investigation into the UN Oil-for-Food Scandal: Why It Lacks Credibility," *Backgrounder*, no. 1819, 1 February (2005).

Gareis, Sven Bernhard and Johannes Varwick, *The United Nations: An Introduction* (New York: Palgrave Macmillan, 2005).

[United Nations] General Assembly Resolution A/RES/616 A (VII) of 5 December 1952.

— —, Resolution A/RES/616 B (VII) of 5 December 1952.

— —, Resolution 1514 (XV) of 14 December 1960.

— —, Resolution A/RES/2202 A (XXI) of 16 December 1966.

— —, Resolution A/RES/S-13/2 of 1 June 1986.

— —, Resolution A/RES/46/151 of 18 December 1991.

— —, Resolution A/RES/50/70B (15 January 1996).

— —, Resolution A/RES/55/2 of 18 September 2000.

— —, Resolution A/RES/58/275-A/58/586 (2003).

— —, Resolution A/RES/58/310-A/58/831 (2004).

— —, Resolution A/RES/59/16A-A/59/529 (2005).

Gilpin, Robert, *The Political Economy of International Relations* (Princeton, NJ.: Princeton University Press, 1987).

— —, Global Political Economy: Understanding International Political Order (Princeton, NJ.: Princeton University Press, 2001).

Glaser, Antoine and Stephen Smith, *Comment la France a perdu l'Afrique* (Paris: Calmann-lévy, 2005).

Gordenker, Leon "The UN System in Perspective: Development of the UN System," in Tobi Trister Gati (ed.), *The US, the UN, and the Management of Global Change* (New York and London: New York University Press, 1983).

Gordon, Joy, "The United Nations and Oil-for-Food: The Facts Behind the Volcker Commission's Interim Report," *UNA-USA Policy Briefing*, no. 5, 10 February (2005).

Gowan, Peter, "US: UN," *New Left Review*, no. 24, November/December (2003): 5-28.

Hargreaves, John D., *Decolonization in Africa* (London: Longman group, 1994).

Hasenclever, Andreas, Peter Mayer, and Volker Rittberger, "Integrating theories of international regimes," *Review of International Studies*, Vol. 26, no. 1 (2000): 3-33.

Higgins, Rosalyn *Problems & Process: International Law and How We Use it* (Oxford: Oxford University Press, 1994).

Hilderbrand, Robert, *Dumbarton Oaks: The Origins of the United Nations and the Search for Postwar Security* (Chapel Hill, NC.: University of North Carolina Press, 1990).

Human Rights Watch, "Rwanda/Zaire: Rearming with Impunity — International Support for the Perpetrators of the Rwandan Genocide," *Human Rights Watch Arms Project*, Vol. 7, no. 4 (May 1995).

— —, Leave None to Tell the Story: Genocide in Rwanda (New York: HRW, 1999).

Hyppolite, Pierre, *Haiti, Rising Flames from Burning Ashes* (Lanham, MD.: University Press of America, 2006).

International Court of Justice, Press Release 2005/23 of 8 November 2005.

International Criminal Court, Press Release 20041004-78-En of 4 October 2004.

James, Harold, *The End of Globalization: Lessons from the Great Depression* (Cambridge, MA.: Harvard University Press, 2002).

Kanya-Forstner, A. S. "Military Expansion in the Western Sudan — French and British Style" in Prosser Gifford and W. M. Rogers Louis (eds.), *France and Britain in Africa: Imperial Rivalry and Colonial Rule* (New Haven and London: Yale University Press, 1971).

Keohane, Robert O., *After Hegemony: Cooperation and Discord in the World Political Economy* (Princeton, NJ.: Princeton University Press, 1984).

Keohane, Robert O., and Joseph S. Nye, Power and Interdependence (Boston: Little & Brown, 1977).

Khan, Shaharyar M., *The Shallow Graves of Rwanda* (London & New York: I. B. Tauris, 2001).

Ki-Zerbo, Joseph, Histoire de l'Afrique Noire: D'Hier à Demain (Paris: Hatier, 1978).

— —, *A Quand l'Afrique?* (Paris: Éditions de l'Aube, 2003).

Kouassi, Edmond Kwam, "Africa and the United Nations," in Ali A. Mazrui and C. Wondji (eds.), *General History of Africa: VIII Africa since 1935* (Oxford, Berkeley and Paris: James Currey, University Press of California and UNESCO, 1999).

Krasner, Stephen D. (ed.), *International Regimes* (Itacha, NY.: Cornell University Press, 1983).

Lewin, André, *Diallo Telli: Le tragique destin d'un grand Africain* (Paris: Jeune Afrique Livres, 1990).

Little, Richard, "International Regimes," in John Baylis and Steve Smith (eds.), *The Globalization of World Politics: An Introduction to international relations* (New York: Oxford University Press, 2001).

Lobe, Jim, "Right-wingers gunning for Annan," *Africa Week,* Special Print Edition, December (2004).

Mandela, Nelson Rolihlahla, *Long Walk to Freedom* (London: Little, Brown & Co.1994).

Martin, Lisa L. and Beth A. Simmons, "Theories of Empirical Studies of International Institutions," *International Organization,* Vol. 52, no. 4 (Autumn 1998): 729-58.

Matanle, Emma, *The UN Security Council* (London: Royal Institute of International Affairs, 1995).

Mazrui, Ali A., "Between Global Governance and Global War: Africa Before and After September 11," *African Renaissance,* Vol. 2, no. 1, January/February (2005): 9-18.

Mehta, Ved, *Mahatma Ghandi and His Apostles* (New York: Penguin Books, 1976).

Melvern, Linda R., *A People Betrayed: The role of the West in Rwanda's genocide* (Cape Town, London & New York: NAEP & Zed Books, 2000).

— —, Conspiracy to Murder: The Rwandan Genocide (London: Verso Publishers, 2004).

Nkrumah, Kwame, *Africa Must Unite* (New York: International Publishers, 1963).

Norwegian Initiative on Small Arms Transfers (NISAT) <http://www.nisat.org/default.asp?page=/database_info/> (25 October 2005.)

Okumu, Wafula, "Africa and the UN Security Council Permanent Seats," *African Renaissance,* Vol. 2, no. 5, September/October (2005): 16-22.

Organization of African Unity, *Rwanda: The Preventable Genocide* (Addis Ababa, International Panel of Eminent Personalities, 2000).

Patil, Anjali V., *The UN Veto in World Affairs, 1946-1990: A Complete Record and Case History of Security Council's veto* (Mansell, UK.: Continuum International Publishing Group, 1992).

Paul, James and Céline Nahory, "Theses Towards a Democratic Reform of the UN Security Council," *Global Policy Forum,* 13 July 2005 at <http://www.globalpolicy. org.> (25 July 2005)

Ratsimbaharison, Adrien M., *The Failure of the United Nations Development Programs for Africa* (Lanham, MD.: University Press of America, 2003).

Richard, Ivor, "Major Objectives and Functions of the UN: The View from Abroad," in Toby Trister Gati (ed.), *The US, the UN, and the Management of Global Change* (New York and London: New York University Press, 1983).

Rothermund, Dietmar, *The Global Impact of the Great Depression, 1929-39* (London and New York: Routledge, 1996).

Ryan, Stephen, The United Nations and International Politics: Studies in Contemporary History (New York: Palgrave Macmillan, 2000).

Sanderson, G. N., "The European Partition of Africa: Coincidence or Conjuncture?" in E. F. Penrose (ed.), *European Imperialism and the Partition of Africa* (London: Frank Cass, 1975).

Sanjian, Gregory S., "Promoting Stability or Instability? Arms Transfers and Regional Rivalries, 1950-1991," *International Studies Quarterly*, Vol. 43, no. 4 (1999): 641-70.

Schlesinger, Stephen, *Act of Creation: The Untold Story of the Founding of the United Nations* (Boulder. CO.: Westview Press, 2003).

Schofield, Victoria, *The United Nations: People, Politics and Powers* (Hove (England): Wayland Publishers, 1979).

Schraider, Peter J., *United States foreign policy toward Africa: Incrementalism, Crisis, and Change* (Cambridge: Cambridge University Press, 1994).

[United Nations] Security Council, Resolution S/RES/169 (1961) of 24 November 1961.

— —, Resolution S/RES/775 (1992) of 28 August 1992.

— —, Resolution S/RES/733 (1992) of 23 January 1992.

— —, Resolution S/RES/814 (1993) of 26 March 1993.

— —, Resolution S/RES/918 (1994) of 17 May 1994.

— —, Resolution S/RES/1373 (2001) of 28 September 2001

— —, Resolution S/RES/1464 (2003) of 4 February 2003.

— —, Resolution S/RES/1498 (2003) of 4 August 2003.

Souaré, Issaka K., "Can the G-8 and International Financial Institutions Help Africa?" *African Renaissance*, Vol. 1, no. 2, September/October (2004): 115-20.

— —, "The Debate on the UN Reform: Near Consensus on the Need for Reform but Rifts on how to go about it," *African Renaissance*, Vol. 2, no. 5, September/October (2005): 10-14.

— —, "France: Unveiling Racism and Police Brutality in the Land of Free," *African Renaissance*, Vol. 2, no. 6, November/December (2005): 130-5.

— —, Civil Wars and Coups d'État in West Africa: An Attempt to Understand the Roots and Prescribe Possible Solutions (Lanham, MD.: University Press of America, 2006).

Spero, Joan E. and Jeffrey A. Hart, *The Politics of International Economic Relations* (New York: St. Martin's Press, 1997).

Stevenson, John & Chris Cook, *Britain in the Depression: Society and Politics, 1929-39* (London: Longman, 1994).

Stoessinger, John G., *The United Nations & the Superpowers: China, Russia & America* (New York: Random House, 1977).

Strange, Susan, "Cavelic dragons: a critique of regime analysis," in Stephen D. Krasner (ed.), *International Regimes* (Itacha, NY.: Cornell University Press, 1983).

Task Force on the United Nations, *American Interests and UN Reform: Report of the Task Force on the United Nations* (Washington, DC.: United States Institute of Peace, 2005).

Tatsuo, Arima, *Future Role of United Nations within the Framework of Global Security: Japan's Perspective* (Paper presented at the 41st Munich Conference on Security Policy, February 2005).

Tharoor, Shashi, "Why America Still Needs the United Nations," *Foreign Affairs*, September/October (2003).

Thatcher, Margaret, *The Downing Street Years* (London: Harper Collins Publishers, 1993).

United Nations, Everyone's United Nations: A complete handbook of the activities and evolution of the United Nations during its first twenty years, 1945-1963 (New York: Department of Public Information, 1968).

— —, *The Blue Helmets: A Review of United Nations Peace-keeping* (New York: Department of Public Information, 1990).

— —, *United Nations and Apartheid: 1948-1994* (New York: Department of Public Information, 1994).

— —, "Report of the Panel of Governmental Experts on Small Arms," UN document A/52/298 (27 August 1997).

— —, Report of the Independent Inquiry into the Actions of the United Nations during the 1994 Genocide in Rwanda, UN document S/1999/1257 of 16 December 1999.

— —, *Côte d'Ivoire: Rapport de la Commission d'enquête internationale pour la Côte d'Ivoire* [available in French only] (New York: United Nations Secretariat, 2001).

— —, Image & Reality (New York: Department of Public Information, 2002). This document is also available at <http://www.un.org/geninfo/ir/ref-frame.htm.> (2 March 2006.)

— —, *The Millennium Development Goals Report 2005* (New York: United Nations Publications, 2005).

Verschave, François-Xavier, *La Françafrique: Le plus long scandale de la République* (Paris: Éditions Stock, 1998).

— —, "Continuation, après le 7 avril 1994 de l'alliance militaire antérieure," in Laure Coret and François-Xavier Verschave (eds.), *L'horreur qui nous prend au visage : l'État français et le génocide au Rwanda* (Paris : Rapport de la Commission d'enquête citoyenne & Éditions Karthala, 2005).

Vogt, Margaret Aderinsola, "Co-Operation Between the UN and the OAU in the Management of African Conflicts," in Mark Malan (ed.),

Whither Peace-keeping in Africa? Monograph no. 36 (Cap Town: Institute of Security Studies, April 1999).

Watts, Arthur, "The Importance of International Law," in Michael Byers (ed.), *The Role of Law in International Politics: Essays in International Relations and International Law* (Oxford: Oxford University Press, 2000), pp. 5-16.

Weintraub, Sidney "US Participation in International Organizations: Looking Ahead," in Toby Trister Gati (ed.), *The US, the UN, and the Management of Global Change* (New York & London: New York University Press, 1983), pp. 184-209.

Weiss, Thomas G., David P. Forsythe, and Roger A. Coate, *The United Nations and Changing World Politics* (Boulder, CO.: Westview Press, 2004).

Woods, Emira, "Somalia: Problems with Current US Policy," *Foreign Policy in Focus*, Vol. 2, no. 19 (February 1997).

Young, Oran R., "International Regimes: Toward a New Theory of Institutions," *World Politics*, Vol. 38, no. 1 (October 1986): 104-22.

Zacarias, Agostinho, *The United Nations and International Peace-keeping* (London: I. B. Tauris Publishers, 1996).

INDEX

A

Abacha, Sani, 218
Abidjan, 99, 100, 102, 103
Abyssinia, 46
Addis Ababa, xv, xviii, 47, 56, 84, 86, 108, 110, 116, 119, 122, 234, 238
Administrative and Budgetary Questions, vii, 210
Advisory Board on Disarmament Matters, 104
Africa in world affairs, xvii, 21
African Groundnut Council, vii, 184
African Group at the UN, 74, 76, 84, 159, 160
African Group of States at the UN, vii, 83, 85
African National Congress, vii, 79
African Union, vii, ix, xii, xiii, 24, 54, 65, 100, 101, 104, 110, 122, 206, 212, 215, 216, 220, 225, 232
Africa-UN partnership, xviii, xx, 24, 71, 208
Afrikaner National Party, 79
Aidid, Mohamed Farah, 127
Algerian question, 73, 74, 75, 118, 203
American dominance, 28, 29
Americo-Liberians, 41

Amnesty International, 24, 106, 120, 121, 232
ANC Youth League, 79
Annan, Kofi, viii, xviii, 59, 89, 99, 120, 157, 159, 168, 174, 175, 176, 177, 178, 179, 183, 187, 190, 191, 202, 223, 224
Apartheid, v, xvii, 24, 42, 74, 75, 76, 78, 79, 80, 81, 82, 83, 84, 85, 86, 87, 88, 115, 118, 119, 125, 171, 198, 201, 207, 229, 240
Argentina, 227
Arusha Accord, 141, 159, 160
Arusha Agreement, 141, 142, 157
Arusha Peace Accord, 143, 159
Asante, 174
Atlantic Charter, 28, 48, 49, 69
Axis powers, 49

B

Baker, Noel, 43
Baradei, Mohamed El, 181, 190
Barre, Siad, 126
Beijing., 29, 70, 86
Bella, Ben Ahmed, 75
Blair, Tony, 184, 218, 219
Brazzaville, 72
Bretton Woods system, 22, 107
Britain, xvi, 28, 29, 33, 34, 35, 38, 41, 43, 46, 63, 64, 70, 76, 78, 81, 84, 87, 95, 170, 173, 174, 183, 184, 198, 201, 203, 218, 225, 237, 239
British Commonwealth, 84

www.ingramcontent.com/pod-product-compliance
Lightning Source LLC
Chambersburg PA
CBHW021542260326

41914CB00001B/132